THE SEPHARDIC WAY
IN DEATH AND MOURN

THE SEPHARDIC WAY IN DEATH & MOURNING

BY RABBI YAMIN LEVY

KODESH PRESS

THE SEPHARDIC WAY IN DEATH AND MOURNING
© Rabbi Yamin Levy 2022

Hardcover ISBN: 978-1-947857-90-2
Paperback ISBN: 978-1-947857-89-6

All rights reserved. Except for brief quotations in printed reviews, no part of this publication may be reproduced, stored in a retrieval system, or transmitted in any form or by any means (printed, written, photocopied, visual electronic, audio, or otherwise) without the prior permission of the publisher.

PUBLISHED AND DISTRIBUTED EXCLUSIVELY BY
Kodesh Press LLC
New York, NY
www.kodeshpress.com
kodeshpress@gmail.com

Set in Arno Pro and Ideal Sans
by Raphaël Freeman MISTD, Renana Typesetting

Printed in the United States of America

The Publication of this Book was Sponsored by
The Khani Family
In Memory of Their Mother

Jila Kimiabakhsh Khani

Jila Khani was a woman of valor
whose life was dedicated to acts of love and kindness.
She was blessed with the gift of giving
and a constant willingness to help others.
She was always ahead of her time. As a leader in the
Sephardic Iranian immigrant community
hers was a voice of wisdom and vision.
She inspired all those who knew her
to be the best they can be.
She never felt the need to prove herself to others.
She was dedicated to her immediate family,
her extended family, her community,
the Jewish people and beyond.

May Her Memory Be a Blessing
Spring 2022
5782

Table of Contents

Author's Preface — xi

Introduction: You Are Not Alone — 1

Chapter 1: *Viduy*: Gateway to Healing — 13

Introduction to *Viduy* · *Mi Sheberakh Tefillah* · Recitation of *Viduy* · A Paraphrase of *Viduy* · Three Components of *Viduy* · Being Proactive When Faced with Terminal Illness · Saying Goodbye · Ethical Will

Chapter 2: Creating a Caring Community — 25

How to Help Others Through Grief · Guide to Making a Condolence Visit · When Are Condolence Visits Appropriate · Leaving the House of Mourning · Comforting Intense Mourning · Points to Remember When Comforting a Mourner

Chapter 3: *Ani Ma'amin* – I Believe — 35

A Belief System · Body and Soul: Life and the Afterlife · The World-to-Come · Nefesh and Neshamah · Rabbi Aryeh Kaplan on Life After Death · Attitude Towards Death · Personal Growth · Vis-à-vis God

Chapter 4: *Kavod HaMet* – Honoring the Deceased — 47

Aninut · When Death Occurs · On Shabbat and Holy Days · Issues that may Arise Immediately After Death · Autopsies · Organ Donation · Amputated Limbs · Summary of the Laws of *Aninut* · Meals During the Period of *Aninut* · Religious Support · The Burial Society (*Chevra Kadisha*) · Preparation of the Deceased for Burial (*Taharah* and *Rechitsah*) · Shrouds (*Takhrikhim*) · Prayer Shawl (*Tallit*) · Transportation of Body / Embalming

Chapter 5: Planning the Funeral Service — 65

Scheduling the Funeral Service · Purchasing a Casket · Flowers · Viewing the Deceased · Cremation · Mausoleum · Laws Relating to *Kohanim* · Suicide and Jewish Law

Chapter 6: The Funeral and Burial — 75

The Funeral Service · Recitation of Psalms · The Eulogy · *Tziduk Hadin* · Escorting the Deceased (*Levayat HaMet*) · Standing While the Body Is Being Moved · Pallbearers · The Burial Service · Filling the Grave · The *Hashkavah* (Memorial Prayer) · Proper Behavior at the Cemetery · Leaving the Cemetery · Accompanying the Mourners Home · Disinterment · Reinternment

Chapter 7: Honoring the Living (*Kavod HaBeriot*) — 89

How We Honor the Living · Who is a Mourner According to Jewish Law? · Empathetic Mourning · Voluntary Mourning · Counting the Seven Days of *Shivah* · Times When *Shivah* Does Not Begin Immediately After Burial · Times When *Shivah* Is Not Seven Days · Burial in Israel · Hearing About the Death After Burial · Double Grief · Tearing a Garment (*Keriah*) · Lighting a Candle · The Meal of Consolation · *Birkat HaMazon* (Grace After Meals)

Chapter 8: Laws and Customs of *Shivah* — 105

Where is Shivah Observed? · Sitting on Lower Chairs · Personal Grooming · Expressions of Joy During Shivah · Torah Study · *Berit Milah* · *Pidyon HaBen* (Redemption of the First-Born Son) · Weddings · Services in the House of Mourning · The Order of Services When Held in the House of Mourning · Leaving the House of Mourning · Services in the Synagogue · The *Kaddish* Explained · Laws of *Kaddish* · Converts and the Laws of *Shivah* · *Shivah* on Shabbat · Concluding Shivah · Various Customs Pertaining to the Conclusion of *Shivah* · Visiting the Cemetery After *Shivah* · If *Shivah* Was not Observed

Chapter 9: *Yom Tov*, *Chol HaMoed*, and the Cycle of the Year   129

When Holy Days Cancel Mourning · If Death Occurs on *Yom Tov* · Counting *Shivah* and *Sheloshim* when Interrupted by *Yom Tov* · Comforting the Mourners on Shabbat and *Yom Tov* · Laws Relating to the Calendar Cycle

Chapter 10: Getting Married When in Mourning   137

When Death Occurs Prior to a Scheduled Wedding · When Death Occurs Immediately After a Wedding · When One Death Occurs Immediately After Death · Second Marriage

Chapter 11: *Zakhor* – How a Jew Remembers   141

The Obligation to Remember · Post-Shivah · Permitted Social Gatherings During *Sheloshim* · Counting the Thirty Days of Sheloshim · Conclusion of Sheloshim · Excessive Grief · Twelve-Month Restrictions for Loss of a Parent · Memorial Services · *Hazkarah* · Visiting the Graves of Loved Ones · Erecting a Monument · The Unveiling Service

Chapter 12: When a Baby Dies: When Saying Hello Means Saying Goodbye   153

Grieving for a Baby · Miscarriage and Stillbirth

Appendix I: Reflections and Meditations   157

Appendix II: Prayers and Psalms   165

Complete *Viduy* in Hebrew and English · Psalms for Funeral Service · *Tziduk Hadin* for Funeral Service · Psalm 91 Hebrew and English · *Hashkavah* for Haham, Man and Woman · *Kaddish Al Israel* · Special *Birkat HaMazon* · *Tziduk Hadin* and *Hashkavot* for Memorial Service · Readings for Memorial Service · *Kaddish* Transliteration

Index   219

Author's Preface

Our *hakhamim* of blessed memory offer a penetrating insight into the psyche of the bereaved by offering a prayer that one may choose to recite after losing a loved one:

> Master of the universe: may it be Your will to repair our estrangement and comfort us at this time of loss. (*Masechet Semachot*, Chapter 10)

The simplicity of this short prayer suggests an almost universal feeling that overtakes the bereaved as they stand before their deceased relative. I have been a rabbi for over 30 years, and I have yet to meet mourners who do not turn to God and who do not want to meticulously observe the rituals as prescribed by Jewish law. In addition to presenting the laws of grief and mourning as observed in the Sephardic tradition I also try to offer guidance for the bereaved and for the community who is responsible to care for their grieving members.

The laws that have to do with death, mourning, and comforting the mourner are subsumed under the general category of *gemilut chasadim*, acts of love and kindness and the biblical commandment to "love your neighbor as you love yourself." HaRambam, Maimonides, writes as follows:

> It is a positive commandment according to the words of our sages to visit the sick, to comfort the mourner, to bury the dead, to carry the dead on one's shoulder, to eulogize the dead,

and to dig his grave. Likewise [it is a positive commandment] to escort a bride to her *chupa*, to make merry the bride and groom and provide them with all their needs. These are acts of *gemilut chasadim*, acts of love and kindness performed with one's body for which there is no fixed measure. According to the rabbis all these commandments are included in the biblical commandment to love your neighbor as yourself. (MT *Hilkhot Avel* 14:1)

We fulfill the mitzvah of loving our neighbor by doing acts of love. This is *gemilut chasadim*. The nature of our human condition is that we often find ourselves in need of help. The Torah steps in and reminds us that we are never alone.

There is another dimension to observing the mitzvah of *gemilut chasadim* as the sage Abba Shaul taught:

> "This is my God, and I will beautify Him" [How does one beautify God?] By imitating Him. As He is merciful and gracious so too you be merciful and gracious. (TB *Shabbat* 133b, Mekhilta, Beshalach 3)

Rabbi Hama bar Hanina expanded upon this lesson and taught:

> What is the meaning of the verse: "After the Lord you shall walk" (Devarim 13:5)? Is it possible for a man to walk after the *Shekhinah*? Has it not been said: "The Lord God is a devouring fire" (Devarim 4:24)? Rather walk after His attributes. As God clothes the naked so too you must cloth the naked. As God visits the sick so too you must visit the sick. As God comforts the mourner so too you must comfort the mourner. (TB *Sotah* 14a)

One imitates God by doing acts of love and kindness. Our sages spared no words in extolling the importance of acts of love and kindness. Indeed, *gemilut chasadim* is one of the three pillars that hold up the entire world (Pirkei Avot 1:2).

AUTHOR'S PREFACE

HaRambam considered *nichum avelim*, comforting the mourner as one of the most important acts of *hesed*.

> It would seem to me that comforting the mourner takes precedence over visiting the sick because comforting the mourner is an act of love to both the living and the dead (MT *Avel* 14:7).

The mourner is incapacitated by his or her grief. In the absence of proper care and concern the mourner can languish and sink into despair. After recovering from his or her illness a sick person will forget they were ever sick. That is not the case with a mourner. The loss of a loved one is permanent. The loss is unchanging and never forgotten. HaRambam, however, while advancing his ruling that "comforting the mourner takes precedence over visiting the sick" did not base himself on a qualitative supposition as the one I just advanced but rather on a quantitative thesis that comforting the mourner is a *chesed* to both the living and to the dead. What benefit could the dead possibility receive from one's act of comfort for the living? The answer is that the deceased needs to make sure that his or her loved ones are cared for. The deceased is not able to care for them so we as individuals and as a community must step in.

According to HaRambam the laws of mourning, while not biblical, are ancient and traditional.

> [The laws of] mourning are not biblical except for the first day alone which is the day of the death and the day of burial. The rest of the seven days are not biblically mandated. Even though it is said in the Torah that Joseph mourned his father for seven days (Bereshit 50:10), the laws of the Torah were given at Mount Sinai where the Halakha was legislated (TB *Shabbat* 135a–b). Moshe our Rabbi instituted for Israel the seven days of mourning for Israel (MT *Hilkhot Avel* 1:1).

Acting as rabbi and teacher, Moshe Rabbenu instituted the laws of mourning for the benefit of the Jewish people. The thrust of this book is that the laws of mourning and the customs associated with grief and comfort are rooted in the psychological needs of the bereaved and their wellbeing.

Before I acknowledge the many people who have helped along the way I will continue an old, yet sacred tradition of stating: *Odeh Hashem Bekhol Levav*, I thank the Almighty with a full heart for His countless blessings including the opportunity to bring this book to light.

I thank all the colleagues, friends and family members who spent time reading the manuscript makings edits and offering suggestions. I am indebted to Laleh Asher Zar whose careful reading of the final manuscript prepared it for publication. Thank you to Gina Kashefi for the design of the cover and her artistic advice. Finally, a warm thank you to Rabbi Alec and Caroline Goldstein of Kodesh Press for their guidance and encouragement. I would like to thank my dear friend and colleague the esteemed Isaac Azose. The text in the appendix is based on the siddur he edited and was used as the original template for *Tefilat Eliyahu Siddur* of the Iranian Jewish Community of New York.

A special thank you goes to my dear friend Pouya Khani who believed in this project and sponsored its publication in memory of his beloved mother Jila Khani. Jila Khani was a dear personal friend and confidant of mine. I learned after her death that I was not unique, and many in our community and beyond the North Shore considered her a dear friend and confidant. She was a special woman who stood up for what was right. She was a distinguished leader of the immigrant Iranian Jewish community of Great neck and Kings Point. This community's success is in no small measure a function of her leadership, vision, wisdom and gracious *chesed*.

I consider myself among the most fortunate authors. I am employed by a supportive and committed community, surrounded by loyal colleagues and friends, and nurtured by a loving family.

Yamin Levy
Great Neck, NY
April 2022

INTRODUCTION

You Are Not Alone

Teach us to number our days, that we may apply our hearts to wisdom.
Tehillim 90:12

If you are reading this book because you are a mourner, I extend to you the traditional words of comfort, *min ha-Shamayim tenuchamu,* "May you find comfort from the heavens above." The death of a loved one, no matter how prepared one may be, is a very profound sorrow. I have learned over the years, from personal experience and as a rabbi that the pain associated with loss is acute and can feel all-encompassing. I have also learned that grief is unpredictable and despite what the experts tell us about the different stages of grief, it is never linear, and everyone grieves differently. This may partially explain why it seems like we are so ill prepared when we are faced with the loss of a loved one.

Our culture finds it particularly challenging to deal with loss. We are so indoctrinated by our consumer culture with the notion that acquiring more things will lead to happiness, that when loss occurs, one is left feeling confused. Procuring what we want has become a very central part of our lives, be it praise and approval, which is something we sought as children and continue to seek as adults, or happiness through the acquisition of gifts, money, and other material goods. This is what makes learning how to accept loss, heal its trauma, and get on with life that much more difficult.

Loss is a part of life; learning to embrace it is a path towards wisdom. Both as individuals and as a community, we must learn how to grapple with loss appropriately. By learning how to grieve in a safe and structured environment, one can potentially transform a painful experience into a magnificent process of growth and enlightenment. Jewish tradition affords the mourner precisely that: a safe and structured environment, as well as a guide on how to navigate the difficult journey through grief and bereavement.

This little book is an exploration of how Judaism's prescribed mourning rituals are a healthy means of navigating the unforgiving journey through grief toward a sense of recovery and resolution. Like a physical wound, grief requires appropriate attention to heal. The death of a human being no matter how elderly he or she may be is always a reason to mourn.

The dead do not praise God, nor do those who go down into silence (Tehillim 115:17).

Life is of supreme value and Judaism's response to death is always sadness and self-reflection. The Jewish laws of mourning and the various customs that have developed throughout the ages afford the bereaved precisely the kind of spiritual response that leads to healing and resolve.

It is through knowledge and understanding of our laws and traditions that these rituals will have meaning for the mourner and will ultimately bring a degree of comfort for the loss experienced by death. Our sages of blessed memory saw *mitzvot* (commandments) as much more than just religious practice. For them *mitzvot* are a lifeline:

> [Someone on a ship] has been thrown [overboard] into the water. The captain stretches out a rope and says to him: "Take hold of this rope with your hand and do not let go, for if you do, you will lose your life!" Similarly, the Holy One, blessed be He, said to Israel: Adhere to the commandments, then, "Ye that cleave unto the Lord your God are alive, every one of you, this day" (Midrash Rabbah, *Shelach Lekha* 27:6).

This is especially evident within the framework of the laws of *avelut* (mourning). The prescribed menu of customs and laws affords the bereaved guidance and gives structure to the grieving process. An appropriate response to the loss of a loved one is *critical* to one's emotional and physical recovery. Some people repress their grief, unable to display emotion. Studies have shown that such a response can be harmful, both physically and emotionally. Others grieve too intensely; they cannot put their loss within a context of reality. This, too, is harmful to the bereaved. The Talmud understood the need for a measured and guided response to grief, as is illustrated in the following story:

> A certain woman was in the neighborhood of Rabbi Huna. She had seven sons. One of them died. She wept over him too much. Rabbi Huna said to her: "Do not do thus!" She paid no heed to him. He said to her: "If you heed me, good; if not, prepare more shrouds" (TB *Moed Katan* 27b).

The story concludes with a tragic ending. The woman does not resolve her grief and dies of a broken heart.

Left to one's own determination the grief of a beloved should be endless. But as the Rabbi advised the woman in the story, one's grief must be framed and contained. That is the role of the laws associated with mourning. By observing the prescribed rituals, we need not ever reflect on whether we have grieved enough or too much. The practice has been tested by time and is the means through which a complete healing can occur.

A subtle, yet critical idea found within the laws of *avelut* is the constant reminder that you are not alone in your grief. You are now a part of the not-so-exclusive club of mourners who have preceded you, who grieve with you, and who will come after you, along with all who mourn for Zion and Jerusalem – all of whom have used the rituals and traditions as an anchor and support on their journey through grief toward comfort and resolution.

Mourning is a communal activity, even when the deceased is not an immediate relative. It is the responsibility of the community to come together and pull one of its fellow members out of the grip of his or her grief. It is therefore essential that the laws of *avelut* be familiar to everyone. These laws are a fundamental part of *gemilut chasadim*, acts of love and kindness, one of the three pillars of our faith. As Shimon the Righteous has stated in *Pirkei Avot* (Ethics of Our Fathers 1:2):

> The world stands on three pillars: Torah, worship, and acts of love and kindness. Rabbi Yehudah further states that one who denies acts of *gemilut chasadim* is as if he or she denies God.

Nichum avelim, comforting the mourner, being present and supportive for a relative, friend, or member of the community who is confronted with loss, is an act of love and compassion, indeed a mitzvah. As is true of all *mitzvot* one must be educated in all the aspects of each specific commandment.

The study of the laws of *avelut*, the laws of mourning, involves a great deal more than a list of that which is permitted or that which is forbidden. In fact, they are an unspectacular reminder that we are all destined to die and that dying is the most natural reality of our existence. Death is one of the only certainties in our lives, and yet we act as if it is something that happens only to others. Years ago, as a young newly appointed rabbi, I announced a new series for my adult education program on death and dying in Jewish law. Two-thirds of my regular participants did not show up. A few of them were honest and said they did not want to think about death. We spend our entire lives in complete denial of the reality of death. It is as if death is something one sees on television or reads about in the papers, but not something relevant to life and living.

Society's obsession with the search for the fountain of youth has given birth to the philosophy that one should not even consider the possibility of mortality, for doing so brings one's own demise closer. I often caution those who share this point of view that one cannot go through life trying to avoid dying. It just doesn't work. By recognizing the existence of death, one intuitively focuses on living and loving, and on being present in the here-and-now.

Then there are those who do not deny death and have a meaningful respect for the idea that our time in this world is limited but live in constant fear of it. Fear of death and fear of the aging process can be all-consuming and debilitating. People spend an inordinate amount of time making themselves miserable over the inevitable. How strange, I often tell myself, that people expend so much energy on their fear of death when one's energies should be spent on how one lives and the quality of life one sets for oneself.

Halakhah: Jewish Law

Jewish Law, *halakhah*, pervades every aspect of Jewish living. It is the structure that holds together the entire enterprise of living as a Jew and a meaningful reflection of Judaism's core values. That is both its strength and its beauty. Rabbi Dr. Walter Wurzburger writes that *halakhah* is not an end but a guide,[1] a means to achieving holiness:

> So that you shall remember and perform all My commandments and you shall be holy to your God (Bemidbar 15:40).

The comprehensive system of Jewish law, *halakhah*, is particular to Judaism and its broad nature is one of its distinguishing features from all other religions. There is no aspect of life that is not instructed by *halakhah*. Its impact on the individual and the society cannot be overstated. No amount of passionate sermonizing or psychologizing can replace the role of Jewish law and Jewish practice, both in the life of individuals and as a model for the larger community and society.

Halakhah, experienced in its fullest state, incorporates two distinct facets. There is the legal aspect of Jewish law and the devotional aspect. To fully appreciate the impact and the powerful effects of a halakhic life and halakhic experience, one must have a healthy commitment to both. The legal aspect of *halakhah* is very specific and involves detailed instructions, rules, and regulations of behavior, while the devotional aspect of *halakhah* entails the yearning to give expression to the intimate and personal desire to know God and be connected with the people of Israel.

---

1. "Covenantal Imperatives," in *Samuel Mirsky Memorial Volume*, ed. Gersion Appel (New York: Yeshiva University, 1970).

Both aspects shape halakhic practice. One without the other is an impoverished experience.

Within the context of the legal and the relational aspects of *halakhah*, Jewish law divides between the laws that are biblically mandated versus those that are rabbinically ordained. In practicality there is no difference – both must be observed; however, as will be seen throughout this book, the distinction has specific, meaningful implications.

Alongside the halakhic process, a culture of customs called *minhag* emerged. *Halakhah* reflects the Jewish people's core values, while *minhag*, in a broad sense, is an echo of the culture and society in which the *halakhah* is being observed. Jews worldwide observe the same *halakhah* but might vary in terms of *minhag*.

The rituals associated with mourning are a blend of *minhag* and *halakhah*. Knowing the difference helps explain how it is that different communities may observe these rituals in a variety of ways and may be useful when deciding what is significant as an observance and what may be considered a minor observance.

There are three different types of *minhag*. First is *minhag* that emerges from *halakhah* (Jewish law) and is rooted in halakhic practice. Alternatively, there are *minhagim* that have no halakhic basis but are established by the practice of the Jewish people and ratified by the *Sanhedrin* (supreme court of Israel). Regarding these two types of *minhag*, Maimonides writes:

> Whoever goes against any one of the regulations of the rabbis is transgressing a negative commandment, since it says in the Torah 'You must follow according to all that they teach you.' This includes amendments, decrees, and *minhag* (customs) that they teach the multitudes to strengthen their minds and improve the world (MT *Mamrim* 1:2).

A third type of *minhag* emerges locally – within a community or even a family, and is often based on local culture and customs of the host society. The first two types of *minhagim* are extremely hard to differentiate from rabbinically ordained *mitzvot*. The third, while still called *minhag*, is significantly less binding.

Halakhah, and the first two categories of *minhag*, expose Judaism's core values while the third kind of *minhag* reflects the community's fears and aspirations. How a community addresses a particular life-cycle moment with joy, or navigates ceremonies through moments of sadness, is often based on the customs of the host culture. The purpose of this kind of *minhag* is to transform ritual into a culturally relevant aesthetic experience.

Most of the *minhagim* associated with mourning are of the third kind. I will do my best to identify such *minhagim* when they are discussed.

Sephardic *Halakhah*, Jewish Law

Jewish law is exclusively based on the Babylonian Talmud, which is a written record of the last Supreme Court of the Jewish people, the *Sanhedrin*. The Talmud was edited and compiled by Ravina and Rav Ashi, two prominent scholars around 500 CE, in the academies of Babylonia (present day Iraq) which was, at the time, the center of Jewish culture and study. The Talmud is not a code of law or a linear narrative, or even a description that provides clear instruction. Instead, it is a compilation of various conversations, discussions and disagreements on a range of topics between Rabbinic scholars who lived up to five hundred years prior sprinkled with stories, ethics and legends, all of which makes it a very difficult literary work to master. Throughout the Middle Ages the Jewish people were dispersed and how the Talmud was interpreted varied between the early Levant and Southern Spanish Sephardic Jewish communities and the European Jewish communities. Sephardic *halakhah*, Jewish law is based on how the Sephardic scholars filtered through and understood Talmudic law.

HaRambam, Rabbi Moshe Ben Maimon, also known as Maimonides (1138–1204) was born in Cordova, Spain and died in Egypt. He was heir to the most authentic Sephardic tradition and devoted his entire life and creative literary and intellectual output to preserve that tradition. His seminal work, the *Mishneh Torah*, is a legal code based on his understanding of the Talmud and covers every aspect of Torah law, including all the laws that have no practical relevance outside of Israel.

In the late 15th century and early 16th century Rabbi Yosef Karo, also from Spain, who later lived and died in Tzefat (Safed), Israel authored the *Shulchan Arukh*. The *Shulchan Arukh* is a code of Jewish law based on the rulings of Maimonides and the rulings of the most prominent legalist of the Ashkenaz European communities of the Middle Ages. He had hoped to create a unified Jewish law for both Sephardic and Ashkenaz Jewry. His vision was never realized but his work remains a pillar of Sephardic Law.

Modern day Sephardic *halakhah* is based on how the contemporary Sephardic scholars who dared to preserve the Sephardic heritage applied the teachings, rulings, and worldviews of Maimonides' *Mishneh Torah* and Karo's *Shulchan Arukh* to contemporary halakhic issues. These scholars include the author of the *Kaf Hachaim*, the nineteenth-century Rabbi Yosef Chaim Sofer from Iraq as well as the twentieth-century scholar, Rabbi Benzion Uziel, the first Sephardic Chief Rabbi of Israel and Rabbi Haim David HaLevi, the former chief Rabbi of Tel Aviv who authored important works such as *Mekor Chaim* and *Aseh Lecha Rav*.

The most extensive, creative, and authoritative Sephardic Rabbinic figure of the 20th century was without a doubt Rabbi Ovadia Yosef, former chief Rabbi of Israel, and author of hundreds of books on Sephardic Jewish law such as the *Yalkut Yosef* series, the six-volume *Yechaveh Da'at* set, the *Yabia Omer Responsa* series, *Hazon Ovadia*, and many other works.

The laws and customs found in this book are based on the rulings of the above Rabbinic works as well as personal consultations with rabbis such as Rabbi Eliyahu Ben Haim, Rabbi Mordechai Eliyahu, z"l, and Rabbi Ratzon Arusi, among others.[2]

---

2. For a more detailed discussion on the subject of Sephardic law read my article titled, 'A Study of Two Traditions: Sephardi and Ashkenaz, in Rutledge Jewish Studies,' edited by Oliver Leaman.

Final Thought

I have learned from death and the reality of its existence some fundamental attitudes on how life should be conducted. Learning to cope with the fear of death and being able to talk comfortably about its inevitability makes for a more meaningful existence and an appreciation of every moment of life. The psychiatrist Viktor Frankl put it beautifully: "The meaning of human existence is based on its irreversible quality" (*Man's Search for Meaning*). Living with the awareness that today may be our last day heightens our level of existence and inspires more noble living. It provides urgency for those things that are important and can no longer be put off until sometime in the future. Hillel the elder stated: *Im lo akhshav ematai*, "If not now, when?" Indeed, a healthy understanding and awareness of our own mortality is not a sign of giving up but rather the seal of courage and wisdom. It is the mark of one who lives life fully, nobly, generously, creatively, and cherishes every moment. While there is a limit to how long we will ultimately live, it is we alone who determine the depth and the quality of our lives. Joshua Liebman writes: "We must make up for the brevity of life by heightening the intensity of life" (*Peace of Mind*, p. 93). So often I am called upon to comfort mourners whose loved one died completely unexpectedly. "Just yesterday he was fine," are the words I hear. Recall what our sages advise us: "A man cannot say to the Angel of Death: 'I wish to arrange my affairs before I die'" (Devarim Rabbah 9:3). Imagine living every moment of our lives with the consciousness of the psalmist: "Teach us to number our days that we obtain a heart of wisdom" (Tehillim 118:17).

In Jewish thought, one can choose life over death. "I shall not die, for I will live," are the words of King David. The righteous, the Talmud teaches, are alive even after their physical death (TB *Berakhot* 18a–18b). And, just as there is life after death, there is also death even while alive – the walking dead, those whose lives lack a dynamic, life-affirming energy. Taking even one breath for granted is to strip existence of meaning!

Learning to live within the framework that life is only temporary is not a depressing idea but a truly enriching experience. Awareness of our own mortality heightens our sensitivities. We learn to deepen our relationship with the familiar and more fully appreciate the new. The things we see we really *apprehend*, and we really hear the things we listen to. Recognizing the fact that we will not always be together brings us closer to our family and friends. We resolve to mend broken relationships and forget petty differences. One learns to forgive not only those who have hurt us, but also, cliché as this may sound, one learns to forgive oneself.

When our focus is on living, meaningful living becomes a priority. Uncovering a sense of life's patterns, coherence, and purpose becomes a part of our consciousness. We realize that "today is indeed the first day of the rest of my life." *Lo amut ki ehyeh va'asaper ma'aseh Yah*, "I shall not die, rather I shall live and relate the wonders of God," becomes one's motto.

Judaism provides us with a complete and perfect religious response to death. It provides us with a means of accepting loss, of mourning and grieving, and of living fully again. In this book I hope to provide mourners with a concise and clear guide to the laws, rituals, and customs of mourning in the Sephardic tradition. Along the way I pray that this book will also educate our communities on the *mitzvah* of *nichum avelim, comforting the mourners,* and help to create an environment where people will develop a renewed respect for life, love, caring, and compassion.

I divided this short book into four sections:

1. The Jewish response to the onset of death and dying
2. The period after death prior to burial
3. The laws and customs associated with *shivah* and *sheloshim* as well as the responsibility of the community to comfort the mourners
4. How we as Jews remember our loved ones

I have tried to make this book readable and accessible. I hope I have succeeded.

It is my heartfelt prayer that one day we will merit to see the fulfillment of Isaiah's prophecy:

Bila hamavet lanetzah u-machah Hashem dima me'al kol panim;
Ve-cherpat amo yasir me'al kol ha-aretz.

May death be swallowed up forever, and may the Lord God wipe away tears from every face and remove the mocking of God's people from throughout the world (Isaiah 25:8).

CHAPTER 1

Viduy: Gateway to Healing

Shema Yisrael, Adonai Elohenu Adonai Echad
Hear O Israel, the Lord is our God, the Lord is One
　　　　　　　　　　　　　　　　– Deuteronomy 6:4

Thus says the Lord: Let not the wise man glory in his wisdom, neither let the mighty man glory in his might, let not the rich man glory in his riches; but let him that glories glory in this, that he understands and knows Me, that I am the Lord who exercises loving-kindness, judgment, and righteousness on earth; for in these things I delight, says the Lord.
　　　　　　　　　　　　　　　　– Jeremiah 9:22–23

Introduction to *Viduy*

Being present while a loved one is in the throes of death can be devastating. It is important to remember that the process of mourning begins only after death. Jewish law forbids funeral preparations while the terminally ill is still alive (*Shulchan Arukh* YD 339:1). While we know that we are all mortal, at moments like these one prays that death will come later rather than sooner, and that until that time both the living and the dying will be spared further pain and suffering. Jewish law insists that one remain full of hope and not submit to despair. The Jewish response to terminal illness is proactive. In addition to seeking out the best medical advice, as the Torah insists, *verapo yirapei*, "and [the sick] shall surely be healed" (Shemot 21:19). Judaism's response to terminal illness has always included both prayer and *teshuvah*, repentance.

Death is often a stage in the continuum of illness, and even when one knows that their loved one has a terminal illness and will not recover, it is appropriate to recite prayers for healing.

The Talmud records the story of King Chizkiah who fell ill and was told by the prophet Isaiah that his illness was terminal. The king turned to the prophet and said: "I received a tradition from my ancestor King David that even when a sharp sword rests upon your neck, do not refrain from pleading with God for mercy." The king then turned to the wall and began to pray. He lived another fifteen glorious years (TB *Berakhot* 10a).

At the center of Jewish practice is faith, *emouna* in Hashem, creator of heaven and earth. *Emouna* dictates that God is good and even when one perceives the world around us as dark and bleak one must dig deep into the recesses of one's being and have *emouna* in God's goodness and God's providence. In addition to *emouna* there is also trust, *bitachon* in God. *bitachon* is more of a spiritual practice than it is a belief. *Bitachon* is a state of calm and equanimity knowing that the universe is in good hands.

King David, in what appears to be a moment of profound despair writes: "I lift up my eyes to the mountains, from where will my help come?" He then immediately responds with "My help is from God, maker of heaven and earth" (Tehillim 121).

Bitachon is the hallmark of the optimist.

Mi Sheberakh Tefillah

The traditional Jewish prayer for healing is called *Mi Sheberakh* which means He who blessed. The *Mi Sheberakh* can be recited in any language. It is traditionally recited in Hebrew.

Mi Sheberakh in English:

> FOR MEN:
>
> He who blessed our forefathers, the pure ones and righteous ones Abraham, Isaac and Jacob, may He bless and heal all who are sick and among them remember and heal (Hebrew name) son of (mother's Hebrew name).
>
> And may the Lord God heal him with a *Refuah Shelemah*, a complete recovery in his entire body and soul: Please God heal him, Please God heal him.
>
> *Ana Adonai hoshi'a na* (twice) We beseech You Adonai deliver us
>
> *Ana Adonai hatzlich'a na* (twice) We beseech You Adonai make us successful.
>
> FOR WOMEN
>
> He who blessed our matriarchs, the pure ones and righteous ones Sara, Rivka, Rachel, and Leah, may He bless and heal all who are sick and among them remember and heal (Hebrew name) daughter of (mother's Hebrew name).
>
> And may the Lord God heal her with a *Refuah Shelemah*, a complete recovery in her entire body and soul: Please God heal her, Please God heal her.
>
> *Ana Adonai hoshi'a na* (twice) We beseech You Adonai deliver us
>
> *Ana Adonai hatzlich'a na* (twice) We beseech You Adonai make us successful.

The recitation of Psalms 23, 119, 121, and 150 is appropriate and can be found in the Appendix of this book.

Our liturgy also provides us with a formal response to terminal illness called *Viduy*. The word *Viduy* means "confession," and it is through the formal text of this response that the process of *teshuvah* (self-reflection) and *tefillah* (prayer) is achieved. In fact, this process is not exclusively associated with death, it is as relevant, if not more so, in life. The Talmud relates the lesson Rabbi Eliezer taught his students:

> "Repent one day before your death." His students asked him, "How are we supposed to know when we will die?" "All the more reason to repent today," replied the teacher, "lest you die tomorrow; and if you repent today, your entire life will be spent in repentance" (TB *Shabbat* 153a).

The primary purpose of *Viduy* is to help one find a sense of peace and equanimity to complete any unfinished business, especially if death is imminent. *Viduy* is an important part of death and dying, and should be facilitated by an experienced rabbi or member of the *chevra kadisha* burial society.

In the strict halakhic sense, *Viduy* is a confessional that is recited immediately prior to death. Rabbi Yosef Karo therefore instructs that it should be presented in a gentle and cautious manner "lest the dying person be distressed by the suggestion of his or her imminent death." Rabbi Yosef Karo further recommends that prior to the recitation of the *Viduy* the terminally ill person should find comfort in the following words:

> Many have confessed but have not died; and many who have not confessed died. And many who are walking outside in the marketplace confess. By the merit of your confession, you shall live. And all who confess have a place in the world-to-come (SA YD 338:1).

The hope is to soften the potential emotional shock and alleviate some of the fear of death.

Rabbi Yosef Karo, in the context of codifying these laws, suggests that the facilitator of the *Viduy* is responsible to create a solemn and sacred space so that the words have their full impact. Both the facilitator and the terminally ill need to be fully engaged in the process and nature of this prayer (SA YD 338:1).

Recitation of *Viduy*

Since the actual text of the *Viduy* is a reflection on the life one has led, the words should be recited not only in the Hebrew but also in a language that the terminally ill can understand. Tragically, if it is already too late and the terminally ill is unconscious or too weak to read the text or even understand what is taking place, the *Viduy* can be recited on the person's behalf by the rabbi or a family member. A suitable text follows. The complete Hebrew version and translation can be found in Appendix II.

A Paraphrase of the *Viduy*

TO BE RECITED WITH A TERMINALLY ILL PERSON

Ruler of the worlds, Master of forgiveness and mercy, may it be Your will, Lord, my God and God of my fathers, that I be remembered for good before Your throne of glory. Look upon my suffering, for there is no unblemished place in my flesh because of Your anger; no peace in my bones because of my sins. And now, God of forgiveness, turn Your kindness toward me, and do not enter into judgment against Your servant. If the time is drawing near for me to die, Your unity will never depart from my mouth, as it is written in Your Torah: "Hear, O Israel, the Lord is our God, the Lord is one." Blessed is the Name of His glorious kingdom for all eternity. I acknowledge before You, Lord my God and God of my fathers and God of the spirits of all flesh, that my recovery is in Your hands and all the events of my life are in Your hands. May it be Your will to heal me completely. And may I be remembered by You, and may my prayers be remembered in front of You like the prayer of Hezekiah when he was ill. But if the time has drawn near for me to die, may my death be an atonement for all the mistakes, sins, and rebellions I have erred, sinned, and rebelled before You, from the day I came into being on this earth until this moment. Grant that my portion be in *Gan Eden*; may I merit the world-to-come, which awaits the righteous. Cause me to know the path of life, satiety of joys with Your countenance, pleasantness in Your right hand forever. Blessed is the One who hears prayer.

We beg You! With the strength of Your right hand's greatness, untie the bundled sins. Accept the prayer of Your nation; strengthen us, purify us, O Awesome one. Please, O Strong One – those who foster Your oneness, guard them like the pupil of the eye. Bless them, purify them, show them pity. May Your righteousness always recompense them. Powerful Holy One, with Your abundant goodness, guide Your congregation. One and only Exalted One, turn to Your nation which proclaims Your holiness. Accept our entreaty and hear our cry, O Knower of mysteries. Blessed is the Name of His glorious kingdom for all eternity.

May the pleasantness of my Lord, our God, be upon us – May He establish our handiwork for us; our handiwork may He establish.

"And it came to pass, in the thirteenth year, on the fifth of the fourth month when I was in the midst of exile, on the river Chebar, the heavens were opened, and I saw divine visions" (Ezekiel 1:1). "In the year of the death of King Uzziah, I saw the Lord sitting on a high and exalted throne, and its lower emanations filled the Temple. Fiery angels were standing above Him. Each one had six wings. With two he would cover his face. With two he would cover his feet. And with two he would fly. Each one called to the other and declared: 'Holy, holy, holy is the Lord, of hosts, His glory fills all the earth'" (Isaiah 6:1).

Hear, O Israel, the Lord is our God, the Lord is one.

The Lord is God. The Lord is God.

The Lord reigns, the Lord reigned, the Lord will reign forever and ever.

Moses is true and his Torah is true. I hope for Your salvation, Lord.

> May the soul of Your servant rejoice, for I lift up my soul to You, Lord.
>
> Into Your hand I entrust my spirit. You have redeemed me, Lord, the true God. May the words of my mouth and the thoughts of my heart find favor before You, my rock and my redeemer.

Three Components of *Viduy*

While the recitation of the *Viduy* is formal and its words carefully measured, there is room in this process for a more spontaneous and personal component. The *Viduy* should be a process whose scope is much greater than simply the recitation of the words given above. To be complete, the *Viduy* should include three components.

1: Redemptive Healing

The first involves personal transformation and the recognition that life is not only about physical health but also about spiritual and emotional well-being – *redemptive healing*.

I have been asked time and time again, but never as poignantly as when Aaron asked. Aaron, a young man, was living with a painful and terminal skin cancer. After services one day, exhausted from the chemotherapy and emotionally a wreck, he asked, "Rabbi, what are the prayers and the *Tehillim* (Psalms) for? Do you really think my cancer is going to be cured?" His words lingered for a moment. I embraced him, looked him in the eyes, and responded in as confident a voice as I could produce, "Yes, our prayers have purpose." We pray, and will continue to pray, for a complete physical recovery. Indeed, we cannot fathom the scope of God's wonders. We will never lose hope. Our sages have stated, "Even when a sharp sword is placed right on a person's throat, one should not desist from imploring the Almighty for mercy." Despair is not an option. *Ein ye'ush, I insisted*, we cannot allow ourselves to give up.

Ours is a tradition that has always sought ways to inspire hope and faith even under the most difficult circumstances. Rabbi Marc

Angel, in his classic work *The Rhythms of Jewish Living: A Sephardic Approach*, offers a penetrating insight into the text of the *Viduy*. "The confession," Rabbi Angel writes, "indicates a tenacity to life. Even when it appears obvious that one will die, he first asks God to heal him." "Aaron," I implored: "Never, *never* give up praying for a complete and speedy recovery."

Over the years I have learned that while we must do everything in our power to seek physical health, we must also learn to heal our emotional and spiritual selves. Praying is not simply about asking God to relieve the physical pain or disease from the body; we also pray so that our hearts will open into a realm of love and understanding. Healing is the clarity we seek to grow, transform, and gain wisdom about ourselves and the world around us. This happens when we enter the unexplored territory of the mind and body – the vast indefinable spaciousness of our very being. This process goes beyond life and beyond death. Here begins the process of letting go of those things that block the heart and clog our emotional arteries. Learning to dissolve the dark fog of anger, fear, forgetfulness, and unkindness that surround us at any given moment is a magnificent gift. Through prayer we learn to open the channels of love and compassion for ourselves and those around us. Our prayers are not complete if they do not include the element of redemptive *refuah* (healing).

11: Introspection

The second component of the *Viduy* includes a close introspection regarding the life we have led vis-a-vis God. In my experience with the terminally ill, I have yet to meet an individual who does not welcome the opportunity to make peace with God. Take Harriette, for example. I knew her for two years before she passed away. She was a woman who never made time for religion and seldom considered God in her day-to-day life. Her life was dominated by her concerns for her family and her business. When death was imminent and I introduced God into her consciousness, she was completely receptive. She was not, as some people suspected, cynical or derogatory. Prayer became a priority, as did the study of Torah and an embrace of some of Judaism's more revered rituals. The last words she uttered in this world we said together; they were the words of the *Shema*, which she recited in a state of peacefulness.

III: Interpersonal *Teshuvah*

Finally, for the *Viduy* to be complete, it must include an introspective regarding the life one has led vis-a-vis other people. There cannot be true *teshuvah*, a real transformation, if one does not attempt to make peace with those whom he or she have had personal contact during one's lifetime.

The terminally ill may at times feel hopeless; however, they are far from helpless. Death does not have to be accepted passively. This is the time to heal the soul and the spirit through personal relationships. Indeed, this is the time to let go of past anger, fears, and disputes, and focus all energies on mending relationships and correcting wrongs. *Viduy* is not complete if it does not include the component that brings healing and peace in one's personal life.

The terminally ill should be encouraged to resolve personal issues and conflicts with those in their lives. Illness and the nearness of death have already altered their perspective and the opportunity is ripe for resolution, even in the most extreme of circumstances. This scene has been repeated throughout my career countless times. The doctors have given the terminally ill patient three to six months to live. That is when I say, "Let's get to work." We identify the people who need to be reached. To some of them it is "thank you" to others it is "I am sorry" and to others it is simply "I love you." The experience can be transformative and profoundly healing.

Oftentimes the resistance comes from the alienated family member. This is tragic. Studies have shown that unfinished business with the deceased does not get buried with them. If it does not surface shortly after their relative's death, it most certainly surfaces later in their own life. The pain begins when feelings of guilt, – "I should have" and "If only" – creep into the psyche, haunting and tormenting the estranged mourner for years and years. No one wants to live with that burden, and now is the opportunity to lighten the weight, to let go of the ugly past and heal the present.

Death is the opportunity for parents and children, siblings, spouses, and extended family members to come together and put an unpleasant past behind them. The same rules of day-to-day life do not apply when a family is confronted with death. Death trumps all. Letting go is the process by which we lighten our burden of anger and heal the pain of relationships that have been neglected or estranged. As a rabbi, I have witnessed the awful pain involved when people go to their grave without having resolved issues with family and friends. There comes a time when one must say "What was, was, and now it is over."

Being Proactive When Faced with Terminal Illness

Dying can be about living. One does not need to mourn the onset of death. Instead, the time and opportunity should be used to deepen and enrich one's life and the life of the person who is living with a terminal disease. As Jews, we never give up hope – we continue to pray until the last breath for a complete healing. Yet a cure is not necessarily all there is. Perhaps the journey is more important than the goal. The faith, the prayer, and the rise of the human spirit are ultimately the purpose of human existence. The last months, weeks, days, or even moments with a loved one can be the beginning of a search for harmony, meaning, and spiritual altitude. Below are some suggestions to help facilitate life in the face of death.

Saying Goodbye

Some people who are approaching the end of their life, like to tell the story of their lives. They like to share who they were and what they did with their lives. Encourage the terminally ill to talk about their life story by asking them questions:

- Describe your childhood.
- How did your parents influence your life?

- What was your greatest accomplishment?
- What was your greatest failure?
- How would you rate yourself in life?

Help the dying person identify practical tasks that should be done.

- Drawing up a will.
- Delegating power of attorney to a spouse or child who can make decisions regarding medical treatment.
- Evaluating a medical directive or a "living will."
- Checking insurance coverage and reviewing financial status.

Use this time to deepen and enrich relationships. Give the dying person the opportunity to share some personal thoughts with different members of the family and close personal friends.

- Have each member of the family go in to see the dying person alone.
- Hold the hand of the dying person.
- Tell the dying person what meaning he or she has given to your life.

In a lifetime we are bound to make mistakes, especially in one's interpersonal relationships. Occasionally we lie, cheat, or hurt another person's feelings. That person may be a parent, sibling, co-worker, or friend. This is the time to reach out and ask for forgiveness.

- Ask the dying person if you can help contact anyone he or she would like to reach out to.
- Is there any unfinished business that has to be resolved?
- Has anyone been hurt as a result of the dying person's actions?

Ethical Will

Illness, and especially terminal illness, causes us to confront our deepest recesses of faith and feelings. It is in this place of inner serenity that one finds clarity and perspective on life and living. The most beautiful moments I have shared with the terminally ill have been the times they tap into that clarity and share something meaningful with me, or with their family or their friends. Moving beyond the illness and transcending the body to share a quality moment with someone special is to give an incredible gift. As the English poet Thomas Campbell wrote, "To live in hearts we leave behind / Is not to die."

The Torah records that when our forefather Jacob felt he was close to death, he called all his children and grandchildren so that he could bless them with the words: "The angel that redeemed me from all evil bless these children; may they carry my name and the name of my parents Abraham and Isaac; and may they grow into a multitude on earth" (Bereshit 48:16–17).

Parents and grandparents are encouraged to express their hopes and desires for the future of their children and grandchildren. They can articulate the values they cherished and the wisdom of their lives. Most importantly, this opportunity should be used to express words of love and admiration for one's children and grandchildren. If this cannot be done in person, an effort should be made to put one's thoughts into writing.

The healing potential through this process can be incredibly profound and dramatic. It is a healing that prepares one for death. This kind of personal preparation and acceptance of the inevitability of death makes the dying process that much more peaceful.

This entire process must be seen as an affirmation of life. No aspect of life in this world is to be taken for granted, not one's enjoyments, health or relationships formed. The *Viduy* process forces not only the terminally ill, but also their survivors, to give meaning to the death process. Death is not something one should fear; rather one should learn to embrace and use it as a means of bringing meaning to life.

CHAPTER 2

Creating a Caring Community

Olam Chesed Yibaneh
Kindness creates worlds
— Psalm 89:3

Acts of kindness are greater than charity since they can be done by both the rich and poor... Charity can only be done with one's money, while acts of loving-kindness can be performed both personally and with one's money.
— Rambam (MT *Avel* 14:1)

How to Help Others Through Grief

Nothing can or should replace the role of a caring and supportive community. This is where Judaism stands apart from other religions and makes all the difference in one's personal and communal life. The community is an essential component in one's quest for spirituality and self-actualization. The sages of the Talmud of blessed memory spared no language in extolling acts of love and kindness. The path towards God is paved, according to the sages, with acts of *chesed*, kindness. The verse in Devarim 13:5 says:

> You shall follow the Lord your God, and Him you shall fear; His commandments you shall observe; His voice shall you hearken to; Him shall you serve; and to Him shall you cleave.

Commenting on this verse, Rashi paraphrases the Midrash and writes as follows:

> "His commandments" [refers to] the law of Moses; "His voice" [refers to] the voice of the prophets; "Him you shall serve" [refers to] the Temple; "Unto Him you shall cleave" [means] cleave to His ways by doing acts of love and kindness, bury the dead, visit the sick, comfort the mourner, as does the Holy One, blessed be He.

Two fundamental principles of Judaism overlap when one speaks of *gemilut chasadim*, acts of love and kindness. The principle of *imitatio Dei*, being God-like, and *ve-ahavta la-reikha kamokha*, "love your neighbor as yourself." Both of these Jewish values merge into one, as the sages of blessed memory taught:

> Said Rabbi Hama bar Hanina: "What is the meaning of the verse, After the Lord thy God ye shall walk" (Deuteronomy 13:5)? Is it possible for a man to walk after the *Shekhinah* [Divine Presence]? Has it not been said: "The Lord thy God is a devouring fire" (Deuteronomy 4:24)? Rather, walk after the attributes of the Lord, blessed be He. He clothes the naked, as it is written: "And the Lord God made for Adam and for his wife garments of skin, and clothed them" (Genesis 3:21). So, you clothe the naked! The Holy One, blessed be He, visited the sick, as it is written: "And the Lord appeared unto Abraham [who was recovering from his circumcision] by the terebinths of Mamre" (Genesis 18:1). So too you visit the sick! The Holy One, blessed be He, comforted mourners, as it is written: "And it came to pass after the death of Abraham that God blessed Isaac his son" (Genesis 25:11); so you comfort the mourners! The Holy One, blessed be He, buried the dead, as it is written: "And He buried [Moses] in the valley" (Deuteronomy 34:6); so you bury the dead! (TB *Sotah* 14a).

How does one achieve true union with God? By being God-like. What does that mean? It simply means to act in ways that reflect compassion and love for other human beings.

In "a caring community" members are no longer individuals, they coalesce with one another, to form a single entity that shares its pains and its joys. The community that is formed connects metaphysically with the larger nation of Israel, past, present, and future. No individual member ever stands alone, especially at a time of sorrow and grief. The members of the community encircle the mourner with their love, warmth, and kindness.

Comforting the mourner, *nichum avelim*, is at the heart of most of the laws and regulations, customs and restrictions that govern *avelut*, Jewish mourning. It is a commandment, a mitzvah, and an opportunity that presents itself over and over. This mitzvah must always be observed, not only when the bereaved is a relative or friend. Read the words of one person who received comfort during his time of need.

> Dear Rabbi Levy,
> Losing my father at such a young age was the most trying and difficult experience I have ever had. I will sorely miss him, his sense of humor, his attention, his kindness. I lost not only a father but a true soul mate. Yet when I think back on the entire experience, I reflect on how fortunate I/we are to be part of a community that cares so very much about its members.
> My mother, my sister, and I would never have survived this trauma had it not been for the support, comfort, and care that was given to us. The food, the visits, the calls, and the cards nourished us and gave us the strength to pick up the pieces and get on with life. Thank you.

I have heard the above sentiment expressed repeatedly by bereaved persons who experienced their loss in the context of an educated and caring community. When the natural tendency of the mourner is to withdraw into loneliness, Jewish law, at precisely this time, calls upon the community to intervene.

Maimonides, also known as HaRambam, one of Judaism's great scholars, a philosopher, and a medical practitioner (1138–1204), writes that the mitzvah of *nichum avelim* takes precedence over other *mitzvot* of *gemilut chasadim*, acts of love and kindness because comforting the mourner is an act of kindness shown not only to the living but also to the dead.

One consequence of the denial of death that is prevalent in our society is that we are often ignorant and unskilled in coping with loss, be it our own or another's. Most people, including those closest to the mourners, do not know what to say when making a condolence visit.

Guide to Making a Condolence Visit

The presence of others can help renew the mourner's strength. Studies have shown that proximity to death and the intimate awareness of the inevitability of one's mortality generates a state of anxiety and feelings of uncertainty. Jewish law insists that the mourner not be left alone and be guided by the community through the mourning process with clear and precise rituals for both the mourner and the comforters.

The house of mourning is open so that the public can come and extend condolences. Traditionally the door is left ajar so that no one needs to respond to a knock or doorbell. Jewish law states that a mourner does not rise to greet anyone, not even a Torah scholar. Similarly, the comforter does not greet the mourner upon entering the house of mourning. Rather he or she finds a seat in front of the mourner (SA YD 385:2). One should not feel pressure to speak. In fact, words, at a time like this are superfluous. Being mindful of where one is and being physically present is far more meaningful than anything that could be said. The companionship of family and friends is the greatest source of support and solace a mourner can receive. Sitting nearby, holding a hand, crying together, listening, and sharing of feelings is the most effective way of comforting a mourner. The bereaved need to have their sorrow acknowledged while recognizing that at this time the pain cannot be erased.

The Talmudic sages recommend that one should not begin the conversation with the mourner. Rather, they should allow the "mourner to speak what is in his or her heart" (TB *Moed Katan* 28b; also, SA YD 376:1). Jewish law further suggests that if the mourner is indeed speechless, one may initiate conversation about the deceased (SA YD 376:1) – no other subject matters. The mourner is weeping, if not externally, then internally. One should find a way to help the mourner express the feelings that are on his or her heart and mind. Assist the mourner by showing genuine concern. Initiating a conversation with the mourner about anything other than the loss at hand may send the message that the mourner's pain is not important, or worse, that you do not know how to care. Being a caring presence and a good listener is more important than any words one might say. Above all, the bereaved need loving people to stand by them during their grief. Not having to suffer alone is the greatest gift one can offer the bereaved. The Jewish laws of *nichum avelim* are designed to prevent the mourner from feeling alone at his or her time of despair and emptiness.

Do not be afraid to ask questions, such as:

- "Could you tell me about the deceased?"
- "What happened?"
- "How did you find out?"
- "What was your relationship like?"
- Or you can simply say, "I'm sorry for your loss."

Grief is a process and the mourner's needs may vary at different times during the course of their grieving. Initially, upon hearing about the death of a loved one, what are ordinarily simple tasks can be extremely difficult for a mourner to handle. Making decisions, answering phone calls, preparing the funeral service, buying groceries, or cleaning dishes – are all necessary tasks that usually go beyond the capability of those who are experiencing the initial shock of the news that a loved one has died. Immediately following the burial, the mourner may still be in shock, and practical help is what is still needed. Organizing services for *shivah* and making sure the mourners have meals prepared is essential.

It is most important to be sensitive about how long one remains when visiting a mourner. Not knowing what to do, visitors sometimes stay too long, or engage in socializing with others in a lighthearted fashion. A house of mourning is not the place to catch up with old acquaintances; one is there to be helpful to the mourner, and if one ceases to be helpful it is time to leave.

When it is not possible to visit the mourners during *shivah*, notes of condolence or a phone call are a way of fulfilling the mitzvah of *nichum avelim*.

Practical Things That Are Helpful to the Bereaved

1. Organize the preparation of meals for the mourners for the entire week of *shivah*.
2. Make sure the mourners have everything they need for Shabbat.
3. Provide childcare for the children of the mourners.
4. Undertake to do grocery shopping for the family in mourning.
5. Ask how you can be helpful.
6. Make sure there will be a *minyan* for services.

When Are Condolence Visits Appropriate?

It is customary and appropriate to extend a condolence visit immediately after burial. While a condolence visit is especially appropriate during the *shivah*, it is also important to look after the well-being of the mourners even after the *shivah* but within thirty days of the death.

Sephardic authorities permit condolence visits on Shabbat and holy days even though there is no public mourning on these days (*Mekor Chaim*, vol. 5 285:33).

Leaving the House of Mourning

Upon leaving the house of mourning, one does not extend the usual farewell to the mourner. Instead, one leaves the presence of the mourner by saying the following words:

> מִן הַשָּׁמַיִם תְּנֻחֲמוּ
>
> May you find comfort from Heaven
>
> The following words are also appropriate:
>
> הַמָּקוֹם יְנַחֵם אֶתְכֶם בְּתוֹךְ אֲבֵלֵי צִיּוֹן וִירוּשָׁלַיִם
>
> May the Lord comfort you among the mourners of Zion and Jerusalem.

When leaving the presence of the mourner, one is not called upon to offer advice or even words of encouragement. Rather the community uniformly uses the formal and prescribed words of comfort. One does not speak as an individual. As individuals we have nothing to say. The wound is too deep, the pain too much to bear. Rather the individual retreats, is humbled, and invokes comfort from heaven.[1]

Confronting Intense Mourning

It is very painful to witness intense mourning. It is tempting to encourage mourners to stop crying, to deny their pain, or to rush them through the painful process of mourning. Accepting another's tears without interfering is a wonderful gift. So is listening without judging. Sometimes this means listening to the same thing over and over again. Saying things like "don't cry" is a cruel injunction for a bereaved person who has few options for expressing their intense feelings. The period of *shivah*, as well as the first thirty days of mourning called *sheloshim*, and the year of mourning are the appropriate times to

---

1. Joel B. Wolowelsky, "A Midrash on Jewish Mourning," *Judaism* 23, no. 2 (Spring 1974).

face the aspects of death and dying that will help the bereaved come to terms with their loss. Therefore, it is important to acknowledge the mourner's loss and the scope of its significance to the mourner. Mourners appreciate the sharing of memories and adding another's anecdotes to their expanding wealth of recollections. If you do not have a story or memory of the deceased, ask the mourner to share one with you.

A careful study of the laws associated with *nichum avelim* informs the student of the extent to which Jewish law understands the physical and psychological toll that loss inflicts on the bereaved. Jewish law expects that anyone in close proximity of death be proactive and fulfill the mitzvah of *nichum avelim*. Even simple acts of kindness and consideration may be of immeasurable value.

Points to Remember When Comforting Mourners

Nichum avelim, comforting mourners, is more than simply a courtesy visit. It is first and foremost a mitzvah that is subsumed under Judaism's core value: Love your neighbor as yourself, *ve-ahavta la-reiacha kamocha*. This is an opportunity to afford the mourner sensitivity and empathy. Everyone is asked to do their part in healing a broken heart.

The following are suggestions for making your visit to a house of mourning a successful one:

- Let the mourner begin to talk and set the tone of your conversation.
- Listen attentively. Remember it is better to be silent than to be talkative.
- Show concern for the mourner's emotional and physical well-being.
- Your conversation should be empathic and not distracting. It is not your job to get the mourner's mind off the loss. If there is going to be small talk, allow the mourner to take the lead.
- Levity may bring you relief, but it is inappropriate for the mourner. Anecdotes about the deceased that are humorous and said with respect are appropriate.

- Do not dwell on your own mourning experiences.
- Do not offer free psychological advice.
- Conclude your words of consolation with hope: "May you be comforted from heaven."

CHAPTER 3

Ani Ma'amin
I believe

The righteous shall flourish like a palm tree, they shall grow like the cedars of Lebanon.

– Tehillim 92:12

A Belief System

A strong belief system is an important means of self-support. Whether or not our beliefs sustain us through a crisis is a personal matter. A well-formulated belief system does not necessarily cancel the urgency of tragedy, even for seriously religious people, and even if the belief ought to resolve certain issues, it does not always impress itself upon us with full vividness. Our perspective on life and our outlook on destiny very much affect how well we cope with loss and pain. There is not a bereavement that I share with the members of my congregation and friends where I am not asked about what Judaism has to say regarding the afterlife and the immortality of the soul. In our attempt to lessen the pain, we seek answers to these questions in the hope that the loss can be given meaning. While we can generally cope with life without giving much thought to death, there is no denying its reality when confronted with the loss of a loved one. At such a time, death requires a spiritual context; otherwise, the pain can become unbearable, and, worst of all, meaningless. I am not suggesting that a belief system will make the pain go away, because it will not. I am also not suggesting that a belief system will shorten the duration of the grief; it will not. The pain is real and must heal naturally. Yet, understanding what our tradition teaches regarding the body and soul, life and death, is not only important knowledge for every thinking Jew, but it also affords the bereaved a context that will be an essential support through personal loss.

Body and Soul: Life and the Afterlife

The Torah, the earliest Jewish text and certainly the most significant, says nothing at all explicitly about life after death or the nature of the soul. It seems that the Torah is exclusively concerned with the collective destiny of the Jewish people as a nation and the personal transformation of the individual in the world of the living. In fact, there is no suggestion of the idea of a soul separate from the body.

Beyond the five books of the Torah, one finds conceptions of an afterlife emerging in the books of the prophets and in some of the psalms. Even then, the concern is primarily with the national destiny of the Jewish people, the messianic redemption, and the resurrection of the dead which remains a fundamental principle within Judaism's worldview.

While the Torah does not speak of a world-to-come for the soul, it does speak of death as a return to the company of one's ancestral family.

> And Abraham expired and died in a good old age and satisfied, and he was gathered to his people (Bereshit 25:8; also 49:29–31; Bemidbar 27:13; I Kings 11:43).

Of course, this is not meant to be understood as a place in the afterlife where the family will gather, but rather as an expression meant to be interpreted either euphemistically or literally, as in the family tomb where other family members are buried. This is the extent of the biblical interest in the afterlife.

The Torah's lack of interest in the afterlife is further evidenced by its constant warning against too much contact with the dead. Whenever a member of the priesthood came in contact with the dead, he was automatically disqualified from performing the service in the Temple. Students of the Torah immediately recognize the relationship between communion with the dead and the pagan and idolatrous practices that the Torah condemns. In the book of *Devarim* you find the prohibitions of child sacrifice and communion with the dead alongside witchcraft and necromancy:

> Let no one be found among you who sacrifices his son or daughter in the fire, who practices divination or sorcery, interprets omens, engages in witchcraft, or casts spells, or who is a medium or spiritualist or who consults the dead. (Devarim 18:10–11).

This attitude toward contact with the dead has to do with the fact that Judaism, from the earliest times, differentiated itself from the prevalent ancient Near Eastern practices of necromancy. Jewish monotheism condemns both physical and nonphysical forms of contact with the world of the dead. Judaism does not believe in ghosts, in superstitious practices, or any form of influence the dead may have on our lives. From the biblical standpoint, communion with the dead was not only a form of political and religious abuse but was also regarded as a form of idolatry. The priesthood was kept distant from performing any rituals associated with death and dying in order to prevent the possibility of abuse at a time when people are most vulnerable.

The World-To-Come

How does one understand the Jewish notion of *Olam Haba*, the world-to-come? There is often confusion when we speak of *Olam Haba* because Judaism distinguishes between the individual's personal eschatology and the Jewish people's national eschatology. While the national eschatology is concerned with the fate of the Jewish people as a distinct entity at the "end of days" and the era of the Messiah, individual eschatology focuses on the fate of each individual after death.

It is no surprise that in Judaism the focus has primarily been on the collective rather than the individual. We draw our greatest strength and worth as individuals from the covenantal community of which we are a part. The Jewish people collectively stood at the foot of Mount Sinai. God engaged them as a nation. Therefore, our tradition emphasizes national redemption as opposed to individual redemption. As individuals who share in the national destiny of our people, we do not ask "What will happen to me when I die?" but rather, "What will happen to the nation of Israel in the future time when God transforms the world?"

Some of the sages within the rabbinic tradition do indeed speak of an individual eschatology.

> My law will guide you in your path in this world; it will watch over you in your sleep, at the hour of death; and when you wake, it will converse with you in *Olam Haba* (*Sifrei, Vayikra* 18:4).

Other statements, however, are not as clear, so it is hard to be certain whether they refer to individual or national eschatology. Take, for example, this often-quoted passage from the Mishnah:

> All of Israel has a portion in the world-to-come, as it is said: "Thy people shall be all righteous, they shall inherit the land forever, the branch of My planting, the work of My hands, wherein I glory" (Mishnah, *Sanhedrin* 10:1).

This passage is referring to a world-to-come that is each individual's destiny immediately after death or in the distant future, at the end of time, when the world will herald the messianic era.

Although the dominant stream in the Bible and early Rabbinic Judaism reflects a national eschatology, this does not mean that a belief in individual afterlife does not exist. In fact, Rabbi Saadia Gaon (882–942 Judeo-Arabic Torah scholar who lived in Egypt, Tiberias, and Babylonia) describes at length the nature of the immortality of the soul (*Emunot VeDeot* 6:13 and 9:5). HaRambam affirms the existence of an immortal soul and *Olam Haba*, a world-to-come, throughout his writings. HaRambam distinguishes between what he calls the *neshamah* and what he calls the *nefesh*. The *neshamah* in Rambam's economy of ideas is that which animates the human being. The *neshamah*, writes Maimonides, "needs the physical body" while the *nefesh* is an independent entity that emanates from God and grows with the human being:

> The *nefesh*, however does not expire because it does not need the *neshamah* or its existence. Rather it knows and understands the knowledge, which is distinct from the shapes, and knows God, and remains in existence infinitely. Solomon wisely said, "And the dust returns to the earth as it was, and the *ruach* returns to God who gave it" (MT *Yesodei HaTorah* 4:9).

HaRambam integrates the philosophical ideas of the immortal *nefesh* with the elaborate images described in the Talmud regarding the afterlife.

> *Olam Haba*, the world-to-come, harbors neither body nor form – save only *nefashot* of the righteous divested of body, as are the ministering angels.
> Thus said the sages of old: "In *Olam Haba* there is no eating, no drinking and no intercourse save that the **righteous are sitting, graced with crowns on their heads and enjoy the luminousness of the *Shekhinah*"** (*Berakhot* 17a). It is clear to you that no body exists there, seeing that there is neither eating nor drinking. The expression "sitting" is figurative, as if saying that they are without effort or fatigue. Additionally, the expression employed, "graced with crowns on their heads" means that the knowledge they acquired (conscious knowledge) is the reason why they have earned *Olam Haba*. Their knowledge is their crowns as Solomon said: "The crown with which his mother has crowned him" (Songs 3:11). But what is the meaning of the phrase "Enjoy the luminousness of the *Shekhinah*?" It refers to their knowing and attaining the truth of the Holy One blessed be He! Something they could not know while in the darkness of their lowly body.

The life spoken of here – because there is no death associated with it, being that death is only incidental to the happenings which befall a body, and as there exists no body, it is called *tzeror hachaim*, as it is said: The *nefesh* of my Lord shall be bound in the *tzeror hachaim* (1 Samuel 25:29). And this reward is such that there is no reward higher than it, and a goodness after which no other good exists, and it is this that all the prophets craved.

How King David longed for *Olam Haba*! As it says: "If I had not believed to look upon the goodness of Hashem in the land of the living" (Tehillim 27:13). Our sages of old have already informed us that it is not within the power of man to clearly understand the goodness of *Olam Haba*, one cannot know its grandeur, beauty, and quantity save only the Holy One blessed be He!" (MT *Hilkhot Teshuvah* Chapter 8).

Related to the subject of the afterlife, Maimonides also explains fundamental issues of reward and punishment and the philosophical implications as related to life and death. For Rambam, while the existence of a soul and a life after death is an absolute fact, it remains a subject beyond human comprehension.

As to the blissful taste of the soul in the world-to-come, there is no way on earth in which we can comprehend or know it (MT *Hilkhot Teshuvah* 8:6).

There is an unbridgeable chasm between the world of the spirit and the world of the flesh.

For Maimonides the body and spirit exist in two separate and distinct realms, and the human beings are limited as to the extent that they can truly appreciate the realm of the spirit. This view is expressed in his commentary on the Mishnah of the tenth chapter of *Sanhedrin* as follows:

Just as a blind man cannot perceive colors, nor a deaf man hear sounds, nor a eunuch feel sexual desire, so bodies [of human beings] cannot attain spiritual delights. And just as fish do not know the element of fire because they live in its opposite, so are the pleasures of the spiritual world unknown to this world of flesh.

While human beings can never truly know the world of the spirit, HaRambam envisioned that they could know the delights of the spiritual world after death through the process of intellectual contemplation of God and the infinite mysteries of the world. It is those who have lived properly, HaRambam writes, who enjoy infinite life as a bodiless soul. Immortality of the soul is not an inherent property of the soul but a consequence of a virtuous life.

Rabbi Aryeh Kaplan on Life After Death

One's need for a belief in the immortality of the soul is as great as any other human need. Yet we are suspicious of religious teachings that simply console the troubled soul. We do not want to close our eyes to the harshness and tragedy of life in this world, yet we are not at peace with the idea that God might have created nothing beyond it.

Numerous attempts throughout the ages have been made to describe what life after death is like. Some are scandalous to reason while others are embarrassing to those who believe in a reasonable theology. I include in this chapter one such attempt written by the late Rabbi Aryeh Kaplan, a popular writer and rabbinic figure of the twentieth century. His idea, which is influenced by Maimonides, is discussed in a small booklet called *If You Were God*, published by the Orthodox Union. His presentation is clear and based solely on Jewish sources, and it represents one view on the issue at hand. The following excerpt from his book is relevant to our discussion on the immortality of the soul.

> What happens then when a person dies?
> We know that the body ceases to function. The brain becomes inert, and the physical man is dead. But what happens to the real you – the human personality? What happens to all this

> information – the memories, thought patterns and personality traits?
>
> When a book is burned its contents are no longer available. When a computer is smashed the information within it is also destroyed. Does the same thing happen when one dies?
>
> Is the mind and personality irretrievably lost?
>
> We know that God is omniscient. He knows all and does not forget. God knows every thought and memory that exists within our brains. There is no bit of information that escapes His knowledge.
>
> What then happens when one dies? God does not forget and therefore all of this information continues to exist, at least in God's memory.
>
> We may think of something existing only in memory as being static and effectively dead. But God's memory is not a static thing. The sum total of a human personality may indeed exist in God's memory, but it can still maintain its self-identity and volition, and remain in an active state.
>
> This sum total of the human personality existing in God's memory is what lives on even after one dies.
>
> – Rabbi Aryeh Kaplan[1]

The concept of immortality of the soul may well be outside the realm of human comprehension: "No eye has seen it other than God." However, our limited understanding of both God and man can provide us with some degree of perception into our ultimate future.

To speak of a concept such as God's memory is indeed very difficult. It involves a deep discussion of the entire transcendental sphere. We therefore give it names that have meaning to us, such as *Gan Eden*, paradise, the world-to-come, the world of souls, or the bond of eternal life. However, the Bible speaks of immortality as a return to God Himself:

---

1. Aryeh Kaplan, *If You Were God*. (Mesorah Publishing 2006).

The dust returns to the dust as it were, but the spirit returns to God who gave it (Eccl. 12:7).

Judaism does not see death as an absolute evil. In fact, the sages interpret the words at the beginning of the Torah when God saw what He had created and "Behold it was very good" (Bereshit 1:31) that God was referring to the angel of death (*Bereshit Rabbah* 9:10). The world-to-come is described in rabbinic literature as "A world where everything is good" (TB *Kiddushin* 39b). The elevated status of the *nefesh* in the world beyond death is described by the sages and reiterated by Maimonides as a place where: "The righteous wear their crowns of glory and enjoy the presence of the divine" (TB *Berakhot* 17a; also MT *Hilkhot Teshuvah* 8:2).

Attitude Toward Death

Jewish tradition puts the seal of life on the chapters dealing with death. As a Jew one believes that it is not death that has the last word, but life. The soul is eternal. Jewish tradition teaches that the grave is not the end. The pain of parting is mitigated by faith in divine providence, which permits no life to be destroyed. The thirteenth principle of faith of Maimonides states: "That the King Messiah will come, and that the dead are destined to be revived." When death robs us of our loved ones, we are comforted by our faith that the essence of our beloved lives on, not only in our hearts and in our memories, but with the Creator of life.

I, as a rabbi and as a human being, am constantly aware of the immense role faith plays in my personal and familial life. The effort of remaining conscious is so extreme, and the awareness of the limited amount of time we have in this world is so constant, that the belief in a life after death remains a profound truth of what I know about God. Do I presume to know exactly what lies ahead for us after death? The answer is no. Yet I know that my belief in God and a purposeful existence remains constant.

Samuel Hugo Bergmann, a twentieth-century philosopher, captured this idea on his eightieth birthday in 1963:

[First] I believe in the Holy One, blessed be He, creator of heavens and the universe. Secondly, we know from this that the world is not subject to blindness.... Thirdly, I do not accept the reality or actuality of death. Our lives are possessed of significance entirely different from that which we usually ascribe to them.... I am saying here that people will live after death and will have to account for themselves.... Everything we do here on earth has an eternal, cosmic meaning.[2]

Personal Growth

Isaiah the prophet, while chastising the people of Israel, makes a remarkable statement: "I have purged you, but nothing came of it, tested you in the furnace but all in vain" (Yeshayahu 48:10). The prophet rebukes the people for learning nothing from the experience of being put through the furnace of affliction. The tragedy, according to Isaiah, is not the pain that was endured; rather, the tragedy is that the suffering was wasted, not leaving the people wiser or better. The prophet of Israel expects one to not only accept pain but use it for personal and spiritual growth. One must use adversity to learn and grow wiser in understanding.

The poet Robert Browning Hamilton expressed this thought in his poem "Along the Road" he wrote:

> I walked a mile with pleasure,
> She chattered all the way,
> But left me none the wiser for all she had to say.
> I walked a mile with Sorrow,
> And ne'er a word said she;
> But, oh, the things I learned from her
> When Sorrow walked with me!

In our hour of sorrow and bereavement, our loss can teach us to live life to its fullest. All life is brief, yet we determine its quality. Because of

---

2. Eli Shai, "Samuel Hugo Bergman: A Partial Portrait." *Ariel* 57 (1984).

its brevity, we must be very discriminating as to how we live it. Rabbi Soloveitchik, of blessed memory, argued that instead of engaging in a futile search for explanations and reasons for evil, we should respond to suffering as a challenge and convert it into a source of some good that otherwise would never have been obtained. He suggests that the entire grief experience is not only a "catharsis of sorrow, but also an experience of self-judgment and penitence".[3] He depicts two areas of penitence. The first is *teshuvah* vis-à-vis our fellow human beings, and the second, *teshuvah* vis-à-vis God.

Man, in Rabbi Soloveitchik's assessment, appreciates and values people and things in hindsight.

In retrospect, man discovers the precise value of someone who is no longer with him or her. This delayed understanding and appreciation is painfully tragic. While the departed was near and could communicate, one is only partially perceptive of their identity. One's awareness of their special qualities, as someone vital and precious to us, comes at the very instant they depart and withdraw into a mist of remoteness. Only then do we inquire with painful longing, "Who was he who brightened my days? What did he mean to me? Why do I feel so bereft and disoriented?"

Rabbi Soloveitchik continues by illustrating why it is that the *avelut* experience is so complicated. We realize how fragmentary our relationship with the deceased was. "Such ex post facto judgments are the saddest of life's experiences. Even those closest to us are elusive."

The mourner bemoans opportunities lost forever and is inspired to intensify and renew relationships with those closest to him.

Vis-à-Vis God

Avelut (mourning) is intrinsically an expression of *teshuvah* (penitence). "The aching heart" writes Rabbi Soloveitchik, "is a contrite heart and a contrite heart seeks atonement." *Shivah* and its restrictions

---

3. "Sitting Shivah is Doing Teshuvah" in *Reflection of the Rav*, edited by Abraham Besdin, vol. 2.

are reminiscent of Yom Kippur, a day when Jews seek forgiveness and renew their relationship with God.

Teshuvah, the act of yearning for God, is similar to the mourners yearning for the departed. "For the penitent," writes Rabbi Soloveitchik, "also mourns the loss of a precious comradeship, the departure of divine closeness." The relationship between God and the mourner, however, unlike the lost relationship between the mourner and the deceased, will be reconciled and renewed. The Torah assures us: "If you search for the Lord your God, you will find Him, as long as you seek Him with all your heart and soul" (Devarim 4:20).

A Final Thought

The meaning one ascribes to life and death is often the key to how well one restructures one's life after a loss. God, God-consciousness, and a spiritual practice affords life meaning. We are placed into this world for a short time. Our destiny is to serve. To succumb we must first conquer; in order to give we must first acquire. To believe one must first understand and to accept one must first know. Perfection is achieved when one can dispense. This may be the meaning of death – the ultimate self-sacrifice to the divine. Death is not a craving for immortality as much as it is reciprocity for God's gift of life.

That the mourner can grieve and recover from a deeply felt loss is indeed an amazing feat, yet human resilience is amazing. Just as a perennial garden that in the fall and winter looks desolate and run-down eventually springs back anew, we too can overcome grief, recover, and restore our lives.

CHAPTER 4

Kavod Hamet

Bila HaMavet LaNetzach
Death will disappear forever

– Isaiah 25:8

Pain is hard to bear....
But with patience, day by day even this shall pass away

– Theodore Tilton

Aninut

No matter how expected the death of a loved one may be, the surviving relatives are always thrown into a state of shock and confusion. The deep sense of loss mixed with feelings of remorse and frustration make for a confusing and debilitating state of mind. Jewish tradition has always understood the value of confronting and accepting the reality of death. Our religious and theological consciousness has always been oriented toward, and rooted in, life-affirming beliefs and actions. Denial of the loss is the antithesis of the religious mourning experience. By facing the issue of death and permitting oneself a complete expression of the emotions associated with loss, there comes healing and resolve.

The rules and practices of mourning begin when the body of the deceased is buried. Until that time, everything associated with the death of a loved one is in a state of disruption – this period between death and burial is called *aninut*. All immediate relatives of the deceased are in a state of *aninut*. The practices associated with *aninut* afford the mourner the ritual structure necessary to deal with the initial emotional state immediately following the death of a loved one.

A person who has lost an immediate relative, such as a father, mother, spouse, son, daughter, sister, brother, half-sister, or half-brother is referred to in Jewish law as an *onen, one who is in the state of aninut* (TB *Moed Katan* 14b; see also MT *Hilkhot Avel* 2:1 and SA YD 374:6). The term *onen* literally means grief-stricken or oppressed. A mourner is an *onen*, or in the state of *aninut*, until the burial of the deceased. Until that time all energies are focused on preparing the final arrangements and funeral service to ensure *kavod hamet*, preserving the honor and dignity of the deceased. The *hakhamim*, sages, were very much aware of the emotional and psychological distress of the bereaved experience. They likened the loss of a loved one to carrying a heavy burden all by oneself. Therefore, Jewish law makes no positive religious demands on one who is an *onen*.

> One whose dead [relative] lies before him is exempt from the recital of the *Shema*, and from prayer, and from putting on *tefillin* and from all precepts laid down in the Torah (TB *Moed Katan* 23b).

Instead, Jewish law expects individuals in a state of *aninut* to occupy themselves solely with arrangements for the funeral so that the heartbreak of the loss of life can be acknowledged and the dignity of the deceased can be appropriately observed. Regarding the *onen*'s exemption from all positive *mitzvot* our sages tell us that there is no virtue in performing commandments that one is exempt from performing at a time of death:

> It has been taught that if he wants to be stringent upon himself and observe *mitzvot* as an *onen* we do not allow him. Why?

Because of *kavod hamet*, honor of the deceased (TY *Berakhot* 3:1; also Tur SA YD 41).

As the above Talmudic passage suggests, the reason the law exempts the mourner from the performance of *mitzvot* goes beyond the practical issue of having enough time to accomplish everything that has to get done before the funeral. Rabbinic law understands the profound psychological trauma of death. Rabbi Soloveitchik describes the ordeal as follows:

> *Aninut* represents the spontaneous human reaction to death. It is an outcry, a howl of horror. One responds to his / her defeat at the hands of death with total resignation and black despair, beaten by the fiend, his / her prayers rejected, forsaken and lonely, one begins to question his / her singular worth (Reflections on Death).

Preparation of the deceased for burial is a great *mitzvah*. It is an act filled with religious meaning and significance. Jewish law mandates that the deceased be handled with great care, honor, and dignity. At a time like this, it becomes irrelevant whether the deceased was a religious person or whether or not the mourners are traditionally observant people.[1] As a people we have a three-thousand-year-old tradition of handling the deceased in a dignified and honorable fashion. It is the way in which our parents buried their loved ones and the generations before them buried their loved ones. We are the next link in following the traditions that have been handed down to us from previous generations.

From the moment of death until the burial of the deceased there is one central and overriding principle that governs the mourner's every action. In Hebrew this principle is called *kavod hamet*, which means providing the deceased with appropriate respect and honor. A human corpse, according to Jewish tradition, is more than just a lifeless

---

1. For a list or rare exceptions see SA YD 345

physical body which can be treated casually. Rather, a lifeless human body is compared to a *Sefer Torah* (Torah scroll) which has become unusable. Because the Torah scroll was once an item used for religious and holy purposes, and still contains holy scripture, it must be treated with respect and reverently buried. So, too, the human being, whose essence in this world was for religious and holy purposes, whose life is imbued with holy sparks, and whose image, the image of God, no less, is an intrinsic part of his or her being, deserves reverent treatment even as a lifeless body (TB *Shabbat* 105b).

Today, because most deaths occur in hospitals or in nursing homes, and the caregivers or their staff notify the families, it is important to know that anything done to the *corpse* requires consent from the next of kin or custodian of the body. It is one's obligation to always exercise this right.

When Death Occurs

Sephardic Jews who follow the rulings of HaRambam and the *Shulchan Arukh* rend their garment and fulfill the mitzvah of *keriah* tearing or rending a piece of garment if they are present at the time the soul expires from the physical body (MT *Avel* 9:11 and SA YD 340:5). Immediately prior to the tearing of the garment, the blessing *Dayan Ha'Emet* is recited (see Appendix II, p. 9). Later codifiers of Jewish law such as Hakham Ovadia Yosef, z"l, one of the former chief rabbis of Israel and foremost Halakhist of the twentieth century, expressed concern that people would not remain with the dying because they would have to rend their clothes. He therefore waived the requirement to rend one's clothing at the time of death so that people would continue to stay at the side of the dying even while death occurs (*Yabia Omer* 4:38).

One should insist that the deceased not be left alone even for a short time unless the body is being preserved in a hospital. As an act of *kavod hamet* the eyes and mouth of the deceased should be shut, the face covered and if possible, the body should be positioned in such a way that the feet are facing the doorway (MT *Avel* 4:1).

In the presence of the deceased, it is forbidden to pray, wear *tefillin*, or study Torah (MT *Avel* 4:6). The recitation of psalms is permitted while in the presence of the deceased (*Yabia Omer*, vol. 6, pp. 103–104). It is not appropriate to eat or drink, smoke, or exchange greetings while in the presence of the deceased. In a large room one must distance oneself at least six and a half feet from the deceased to do any of the above.

On Shabbat and Holy Days

If death occurs on Shabbat or on a Jewish holy day, only a minimum of arrangements may be made, specifically, those that are limited to the immediate needs and honor of the deceased.

- On Shabbat and holy days, one does not rend one's clothing nor should any desecration of the Shabbat and holy day take place (SA YD 340:1).
- On *Chol HaMoed*, the intermediate days of Pesach and Sukkot, one may observe *keriah*, tear one's garment (*Yalkut Yosef*, vol. 7 4:17).
- On Shabbat and holy days, the body of the deceased should not be moved, and certainly not transported.
- The body should be covered, and someone should remain with it until the conclusion of the Shabbat or holy day.

Immediately following the Shabbat or holy day the *chevra kadisha*, burial society, is informed, and they make the necessary arrangements. If the hospital or nursing home does not allow the body to remain on its premises until the end of Shabbat or the end of the holy day, a non-Jew should be asked to contact a funeral home that hires non-Jewish employees, to pick up the body. The body should remain with the non-Jewish caretakers until the conclusion of the Shabbat or holy day.

Issues That May Arise Immediately After Death

Questions relating to autopsies, organ donations, and amputated limbs may arise, and it is important that the family consult their rabbi before making decisions on these matters. Below is a brief examination of some of the issues relating to such matters.

Autopsies

An autopsy is a careful examination of the internal tissues and organs of a dead body. There are several possible reasons for performing an autopsy. Among them is a desire to better understand the cause of death or to further the cause of medical research. The dissection of the human body for reasons that have no medical benefit is considered a desecration of the human body. The prohibition against desecrating dead bodies, and the correlation of showing respect and honor to dead bodies, are based on the principle that was stated earlier, *kavod hamet*, showing respect for the dead body.

The human being is the totality of body and soul. In Judaism, the body, even soulless, has value and deserves appropriate dignity and respect. The physical body is regarded as having unique value. The fact that one performs *mitzvot* with the body and that one's body is a vehicle for the worship of God, reflects its everlasting and supreme worth. The operative legal principle is as follows: **anything that would not be done to a person while they were alive cannot be done to them after they are dead.**

An extension of the principle of *kavod hamet* is the prohibition of receiving any benefit from the dead body, *hana'ah min hamet* (SA YD 349). It is forbidden by Jewish law to benefit from another human being without the other person's consent. The body is more than just an object that can be used or exploited. The human body *is* the person. The relationship to the human body, even a dead body, must be the same as the relationship to the living person. Therefore, an autopsy cannot even be considered if the deceased did not consent to it before his or her death. In Israel, however, the former Sephardic Chief Rabbi, Rabbi Benzion Uziel, *z"l*, ruled that Jewish law would permit autopsies for educational purposes and the advancement of medical research if they were carried out with the proper respect for the body and with prior consent from the deceased (*Teshuvot Mishpetei Uziel* YD nos. 28, 29).

Having made the case for prohibiting autopsies outside the state of Israel, it should be stated that there are extenuating circumstances in which an autopsy would not only be permitted but required. If the argument could be made that there is a legitimate possibility of saving a human life by performing the autopsy, it would then be permitted. Two such examples could include: (1) If the autopsy can reveal the cause of death and in turn save other lives; (2) When an autopsy may assist in the investigation of a murder and by doing so save the lives of other potential victims.

Rabbi Yaakov Ruza, the chief *posek* for the Tel Aviv area *chevra kadisha* and coroner's office, shared with me how some years ago, a forty-eight-year-old man unexpectedly died of heart failure. His father had died the same way, and there was concern that this might be a congenital genetic disease. Rabbi Ruza was inclined to go along with the doctor's advice that an autopsy should be performed. Before he made such a decision, he consulted some other leading halakhic authorities. Two of the three he consulted advised against an autopsy, but Chief Rabbi Mordechai Eliyahu, former Sephardic Chief rabbi of Israel, insisted that an autopsy must be done. Rabbi Ruza followed Chief Rabbi Mordechai Eliyahu's ruling, and as a result twelve family members may have been saved from congenital heart disease.

When a doctor insists that an autopsy is necessary, it is important to know that alternatives to full autopsies can be explored. For example, in Israel, specific-organ biopsy is a common procedure that often provides the same results as an autopsy (*Iggerot Moshe* YD, vol. 2, end of chapter 151). In discussions with Dr. Harvey Shiller, chief pathologist at Providence Hospital in Seattle, I learned that similar options are available in the United States. The family of the deceased can request limited autopsy of certain organs, and/or biopsy of organs or tissues.

Other notable examples of when autopsies would be permitted are recorded in the responsa literature of the rabbinical authorities who deal with medical questions in Jewish hospitals in Israel.

Organ Donation

Jewish tradition has always recognized the supreme importance of *pikuach nefesh*, the obligation to save a human life if it is in our power to do so. This commandment is stated in the Torah both in the negative: "Do not stand idly by the blood of your neighbor" (Leviticus 19:16) and in the positive: "Return your fellow's lost possession (his or her life)" (Deuteronomy 22:2). Thus, when the opportunity presents itself, one must do everything in one's ability to save a life provided one's own life is not at risk.

With the increased success rate of organ transplants, contemporary halakhic authorities have been discussing what might appear to be objections to organ donations considering the great potential for *pikuach nefesh*.

The most significant objection to organ donations in Jewish law regards assessing the time of death. Organs used for transplants must be taken while respiration and circulation are ongoing. The only time when this can happen is when brain-death has been established and the organs are being perfused by external means. Rabbi Moshe Tendler, z"l, a leading halakhic authority in the Orthodox community, Rosh Yeshiva and biology professor at Yeshiva University, has ruled that brain death is indeed death according to *halakhah*.

Recently this issue has received significant attention in the Jewish media, most notably with the tragic death of two talented young leaders in the Jewish community. They both died in Israel and their organs saved and enhanced the lives of others.

In 1986 Sephardic Chief Rabbi Ovadia Yosef ruled that transplants were a *mitzvah* for the living and though the dead are not obligated to perform *mitzvot*, an organ donation was an honor for the dead. The Rabbinical Council of America, in 1991 approved organ donations and the acceptability of brain-stem death, which makes the donation of organs possible.[2]

---

2. This is an issue that continues to be debated. For more information see *Jewish Medical Ethics* edited by Dr. Fred Rosner and Rabbi David J. Bleich.

Assuming one rules with those who consider brain-stem death a halakhic death, the next obvious objection has to do with laws relating to *kavod hamet*, treatment of the body after death. As was mentioned earlier, *halakhah* prohibits desecration of the body and gaining any benefit from the body. The potential to save another life, however, overrides any of these concerns.

A secondary concern relating to the above issue might be the delay of burial. Once again if an organ of the deceased can save an immediate life or enhance another person's quality of life (e.g., eyesight), then delay of burial would not be a serious enough objection to withhold the donation of organs. The emphasis here is the immediacy issue. The organ must be used immediately and not frozen for future use or for experimentation.

Another objection raised in the literature suggests that a dead person is not obligated to observe *mitzvot* and thus not required to save another person's life. This of course is easily obviated if the deceased declared his or her desire to donate organs or if the "patient advocates" deemed that the deceased would have wanted to save another person's life.

Amputated Limbs

According to Jewish tradition, the entire body is to be buried after death. Therefore, if an individual dies with severed limbs, the limbs must be buried with the deceased.

- If a limb or limbs were amputated before death, they should be buried in the eventual grave of the individual.
- If the individual does not have a grave, the limbs should be buried in a Jewish cemetery. There is no special service associated with the burial of limbs.

Especially the article written by Rabbi Nachum Rabinovitch, pp. 383–389, and the article by Dr. Fred Rosner, pp. 389–409.

Summary of the Laws of *Aninut*

The following are some of the laws relating to the stage of *aninut*:

- One whose father, mother, son, daughter, sister, brother, half-sister, or half-brother died is termed an *onen* from the time of death until interment.
- An *onen* may not eat meat or drink wine or liquor (SA YD 341:1).
- An *onen* may not attend a festive meal or celebration.
- An *onen* is denied the luxuries of self-adornment, bathing for pleasure, shaving, and taking a haircut (*Kaf Hachaim* 341).
- An *onen* may not indulge in conjugal relations (*Kaf Hachaim* 341, also MT *Avel* 4:6).
- An *onen* may not engage in work or business (Ibid.).
- An *onen* is exempt from all the *mitzvot aseh* (positive commandments) of the Torah and does not recite the *hamotzi* blessing or the *birkat hamazon* (Grace after the meal) (*Yabia Omer*, vol. 4 YD 25:2).
- An *onen* does not recite the morning blessings. However, after burial, the morning blessings can be recited all day and all evening. In the evening, the blessing on the Torah is not recited (*Yechaveh Da'at* 4:4; *Yabia Omer*, vol. 5 chapter 10).
- An *onen* may not study Torah (SA YD and Rambam, *loc. cit.*).
- An *onen* is exempt from prayers and specific positive commandments. He must, however, observe all the negative commandments (MT *loc. cit.*).
- Hakham Ovadia Yosef rules that the *Onen* may wear *tzitzit*, *tallit*, and *tefillin*, but does not recite the blessings (*Yalkut Yosef*, vol. 7, p. 50, fn. 3 also *Yalkut Yosef*, 3:9). Many communities, however, follow the *Shulchan Arukh* who rules that an *onen* does not wear *tallit* and *tefillin*.

Meals During the Period of *Aninut*

It is forbidden to eat in the presence of the deceased. This applies to everyone including the mourners. The *onen* is not permitted to eat a regular elaborate meal at a table with company. Instead, the *onen* should eat alone at a separate table (SA YD 341:1).

Shabbat

- On Shabbat the *onen* may eat meat and drink wine and must observe all the Shabbat commandments. The *onen* must abstain from matters of private enjoyment (e.g., conjugal relations and the study of Torah) even on Shabbat (SA OH 71).

Holy Days

- On Sukkot the *onen* eats and sleeps in the *sukkah* without reciting the blessing. If this is difficult, however, he is exempt from the *mitzvah* (*Yabia Omer*, vol. 4, p. 297).
- On Pesach the *onen* must observe all the *Mitzvot* of the *Seder*. He or she does not recite the blessings and must respond *Amen* to someone else's blessings. The same applies to the recitation of the Haggadah and the *Hallel* (*Hazon Ovadia*, vol. 2, p. 185 and footnotes).
- The *onen* must recline on the night of Pesach to fulfill the *mitzvot* of the *Seder* (*Yalkut Yosef*, vol. 7 3:6).
- An *onen* must observe all communal fast days (*Yalkut Yosef*, vol. 7 3:7).
- On Hanukkah an *onen* should have someone else light the Hanukiah on his or her behalf (*Kaf Hachaim* 341:103; also *Gesher Hachaim*, vol. 1 18:16).
- During *Sefirat Ha'omer*, the counting of the *omer*, the *onen* does not count the *Omer* in the evening prior to burial. On the next day, after the burial, the *onen* counts without a blessing and that evening continues to count with a blessing (*Yalkut Yosef*, vol. 7

3:14). If the burial is postponed and the *onen* missed an entire day of counting, the remaining days of the *omer* are counted without a blessing.

- The custom in some Sephardic communities is that the *onen* recites *Kaddish* with the hazan for the relative who has just passed away (*Yalkut Yosef*, vol. 7 3:17 and footnotes).

Religious Support

One should call the rabbi immediately upon learning that a dear one has passed away. The rabbi will in turn notify the *chevra kadisha*, the community's burial society. The rabbi is a trained professional who knows how to deal with issues related to grief and loss. Consult with your rabbi on all matters that you may face at this time.

The rabbi will also want to spend some time with the mourners and close relatives to learn more about the deceased. The information he is provided will help the rabbi prepare for the funeral service. The bereaved should be honest and open with the rabbi. The different relationships with the deceased should be discussed, as well as both the good times and bad times. The mourners could share with the rabbi what they loved and admired about the deceased and what they found difficult about him or her. Meeting with one's rabbi at a time like this can be very helpful and comforting for the mourners and the others who share the grief. This is a time when the bereaved will need someone to talk to, a time for them to ask questions regarding death, life, the afterlife, and the rituals associated with death.

The rabbi will want to know the following information:

- The Hebrew name of the deceased.
- The Hebrew name of the deceased's mother and father.
- The exact time of death.

The Burial Society (*Chevra Kadisha*)

The burial society, also known as the *chevra kadisha* or brotherhood, is a nonprofit organization of volunteers who are familiar with Jewish funerary traditions and are willing to help the mourners with all the burial preparations. In some Sephardic communities, the members of the *chevra kadisha* visit the critically ill and recite prayers for healing on their behalf. In these communities the *chevra kadisha* will make sure that one of its members is present at the time of death. From that moment on, they take care of all the necessary preparations.

The *chevra kadisha* is responsible for picking up the body, for the rituals of *rechitsah*, washing the body and *shemirah*, watching over the deceased (see below), and for transporting the body to the chapel for the service, and from the service to the cemetery.

The *chevra kadisha* has the responsibility of providing burial for all members of the community, rich and poor alike. It operates as an independent organization whose officers represent a cross-section of the larger community.

Ideally, the *chevra kadisha* consists of trained volunteers and professionals who act with great efficiency, dignity, and discretion. Members of the community should be encouraged to join the *chevra kadisha* or brotherhood as well as to support it financially

The following are some questions you will be asked by the *chevra kadisha* before the deceased is picked up:

- Full legal name of the deceased, full Hebrew name of the deceased, including Hebrew names of their mother and father.
- Social Security number of the deceased.
- Family contact.
- Current location of the deceased.
- Synagogue affiliation.
- Has the death certificate been signed yet?
- Is there any intervention required by an official (e.g., autopsy)?
- *Tallit* of the deceased.
- Name of cemetery.
- Date and time of funeral service.
- Name of officiating rabbi.

Preparation of the Deceased for Burial

The following sections will address certain issues that relate to preparing the body for burial.

Staying with the Deceased (*Shemirah*)

Once again, *kavod hamet*, preserving the sacred dignity and the reverence for the human body, is the governing principle for all the rituals and traditions when responding to death. Therefore, from the moment of death until the burial, the deceased may not be left alone. The family should make sure that someone always remains at the side of the deceased until a member of the burial society, or the rabbi arrives. Once the burial society takes over, a *shomer* (watcher) is assigned to stay at the side of the deceased. The *shomer* recites psalms and is forbidden to smoke or eat in the presence of the deceased (*Yabia Omer* vol. 6 OH 30:6, p. 103) The *shomer* remains awake throughout the entire night. While it is preferable that the *shomer* be a member of the family or a personal friend, this is not always possible.

Preparation of the Deceased (*Taharah* and *Rechitsah*)

The *chevra kadisha* is responsible for preparing the deceased for burial. The preparation involves three parts: *rechitsah*, washing of the body; *taharah*, a ritual cleansing; and *halbashah*, dressing the deceased in the appropriate shrouds. While engaged in these three steps of preparation, those attending to the procedure recite the appropriate biblical verses or prayers. Experienced members of the *chevra kadisha* who have had the appropriate training should conduct these procedures. The only ones excluded from the performance of this *mitzvah* are *Kohanim* because of their religious prohibition of being in close contact with a dead body.

Rechitsah, *taharah*, and *halbashah* for a man are done only by men, and for a woman only by women. Under no circumstances should a man participate in the preparation of a woman (SA YD 352:3). Only under extenuating circumstances and after consultation with a rabbi may a woman participate in the preparation of a man. Lastly under no circumstances can it be performed by a non-Jew.

These preparations should take place as close as possible to the time of the funeral service. Ideally, no more than three hours should elapse between the preparation of the deceased and the funeral service.

Throughout the preparation of the body, the utmost respect for and dignity of the deceased must be preserved. This is maintained by adhering to the following rules:

- The attendants are not permitted to eat, drink, or smoke while in the presence of the deceased.
- The attendants are not permitted to engage in idle conversation or matters that do not directly pertain to the preparations of the deceased.
- The body of the deceased is never exposed except for a very short time when a particular body part is being washed.
- The body of the deceased must be handled with the utmost care.
- The body of the deceased is never placed face downward.

Throughout the washing of the body, various prayers and biblical verses are recited, depending on what part of the body is being cleansed. There are appropriate readings for the washing of the different body parts and for the dressing of the deceased. When the deceased is a man, the procedure concludes by placing his *tallit* (prayer shawl) into the coffin.

Shrouds (*Takhrikhim*)

The Babylonian Talmud records how Rabban Gamliel, the preeminent leader of his generation (80 CE–118 CE) and a wealthy man, instituted the practice that every Jew, rich or poor, must be buried in similar simple shrouds to prevent families from vying with each other in providing elaborate garments for the dead, and shaming those who could not afford elaborate garments.

At one time, funerals in Israel became so costly that the expense was harder for some relatives to bear than the death itself. Some relatives even abandoned the corpse and ran away. Such tragedies ended when Rabban Gamliel left orders that his body be carried to the grave in a simple linen garment. From then on, everyone followed Rabban Gamliel's example....

Said Rabbi Papa: "And now it is a general practice to carry out the dead even in rough cloth worth only a *zuz*" (TB *Moed Katan* 27a).

The shrouds (*takhrikhim* in Hebrew) are handmade, clean, white, garments (SA YD 352:2). They are usually made of cotton, linen, or muslin. They symbolize simplicity and purity. The High Priest also wore simple white linen garments when he entered the Holy of Holies on Yom Kippur. The lesson is penetrating: Our lives should be led with humility and modesty. One faces his or her Creator in the same way one entered this world, humble and contrite. Before the Master of the Universe there is no wealth or status.

Prayer Shawl (*Tallit*)

It is the custom of most Sephardic communities outside of Israel to bury men wrapped in a *tallit* or prayer shawl (*Gesher Hachaim* 10:5). In Israel the deceased is wrapped in his *tallit* until the burial, but immediately prior to the interment it is removed and returned to the family.

Interring the deceased with his *tallit* is a custom that can be traced back to the early Middle Ages and should be observed in the fashion that the Sephardim have been doing for centuries. The Sephardim do not cut or remove the fringes of the *tallit* before burial. In fact, *Maran* in the *Shulchan Arukh* states: "The deceased is buried with a *tallit* that has *tzitzit*" (SA YD 350:2).

At some point before the funeral, the family should make sure to supply the *chevra kadisha* with the *tallit* the deceased wore throughout his lifetime. If the deceased did not own a *tallit*, or it cannot be found before the funeral, the *chevra kadisha* will supply another *tallit* or a *tallit* can be purchased for this purpose.

Transportation of the Body / Embalming

Transporting the corpse a long distance for burial presents a problem. There is a legitimate concern on the part of state and government officials regarding the decomposition and odor of decaying human remains in airports and airplane cargo, especially if transported in wood caskets.

Jewish law does not, under any circumstances, permit a process called embalming the body. In this procedure all the blood is drained from the body and replaced with a chemical.

Today the *chevra kadisha* that transports bodies long distances and on airplanes use a sealed ziegler case or a metal-lined container which is leak-proof and odor-resistant.

When the body is transported, care should be taken to make sure that it is always accompanied by a Jew.

CHAPTER 5

Planning the Funeral Service

Ve-nachacha Adonai tamid
And the Lord will guide you continually

— Isaiah 58:11

No one ever told me that grief felt so much like fear
— C.S. Lewis, *A Grief Observed*

Scheduling the Funeral Service

It is regarded as a sign of great disrespect to the deceased if the body is not buried immediately. Human beings are created in the image of God and must be accorded the utmost of respect. The importance of burying the dead immediately is reflected in numerous *halakhot* (laws) that mandate us to forgo whatever we may be doing at any given moment to bury the dead even when the deceased is not a relative or an acquaintance. The importance of this mitzvah is highlighted by the *halakhah* that even the High Priest, on his way to perform the service on Yom Kippur, the holiest of days, must defile himself and forgo performing the service in order to bury the dead. This obligation comes under the heading of a *met mitzvah she'ein lo kovrim*, a corpse that is unburied and no one else is taking responsibility (TB *Nazir* 43b).

The Torah states regarding the death sentence of a criminal:

> His body shall not remain for the night on the gallows; rather you shall surely bury him on that day, for a hanging person is a curse of God (Devarim 21:23).

The Talmud deduces from this verse that if the Torah shows such consideration for a criminal, it should surely apply to an innocent person (TB *Sanhedrin* 46a). In another Talmudic teaching Rabbi Shimon Bar Yochai (160 CE) stated that one who does not bury his or her dead immediately transgresses a negative commandment (TY *Nazir* 7:1). HaRambam rules in accordance with the Talmudic sentiment:

> We do not delay the burial of the dead. Instead, we hurry to bury the deceased immediately. Hastening the burial is praiseworthy. For one's father and mother, by contrast, it is demeaning (MT *Avel* 4:7).

Based on the above ruling, burial within twenty-four hours following death is the norm in the Jewish tradition. There are exceptions to the rule of immediate burial. One exception has to do with *kavod hamet*, showing honor and respect to the deceased. If, for example, the presence of a close relative, a dignitary, scholar or a rabbi will bring honor to the deceased, and that person needs to travel a long distance to take part in the service, and is doing everything possible to arrive as soon as possible, the funeral can be delayed. Other exceptions include legal delays in the funeral service due to government regulations and situations where the burial will take place overseas. The only other times a burial would be delayed is when death occurs immediately before Shabbat or on a holy day on which funerals are not permitted. In such a case, the burial is postponed until after the Shabbat or holy day (*Yabia Omer* vol. 4, p. 305 based on SA YD 357:1).

Purchasing a Casket

Traditionally the Jewish people have always used a casket made entirely of wood so that the body, shroud, and coffin decompose at approximately the same rate. The interior of the casket should not be lined. In some communities it is the custom to drill holes in the bottom of the casket to fulfill the passage "From dust thou art, and unto dust thou shall return" (Bereshit 3:19). In the Syrian communities of Brooklyn, New York, and Deal, New Jersey, it is the custom to uncover the casket and fill it with earth.

Most communities offer one standard casket, suggesting that all are buried equally and with simplicity. In his autobiography, Ed Koch, the former mayor of New York, describes his experience with finding an appropriate coffin for his mother.

> We needed to pick out a casket. We told the director we were looking for something in the Orthodox tradition and he ushered us into a room with twenty-five-hundred-dollar caskets.... He knew we were looking for something simple, but he figured he'd work his hard sell on us just the same. He took us into several rooms and in each room the caskets cost less.
> He didn't skip a room. He probably thought our resolve would weaken and we would be shamed into buying an expensive one.
> Finally, he took us into the basement, where he showed us two pine boxes, which is what we had told him we wanted in the first place. My mother would not have appreciated an expensive casket... besides, an Orthodox funeral requires a simple wooden casket without nails or ornament.... Yet... even here in the basement, he wanted to sell us the more expensive of the pine caskets.... We were so humiliated by the ordeal that we said yes [to the more expensive one]. We couldn't resist any further. I've never forgotten that. That man made us feel cheap and we succumbed (*Citizen Koch: An Autobiography*).

This passage illustrates the wisdom of our ancient traditions and customs. This is the time when we need the tradition to help us make decisions as to what will appropriately honor our loved ones.

Flowers

The impermanent beauty of flowers, another of God's creations, lends unique beauty to any occasion, whether it be one of joy or sorrow. While Sephardic custom permits the use of flowers to adorn and show respect to the deceased (*Yabia Omer*, vol. 3 YD 24; *Yalkut Yosef*, vol. 7 chapter 7:1), it has never been considered an ideal custom.

The primary reasons that flowers are discouraged include: (1) floral tributes at funerals are primarily a non-Jewish custom, and it would not be appropriate to model our service on gentile services; (2) floral decorations are expensive, and since their ephemeral beauty is short-lived, a charitable donation to a worthy cause is regarded as more meaningful; (3) the Jewish funeral service is traditionally distinguished by its simplicity and modesty, and allowing the use of flowers would run the risk of turning the chapel into an ostentatious display of elaborate floral decorations that would not fit the spirit of the traditional service.

If floral decorations are displayed in good taste, there are solid halakhic grounds for permitting their use. Rabbi Ovadia Yosef, a contemporary Sephardic halakhic authority, writes:

> Those who have the tradition to adorn the casket of the deceased with flowers... have a halakhic basis for their custom....
>
> However, whenever possible, if the family will listen to their rabbis' advice, they should be discouraged from displaying flowers at the chapel or cemetery (*Yalkut Yosef*, Ibid.).

In place of floral gifts, the family and friends of the deceased should be encouraged to pay tribute to the deceased by sending donations to a worthy charity in memory of the deceased. Charitable donations are a meaningful memorial and benefit the living. If people insist on flowers, they do not have to be discouraged, and they can display the flowers at the service in a non-ostentatious fashion.

Viewing the Deceased

Placing the dead body of the person we love on display does not constitute appropriate *kavod hamet*. The mass of lifeless flesh represents the antithesis of *tzelem Elohim*, the image of God. No amount of cosmetics, mechanical devices, chemical injections, or fancy clothing can bring dignity to a dead body. Therefore, the body is covered with a sheet immediately after death occurs. It is forbidden to manipulate or beautify the dead body for cosmetic purposes.

In many Sephardic communities, the immediate family may see the deceased prior to burial. This is practiced in a very private fashion, and under no circumstances is the body manipulated or altered. In some communities, as a sign of love and respect, the sons and daughters of the deceased will kiss the hand of their father or mother prior to the funeral service.

Cremation

Jewish law states that the body of the deceased must be buried in the earth. It is therefore forbidden under any circumstances to cremate the dead. Even if the deceased willed a cremation, the family must ignore the wish and observe the tradition that has been passed on from generation to generation. Cremated ashes cannot be buried in a Jewish cemetery.

Mausoleum

The requirement for burial refers specifically to burial in the earth. In certain cities, due to the dampness of the ground, a mausoleum is built around a plot of earth. This kind of mausoleum is permitted.

Mausoleums that are built above ground and not surrounded by earth are not permitted according to Jewish law. Even if the deceased willed such a burial, his or her will is denied. The only exception to this rule is when civil law requires burials above ground due to the unstable and shifting nature of the land.

Laws Relating to *Kohanim*

The title of *kehunah* refers to a male *kohen*, a member of the priesthood. This status is passed down from father to son and is retained as long as the male adult is either single or married to a Jewish woman. Chapter twenty-one of *Vayikra*, also known as the Holiness Code, mandates the regulations governing the behavior of *kohanim*. It was designed to ensure the highest level of sanctity for the spiritual leaders of the Jewish people.

The Holiness Code prohibits the *kohen* from having contact with the dead. The exception to the Holiness Code of the *kohen* is when the deceased is an immediate relative of the *kohen*, such as his wife, mother, father, son, daughter, brother, or unmarried sister. These exceptions do not apply to the High Priest, the *Kohen Gadol*. In such instances the Torah obligates the *kohen* to participate in the mitzvah of burying his relative. The biblical Holiness Code of the priestly family was a radical departure from ancient Near Eastern traditions that oftentimes involved elaborate rituals around death, at which time the pagan priests would exploit the vulnerable mourners. The Torah, in contrast, mandates that the *kohen* completely disassociate himself and his office from death and all rituals associated with death and dying. By doing so, the Torah redirects the function of the *kohen* and focuses on his role as teacher and spiritual guide. Therefore, a *kohen* is not permitted to carry, move, or touch a dead body or a detached limb of a human being. He is also not permitted to be present under the same roof with a corpse or limb. Jewish law mandates that if death occurs while a *kohen* is in a house or building, he must immediately leave the premises (SA YD 372:1). At a funeral service, a male *kohen* may not enter the chapel or any of its rooms if the deceased is in the building. To pay respect to the deceased, a *kohen* must listen to the service from outside the chapel. Some chapels have a special room for *kohanim* which is adjacent to the room where the service is held but is constructed in such a way that it does not share the roof of the larger building and has a completely separate entrance.

Similarly, a *kohen* cannot enter the cemetery grounds. It is the custom in most Jewish cemeteries to bury *kohanim* at the entrance of the cemetery so that the family can visit the grave without stepping on the cemetery grounds.

The only other time a *kohen* may defile himself by participating in a funeral service is in an extenuating circumstance when there is no one else to attend to the preparations and burial of a dead person. This, as was mentioned earlier, is referred to as *met mitzvah*, and it is deduced from the verse *lenefesh lo yitamah be'amav*, "He shall not defile himself amongst his people." The clause "amongst his people" is understood to mean only when he is among his people is he forbidden to defile himself. But when there is no one else available to attend to the corpse, he must defile himself and bury the body to preserve *kavod hamet*, the dignity and honor of the deceased.

Summary of Laws Relating to *Kohanim*

- A *kohen*, even under the age of thirteen, should follow the restrictions of the Holiness Code (*Mekor Chaim*, vol. 5, chapter 284)
- A *kohen* may not enter any area that is under the same roof as a dead Jewish body. If a *kohen* is informed that a Jew has died in his apartment building or office building, he should leave the premises immediately.
- A *kohen* may not touch or carry a corpse, or even the smallest part of a lifeless body or limb.
- A *kohen* may participate in the burial of the following relatives: wife, mother, father, son, daughter, brother, unmarried sister (*Yalkut Yosef*, vol. 7 30:1).
- When a *kohen* enters the cemetery grounds for the burial of an immediate relative, he must leave the cemetery grounds immediately following the interment (SA YD 373:6).

Suicide and Jewish Law

Because of the absolute sanctity of human life, it is strictly forbidden to take one's own life. As a Jew, one is charged with preserving life and with sanctifying God's name throughout one's lifetime. The right to choose to die is not in one's hands. Only God can exercise such a right. When one defiantly rejects God's will and takes one's own life, death not only loses its atoning qualities but is regarded as a serious transgression. The rabbinic teachings in *Ethics of the Fathers* makes this point in absolute terms:

> Do not allow your natural impulse to convince you that the grave is a refuge for perforce you were formed; perforce you were born; perforce do you live; perforce you shall die; and perforce are you destined to give an account and reckoning before the Supreme King of Kings, the Holy One, blessed be He (*Pirkei Avot* 4:29).

No matter how noble one may view the act of suicide, it can never be condoned. Active euthanasia, even intended solely for the purpose of ending suffering, is categorically forbidden. On some level, Judaism considers suicide to be more heinous than murder. Rabbi Bahya Ibn Pakuda writes in his seminal work *Duties of the Heart*, "The closer the relationship between the killer and the killed, the more heinous the crime, and man is closest to himself" (*Duties of the Heart*, chapter 4).

Because suicide is a denial of God's supreme will over His creations, the bereaved are generally required to follow a different pattern of mourning for a person who commits suicide. The general principle is that *kavod hamet*, the usual honor afforded the deceased is denied to a person who commits suicide because of the nature of this crime. While honor to the deceased is denied, all the rituals that show honor to the bereaved are observed.

A person who commits suicide, God forbid, is buried away from all other Jewish graves. Most cemeteries reserve a row at the end of the cemetery along the fence for suicides. Under these circumstances, no formal eulogy is delivered, and *keriah* and *shivah* are not observed (*Yalkut Yosef*, vol. 7 33:1; also, *Yabia Omer*, vol. 2 chapter 24 and vol. 6 chapter 36).

Kaddish and *Hashkavah* are recited for one who commits suicide. Relatives should also observe *hazkarot* memorial services in memory of the deceased (*Yalkut Yosef*, vol. 7 33:2).

What Is Halakhic Suicide?

The above laws take effect if it has been determined that the deceased did, in fact, commit suicide. Jewish law has its own criteria for determining whether a death was a suicide, independent of police records or court rulings. Below are some of the factors involved in such determinations according to Jewish law:

- Can it be ascertained without a doubt that the death was in fact a suicide? If there is any doubt at all, Jewish law does not assume suicide (SA YD 345:2).

- Might the deceased have been insane to any degree, even temporarily, while committing suicide? If that is the case, the above laws of suicide do not apply.

- Was the deceased under the influence of drugs, alcohol, or any substance? Once again, if it can be determined that the deceased was under the influence of some drugs or substance, then the death is not considered to be a halakhic suicide.

- Was the deceased motivated by extreme pain, suffering, or anxiety? If so, we assume that the deceased had no control over his or her actions and thus the death was not, in fact, an actual suicide.

- Was the death instantaneous, or was it lingering, during which time the deceased may have tried to alter the course of events and repent? (*Yalkut Yosef*, vol. 7 33:1). If so, we assume that the *teshuvah* (repentance) was sincere, and even though he or she died, we regard the deceased as a *ba'al teshuvah*, a person who has repented.

- Is it possible that the deceased committed suicide as a means of repentance? If this is true, we mourn his or her death even though the act is not condoned (Ibid.).

Based on the above information, the rabbi decides whether or not the situation presented is indeed a case of suicide. As was mentioned earlier, the rabbinical decision is independent of any police or court ruling. In practice, a person who commits suicide is rarely deemed a halakhic suicide. Most authorities are of the opinion that nobody in his right mind would kill himself – or herself. If the person were completely rational, suicide would not be a possibility. The very fact that the deceased committed suicide is enough evidence to deem him or her at least temporarily insane. For this reason, suicide is non-existent in Jewish law and the deceased is always accorded a respectful and dignified Jewish burial.

CHAPTER 6

The Funeral and Burial

Imo Anochi be-tzarah, I am with him at his time of grief.
— Tehillim 91:15

Though I walk through the valley of the shadow of death, I fear no evil for You are with me....
— Tehillim 23:4

The Funeral Service

The traditional Sephardic Jewish funeral service is kept simple and to the point. Its purpose is not to comfort the mourners. On the contrary, our sages of blessed memory, taught:

> There can be no comfort for one whose deceased lies before him (*Pirkei Avot* 4:23).

Rather, the service is intended to further offer *kavod hamet*, honoring the deceased through the recitation of *tehillim*, the gathering of family, friends, and the community, and sharing memories and the good deeds the deceased performed during his or her lifetime. All of this in order to express how the departed will be missed.

The basic structure of the funeral service is as follows:

- The service begins with the recitation of *tehillim* 49, 16 and 23.
- The deceased is eulogized by friends, family, and the rabbi.

- The recitation of *Tziduk Hadin*, an affirmation that God is just and righteous.
- Some communities recite *Kaddish* after the eulogy and *Tziduk Hadin*.
- The body of the deceased is escorted to the cemetery or gravesite.
- Burial Service.

Recitation of Psalms

The *tehillim* selected for reading at the funeral service give expression to the thoughts, feelings and emotions which emanate from the heart of one who seeks solace and comfort at a time of loss. While the Book of Tehillim is popularly known as the book which was written by King David, the Talmud teaches that there were at least ten different authors (TB *Bava Batra* 14b). Tehillim stands out from the rest of the Bible, the *Tanakh*, in one important respect. The Torah and the *Nevi'im*, the books of the prophets, give voice to God's message for mankind while the Book of Tehillim gives voice to man's message to God. While the other books of the Bible describe God reaching out, as it were, through his prophets, to draw mankind near to Him – the Book of Tehillim describes man's soul reaching out to God, yearning for knowledge and wisdom, nearness, and comfort.

The Book of Tehillim reminds us that all of life's experiences – the moments of joy and victory as well as the moments of affliction and bitterness – can be used as a means of striving toward better clarity of thought and purity of soul to resolve before our Creator. All of life's experiences can inspire song and poetry. Tehillim serves as a means of presenting-up to God the sentiments of all those who turn to God for consolation and strength, inspiration and devotion. Unconditional trust in God is the dominant theme throughout the Book of Tehillim. The words "Though I walk through the valley of the shadow of death, I will fear no evil, for You are with me, Your rod and Your staff, they comfort me" (Tehillim 23) is a message that one hopes and prays would resonate with the mourners at the time of their loss.

While the choice of Tehillim selected for the funeral service may vary from community to community, most begin with *tehillim* 49, 16, and 23. Other *tehillim* that may also be recited include Tehillim 1, 15, and 90. The Hebrew and English texts of these Tehillim, together with commentaries, can be found in Appendix 11.

The Eulogy

The eulogy is often the focal point of the funeral service. It is important that at least one eulogy be prepared and delivered by an experienced and capable person, preferably a rabbi. The Talmud states in strong terms that one who is lax in the preparation and delivery of a eulogy deserves to be buried alive (TB *Shabbat* 105b).

Rabbi Joseph B. Soloveitchik, of blessed memory, writes that the *hesped*, the eulogy, has a twofold objective. Its first objective is to make people weep, as is clearly stated in the Talmud: It is obligatory for the eulogizer to raise his voice and speak in terms which will break the heart (TB *Berakhot* 6a).

Rabbi Soloveitchik explains that:

> The *halakhah* did not like to see the dead interred in silent indifference. It wanted to hear the shriek of despair and to see the hot tear washing away human cruelty and toughness.[1]

The second objective of the eulogy is "informative and instructional." Through the eulogy we tell the life story of the deceased. We ask the question: "Who was this person?" No matter how well we think we knew the deceased during their lifetime, ultimately, we are each a "sealed book," even to those closest to us, until our last hour. Rabbi Soloveitchik continues:

> Anonymity is an integral part of the human existential destiny. *Sof davar hakol nishma*, "the end of the matter, all is heard" (Ecclesiastes 12:13). Only at the conclusion of the *Davar*, the human career, only at the end of the life story of man or woman,

---

1. *Tradition* 17 no. 2 (Spring 1978), p. 73.

do people become inquisitive. Only then do they begin to inquire about him or her. Who was he or she? Only then *hakol nishma* – all kinds of questions are asked (Ibid.).

Jewish tradition insists that a person be mourned appropriately. The Talmud tells us:

> R. Simeon b. Pazzi said in the name of R. Joshua b. Levi in Bar Kappara's name: "When one sheds tears for a worthy person, the Holy One, blessed be He, counts them and lays them up in his treasure house, for it is said: 'You count my grieving: Put my tears into Your bottle; are they not in Your book?'" (TB *Berakhot* 6a).

The purpose of the eulogy is to show honor and respect for the deceased by expressing his or her good deeds and positive qualities, and to show how much he or she will be missed. The eulogy and remembrances of the deceased have a dual purpose. They function as another way of expressing *kavod hamet*, honor of the deceased, but they also function as a way of bringing comfort to the mourners (TB *Sanhedrin* 46b and *Torah Temimah* on Bereshit 23:2).

It is very important to give the rabbi, or whoever will be delivering the eulogy, accurate information about the deceased. There is a tendency at times to exaggerate the qualities or glorify the traits of one who has just passed away. The *Shulchan Arukh* states that while one should not overstate the qualities of the deceased especially if those in attendance will know they are an exaggeration, one should describe and embellish the finest and best qualities of the deceased (SA YD 344:1). An experienced rabbi knows how to gather the appropriate information needed to uncover the unique qualities and special virtues of the deceased.

Times When the Eulogy Is Scaled Back

Every person is deserving of an appropriate eulogy. There are times, however, when the deceased leaves special instructions regarding his or her eulogy. If the deceased clearly wished that no eulogy be delivered, that wish should be honored.

There are certain times of the year when it is appropriate to scale back the delivery of a eulogy because excessive sadness and wailing is forbidden. The principle governing this law asserts that the joy of the community subsumes the individual person. Other opportunities for remembering and reflecting upon the life of the deceased can be created for example at the *sheloshim*, the thirty-day memorial service, or at a later time.

If the Funeral Occurs on Any of These Days the Eulogy Is Scaled Back:

- During *Chol HaMoed* of Pesach or Sukkot.
- During Hanukkah, Purim, or Rosh Chodesh (New Moon).
- On the eve of any of the Jewish holy days and on Friday.
- During the entire month of Nissan.

Tziduk Hadin (Prayer Affirming God's Righteousness)

The prayer *Tziduk Hadin* consists of various verses from the *Tanakh*. It is a prayer that affirms our faith in God and in His divine justice. It begins with the words:

> You are righteous, O Lord, and upright are Your judgments (Tehillim 119:137).
>
> The Lord is righteous in all His ways (145:17).

This declaration of sorts acknowledges the fact that we do not and cannot ever understand God's ways and despite this, our faith does not waver. Life and death are in the hands of the Almighty, and that will always remain a mystery we cannot fully fathom. At a time of loss, one's life is put into perspective; we accept our lot and reaffirm our belief that *God* provides and takes away life. The earliest appearance of such a theme is found in the book of Devarim, *Perashat Ha'azinu*, the Song of Moses, and it is later used throughout the *Tanakh*:

The Rock [a reference to God] – perfect is His work, for all His paths are just; The Lord is a God of faith without iniquity, righteous and fair is He (Devarim 32:4).

The first recorded association of this general theme with death and mourning dates to the Talmudic period. The Talmud records that at the end of the Jewish revolt against the Roman empire while the fortress of Betar was falling, toward the end of the summer of 135 C.E., Rabbi Hanina ben Teradion was captured. Condemned to death for teaching Torah, he was wrapped up in a parchment Torah scroll and burned alive at the stake. Rabbi Hanina ben Teradion's entire family was also taken to be martyred, and the Talmud reports that they uttered the above verses, which later formed the basis of the *Tziduk Hadin* prayer (TB *Avodah Zarah* 18a).

Indeed, our tradition mandates that these words be stated on behalf of the mourner as a departure for healing and resolution. Human beings yearn for life, yet we are reminded at a time of bereavement that it is only God who controls life and death, and that ultimately death will be our end.

Like *keriah* the blessing *Dayan Ha'Emet, and Tziduk Hadin* should be recited at the time of death (SA YD 339:3). Today, in most Sephardic communities, the accepted custom is to recite the *Tziduk Hadin* prayer at the conclusion of the funeral service. It is also recited prior to the *Hashkavah* at the end of *Shacharit* during the entire week of *shivah*.

Below is an English translation of the *Tziduk Hadin* prayer. For the complete Hebrew text, see Appendix II.

> You are righteous O Lord, and upright are Your judgments.
> The Lord is righteous in all His ways, and pious in all His deeds.
> Your righteousness is an everlasting righteousness, and Your Torah is truth.
> The judgments of the Lord are true, being righteous together.
> Since the word of the King reigns,
> Who could say to Him, what are You doing?

He is One, and who could possibly answer Him back?
Whatever His essence desires, He does.
There are those who are great and those who are small, and
the servant is free of his master.
Behold, He has no faith in His servants, and to His angels He
attributes folly.
Certainly, the human, who is but worm, the son of man, who
is but maggot.
The Rock, perfect is His work, for all His ways are just, trustworthy God, never unjust, righteous and upright is He,
the Judge of truth, who judges righteously and truthfully.
Blessed is the Judge of truth, for all His judgments are
righteous and true.

The words of the *Tziduk Hadin* afford the mourner a sense of connection to one's faith, to a historical past, and to a caring community. Like the *Kaddish*, the *Tziduk Hadin* prayer is recited with a *minyan*, a quorum of ten men. This is a reminder that the mourner is not alone in his or her grief.

Escorting the Deceased, *Levayat Hamet*

A *chesed shel emet* is an act of kindness that is distinguished from other acts of kindness in that it is also an act of complete sincerity and *truth*. The term designates acts of kindness and love that are done without expecting or ever receiving anything back – not even a thank you. The mitzvah of accompanying the deceased to burial, *levayat hamet*, is referred to as an act of *chesed shel emet*, a sincere act of kindness. Yaakov Avinu, Jacob our forefather, referred to it as such. On his death bed Yaakov Avinu called his son Joseph and asked that he do for him a *"chesed"* and *"emet"* and have him buried in the land of Israel with his father and grandfather (Bereshit 47:29; see also TB *Berakhot* 18a). In fact, our sages liken the accompaniment of the deceased to his or her final resting place to accompanying God (TB *Berakhot* 18a).

The importance of escorting the deceased to the cemetery is underscored by the fact that one is permitted to cancel Torah study in order to observe this mitzvah (SA YD 361:1). This is especially true if the deceased was a Torah scholar and teacher. The rule of canceling Torah study does not apply to a Torah teacher whose absence would mean canceling Torah study for students. Therefore, every effort should be made to accompany the family to the cemetery.

The tradition is to have the hearse carrying the body leave the funeral home slowly, symbolically suggesting how difficult it is to part. Those in attendance follow the hearse a few feet prior to getting into their cars fulfilling the mitzvah of *levayat hamet*, escorting the deceased (*Siddur Bet Oved* by Rabbi Yehuda Shemuel Ashkenazi, p. 442).

As one escorts the body to its final resting place Tehillim 91 is chanted (text and translation can be found in Appendix II, p. 6), followed by the words:

> He the merciful One atones iniquity, and does not destroy, He withdraws His anger, and does not arouse His rage, Adonai deliver us, the King will answer us on the day we call.

Standing While the Body Is Being Moved

Those who are present must stand when the dead body is moved from place to place. Standing is not only a sign of respect for the deceased but a show of respect for those performing the mitzvah of *chesed* (kindness) (SA YD 361:4).

Pallbearers

The handlers of the casket, or those carrying the bier, as well as those waiting to replace the pallbearers are performing an important mitzvah and giving honor to the deceased. It is therefore important that the pallbearers selected for this task be Jewish (Mishnah, *Berakhot* 3:1).

A good indicator of how esteemed this mitzvah was in the eyes of our sages is related by the fact that the pallbearers are exempt from the mitzvah of reciting the *Shema* if they are needed for the task (SA YD 358:1; also OH 72:1). The rest of the participants are required to recite the *Shema* but are exempt from reciting the *amidah* because the *amidah* is rabbinic while the recitation of the *Shema* is biblically ordained.

Blessing Before Entering the Cemetery

Before entering the cemetery, if one has not been there for more than thirty days a blessing is recited. Usually, one person recites the blessing on behalf of all those that are present (*Yalkut Yosef*, vol. 7 6:18).

The blessing is as follows:

> Blessed are You, Lord our God, King of the universe, who fashioned you with justice, nourished and sustained you with justice, took your lives with justice, knows the sum total of all of you with justice, and will restore and resuscitate you with justice. Blessed are You, who resurrects the dead.
>
> (Hebrew text is in Appendix II.)

Burial Service

Upon arriving at the cemetery, the pallbearers carry the casket to the gravesite, with the feet of the deceased always directed forward. At the gravesite the casket is turned around and buried with the head forward.

As the casket is escorted, Tehillim 91 is chanted followed by the words:

> And He, the merciful one, will forgive iniquity and not destroy man. He will frequently turn aside His anger and not arouse all His wrath.

Once at the grave, the casket is immediately lowered. The rabbi may use this opportunity to say a few closing remarks. In some communities it is customary for the rabbi or the person officiating to symbolically ask the deceased, on behalf of those present, to forgive any pain caused during his or her lifetime or for any disrespect while preparing the burial. In some communities, *hakafot*, a procession encircling the grave seven times, may be enacted.

Filling the Grave

Hashkavah, the memorial prayer, cannot be recited until the entire casket is covered with earth. It is a mitzvah for relatives and friends to assist in the burial of a loved one by helping to fill the grave with earth. For some this may seem difficult, but it is the last opportunity to do a physical act of love and kindness for the departed. This too is considered a *chesed shel emet*. By physically burying the deceased, we not only fulfill the mitzvah of *kavod hamet* but we also provide visible opportunity for the mourners to see, accept and embrace the death of their loved one. A healthy readjustment to society requires acceptance of the reality and finality of death.

The accepted custom is to do more than simply the minimum of covering the casket with earth. I make a point of encouraging family and friends to fill the entire grave with earth before leaving the cemetery.

I once officiated at the service of an elderly man in Seattle who never married. As a result, he had no children, but he had numerous loving nephews and nieces. As the family and friends were filling the grave with earth, one young man, clearly not Jewish, refused to give up his shovel and allow others to fill the grave. I approached and asked him what he was doing. He answered that he owed this act of respect to the deceased. I must have looked puzzled because an explanation followed. The deceased had employed this man's father, and many years earlier, when the man's father had died, the deceased had attended the service. This being a non-Jewish service, the burial of the body was left to the custodians of the cemetery. The deceased, however, stayed behind after everyone left and personally buried his friend. When the young son asked the deceased what he was doing, he responded by saying: "I'm showing your father the utmost respect because I loved him, and when I die, I want you to do the same for me." The man had promised he would, and on that day, he kept his promise.

Handing Over the Shovel

Another custom associated with the burial service is to take the shovel or digging utensil and not pass it from hand to hand. Rather the shovel is inserted back into the ground after it is used for the next person to take and use (*Hokhmat Adam* 158:30). The reason for this custom is to symbolically avoid making the person who is handed the shovel the messenger of the previous person. Each person performs the mitzvah individually, by personally picking up the shovel himself or herself.

While earth is being shoveled into the grave the following words are said:

> From dust you are created, and to dust you shall return.
> And He, the merciful One, will forgive iniquity and not destroy man.
> He will frequently turn aside His anger and not arouse all His wrath.

The *Hashkavah* (Memorial Prayer)

Although the version of the *Hashkavah* may slightly vary between communities, the central themes are identical. The themes of the memorial prayer include an affirmation that God is compassionate and merciful, and that the deceased is no longer in the community of the living. Now he is among the community of the holy and righteous who have preceded him or her in death.

The Moroccan Sephardic communities have a custom not to name the deceased in the *Hashkavah* until after the *shivah* period. Instead of using the name, reference is made to the deceased by saying *haniftar lebet olamo*, "He/she who has gone to his/her eternal home."

Customs vary among the many Sephardic communities as to whether one should reference the deceased with a mother's name or father's name (*Yalkut Yosef*, vol. 7 23:22). One should follow the custom of the community to which they belong.

At the cemetery:

- Some communities have the custom, following the *Hashkavah*, of having the children rise to ask *mechilah* (forgiveness) from the parent.
- The Syrian communities have the custom of blowing the shofar immediately following the *Hashkavah*.

- Some have the custom of using this opportunity to recite *Hashkavah* for the parents of the deceased, if appropriate, or for any close relatives who may have preceded the deceased in death.

The complete text of the *Hashkavah* can be found in Appendix 11.

Proper Behavior at the Cemetery

It is important that people show appropriate respect at the cemetery. The cemetery is not a place for frivolous behavior and idle talk. One should maintain a sense of solemnity and respect. It is forbidden to eat or drink in the cemetery proper. Those in attendance at the cemetery should be encouraged to dress appropriately and modestly.

There is a principle that one should not indulge in religious activities in the presence of the dead. Therefore, one should not study Torah at the cemetery or carry a *tallit* or *tefillin*. Men who customarily wear the fringes of their *tzitzit* outside their garments should make a point of concealing them while in the cemetery (SA YD 367:4, OH 23:2)[2].

Leaving the Cemetery

After leaving the cemetery, those in attendance should ritually wash their hands. At the exit of the cemetery, there is usually running water for this purpose. Some have the custom of reciting the words of Isaiah:

> May He swallow up death forever and may the Lord God wipe away tears from upon every face and remove the scorn of His people from the entire world, for the Lord has spoken (Yeshayahu 25:8).

---

2. For a discussion on the nature of visiting cemeteries see Yamin Levy and Amichai Levy, "Solemn Space: Praying at Cemeteries and the Prohibition of *Loeg L'Rash*" in *Rav Shalom Banayikh: Essays presented to Rabbi Shalom Carmy in Celebration of Forty Years Teaching*, Edited by Hayyim Angel and Yitzchak Blau, Ktav Publishers 2012.

After washing, the hands should not be dried with a towel or kerchief but should be left to dry naturally (*Kaf Hachaim* 4:8).

Accompanying the Mourners Home

It is appropriate to accompany the mourners from the cemetery back to their home (SA YD *Bet Yosef* 378). Once the funeral service is over, the mourners should not be left to grieve alone. Returning home with the mourner affords them an anchor, a sense of belonging, and important comfort.

Disinterment

Disinterment and the opening of the casket after burial, may never be undertaken without first consulting an authority on Jewish law. Jewish law completely prohibits such an action except for certain unusual circumstances (*Yalkut Yosef*, vol. 7 32:1 and 32:7). Even disinterment for the purpose of reinterment in another grave is strictly forbidden.

The Following Are Cases Which May Be Considered by Rabbinical Authorities as Exceptions to the Rule Stated Above:

- When a deceased has been buried with the intent of being reinterred in another grave at a later time. The Spanish and Portuguese community inter all their dead with the condition that they may have to be reinterred, if needed at a later time.
- If, after burial it was found out that the deceased wanted to be buried alongside their spouse and by doing so would facilitate visiting the graves of parents (*Yalkut Yosef*, vol. 7 32:1).
- If a man or a woman was buried in a wrong grave and the family wants to bury their parents next to each other (Ibid. 32:2).
- If the deceased will be reinterred in Israel (Ibid. 32:3–5).
- If the government appropriates the land for construction (Ibid. 32:10).

- If the gravesite will be destroyed by water or other natural disasters (Ibid. 32:13).
- If the deceased is being moved from a non-Jewish cemetery to a Jewish cemetery (Ibid. 32:9).

These and other such exceptions to the above rule are decided based on numerous factors, many of which are too complicated for the scope of the discussion here. Competent rabbinical council should be sought before making any decision on these matters.

Note that even when reinterment is permitted, a period of twelve months should have elapsed before disinterment is undertaken. Our sages regarded the transfer of bones as less of an assault on the dignity of the deceased than the transfer of a decomposing body.

If a body is disinterred, the grave and the monument cannot be sold or reused (*Gesher Hachaim* 26 3:2). The principle that governs this law is that one cannot benefit from the deceased. This includes the grave, casket, shrouds, and monument of the disinterred. The only way to reuse any of these items would be if they were used by indigent individuals in the community who could not otherwise afford a grave or monument.

Reinterment

An entire day of mourning must be observed at the time of reinterment of the remains of one's father, mother, or close relative (*Yalkut Yosef*, 32:10). This includes the prohibitions against wearing shoes, sitting on chairs or couches, marital relations, bathing, and so on (SA YD 403:1). Similarly, *keriah* and *seudat havra'ah* are performed immediately following the reinterment. The day of mourning concludes with nightfall.

The utmost respect must always be shown to the remains of the body. If the remains will be traveling a distance, they must be accompanied by a *shomer* (SA YD 403:10).

CHAPTER 7

Honoring the Living (*Kavod Haberiot*)

Shomreini El ki chasiti bakh
Watch over me, Almighty, for I have taken refuge in You
– Psalm 16:1

Love doesn't die, people do. So, when all that is left of me is love, give me away.
– Rabbi Allen S. Maller

How We Honor the Living

Grief, like a wound, requires proper attention to heal. Appropriately mourning the loss of a loved one is the natural way to resolve grief. That the mourner will ultimately recover from the sorrow of loss may seem to be an insurmountable feat, yet people do recover. This is nature's way. Forests burn down and eventually grow anew. The Jewish response to death is not only about loss and mourning but also about recovery and restoration. Though at times it may seem preposterous, even in the most excruciating circumstances the bereaved conquer their grief, they heal and even grow from the experience.

I have learned many lessons about grief from those who have trusted me as their rabbi. One of those lessons is that the only grief that does not end is the grief that was not mourned. People seek creative ways to avoid feeling the pain of loss and act as if nothing has happened. I have seen it repeatedly; no one succeeds in permanently denying the effects of death. Fear is probably the number-one barrier to mourning. It may be the fear of rejection by others brought on by being honest and open about one's feelings. Some fear that if grief takes hold, it will never let go. For this reason, our sages, of blessed memory, transmitted laws, practices, and customs that govern our treatment of death and the experience of mourning. The Jewish way of responding to death mandates laws that govern not only the behavior of the mourner, but the behavior of the community. Until this point in the mourning process, the entire focus has been on *kavod hamet*, maintaining the utmost respect and dignity of the deceased. From burial onward, the focus is now on *nichum avelim*, comforting the mourners. The community must be a supportive anchor for the mourners and allow them the opportunity to express their grief in a safe, sensitive environment. Judaism, through *shivah*, the seven-day period of mourning, offers the mourner a structure for open and uninhibited grief, allowing for an adequate response to the death of a loved one and a healthy way of coming to terms with loss.

Shivah is a Hebrew word that literally means "seven." It refers to the seven days immediately following the burial of a relative that are set aside for the full expression of grief. The tradition of *shivah* dates back to before the giving of Torah, as is evident from the story of Joseph, who mourned his father's death for seven days.

> And they came to the threshing floor of the thornbushes, which is on the other side of the Jordan, and they conducted a very great and impressive eulogy, and he observed for his father a mourning of seven days (Bereshit 50:10).

Jewish tradition recognizes the need of those in mourning to face their loss and not pursue regular daily living as if nothing unusual has taken place. During this period the mourner is placed in a safe and supportive atmosphere with family and friends to deal with the difficult realities of life and death. The period of *shivah* is designed to allow the mourner the opportunity to reflect upon moments and memories with the departed and gradually prepare the stage for a healthy transition to normal living.

It is the family, friends, and community volunteers who join the mourner in his or her grief and lend support and strength that makes the *shivah* experience meaningful. The family and friends are there to cater to the mourner's every need, be it physical or emotional.

Who Is a Mourner According to Jewish Law?

Mourning practices, according to Jewish law, are not optional. According to the Sages of the Talmud one is required to observe the laws of *shivah* for the following immediate relatives: father, mother, spouse, son, daughter, sister, brother, half-sister, and half-brother. Rabbinic law requires that *shivah* also be observed for one's maternal half-brother, married sister, and half-sister. Boys under the age of thirteen and girls under the age of twelve are not required to observe commandments. Regarding the rituals of mourning, however, if they can understand the situation, they should be encouraged to observe the laws of mourning (TB *Moed Katan* 14b, MT *Avel* 2:1 and SA YD 374:4).

Empathetic Mourning

A father or mother-in-law are not, according to *halakhah*, a relationship that requires the observance of *shivah*. Sephardic custom, however, expects that one observes some of the mourning practices for their father-in-law or mother-in-law as well as stepmother or stepfather. Although they are not halakhically required to mourn the death of the deceased, this group of mourners must mourn with the bereaved. The nature of this mourning is best described by Rabbi Yosef Karo in the *Shulchan Arukh*. He states as follows: "Whomever one mourns for, one mourns with" (SA YD 374:6; MT *Avel* 2:4).

In other words, the empathetic mourner joins their spouse or parents as a sign of respect and support. It affords the mourner comfort and support knowing that those closest to them are also observing some form of mourning. This level of mourning is not practiced by Ashkenaz Jewry (Rema 374:6). The empathetic mourner's *shivah* obligations are limited until the conclusion of the Shabbat following the burial. It is generally assumed that parents would not want their children mourning, therefore empathetic mourning does not apply when mourning the death of a grandparent. Similarly, one does not observe the laws of *shivah* for a son-in-law or daughter-in-law (MT Avel 2:4). Since empathetic mourning is a sign of respect and support for the mourner, its rituals are only observed in the presence of the mourner but are not relevant if the mourner is in a distant location or city.

Voluntary Mourners

How does Jewish law respond to the loss of a beloved person when the deceased is not one of the nine immediate relatives (see above) whom one is required to mourn and they don't fall into the category described above of empathetic mourners? The loss of a beloved rabbi or teacher, or of a grandparent or a dear friend can at times be as painful, if not more so, than the loss of an immediate relative. Within the framework of the laws of *avelut*, Rabbi Moshe Isserles, the chief Rabbi of Krakow between 1525 and 1572, formulated the need for a category that he called voluntary mourning (Rema 374:6). He understood that the traditional response to death was more than formulistic, but also therapeutic. He therefore created a religious response to the death of a beloved person who was not a halakhic relative. The only restriction placed on voluntary mourners is that they may not violate any Torah commandments. The exemption afforded the mourner from the daily study of Torah does not apply to the voluntary mourner.

Counting the Seven Days of *Shivah*

Shivah begins immediately after burial, more specifically once the grave is filled with earth, and lasts seven days. Jewish law considers a portion of the day to be a complete day. Therefore, even if the interment was completed in the late afternoon before sunset, that period is considered day one of *shivah*. Similarly, the observance of a minimum amount of *shivah* on the seventh day is considered a complete day. In other words, shortly after morning services on the seventh day of *shivah*, those present extend their last condolences and the mourners rise from their mourning (SA YD 395:1).

The total number of days the mourner observes for *shivah* are seven halakhic days but not necessarily seven full days.

Times When *Shivah* Does Not Begin Immediately After Burial

Holy Days or *Chol Hamoed*

If the death occurred during a holy day the burial takes place on *Chol HaMoed*, the intermediate day. *Shivah*, however, does not begin until *Motza'ei Yom Tov*, immediately with the conclusion of the holy day (SA YD 399:2). In such a circumstance the *shivah* does not begin after burial but rather after the holy day. Outside of Israel the last day of the holy day is counted as the first day of *shivah* even though the actual *shivah* practices begin with the conclusion of the holy day.

Burial in Israel

It has become a much more common occurrence for families to bury their loved ones in Israel. In such a situation the mourners who accompany the casket begin *shivah* after the burial. The mourners who remain behind begin *shivah* when the body leaves their presence (SA YD 375:2). Today however, with the advent of video conferencing, even mourners who remain behind begin their *shivah* immediately after burial.

When the Mourner Is Not at the Burial

If one will not be able to attend the funeral of an immediate relative, *shivah* begins at the exact time the burial took place. If, however, it is unclear when the burial will take place, *shivah* begins immediately upon hearing the news of the death (*Yalkut Yosef*, vol. 7 24:6).

When Burial Is Delayed

If the deceased was going to be buried in another city and the mourners who stayed behind began their *shivah* period, but a delay occurred and the deceased was not buried as scheduled, the mourners should not interrupt their mourning period. After burial, the mourners do not need to sit *shivah* again.

No Corpse

If, tragically, there is no corpse and news of the death was reported within thirty days of the death, the mourners begin *shivah* immediately upon hearing the news (*Yalkut Yosef*, vol. 7 24:7)

Times When *Shivah* Is Not Seven Days

Jewish holy days are considered moments of national celebration and as per Jewish law the individual must always count oneself along with the larger community. Therefore, if one of the major holy days occurs during *shivah*, the *shivah* is considered complete with the onset of the holy day (SA YD 399). Even if mourning began only one hour before the holy day, that one hour is equivalent to the observance of the full seven days of mourning and counts as seven days toward the thirty-day memorial. This will be explained in further detail later on.

Hearing About the Death After Burial

One is obligated to sit *shivah* even when the news of the death of a relative arrives after the burial, if it is within thirty days of the death according to the local time of the person who receives the news (*Yalkut Yosef*, vol. 7 34:7). Even if the news arrives on the thirtieth day one must sit *shivah* (*Yabia Omer* vol. 5 EH 7:4, p. 290). If, however, the news of death arrives after the thirtieth day from the time of death, then one sits *shivah* for only one hour based on the principle that was discussed earlier, "a portion of the day is considered an entire day" (SA YD 402:1 based on TB *Moed Katan* 20a and *Pesachim* 4a). The above also applies when the news involves one's parents. However, while the *shivah* restrictions do not apply when one is notified of a parent's demise, all the thirty-day restrictions of the *sheloshim* period go into effect, such as not getting a haircut, not shaving etc.

Double Grief

If two or more family members die on the same day, God forbid, the mourners observe only one *shivah* period for all those who passed away (*Bet Yosef* YD 375). If, however, a second family member dies while one is already sitting *shivah* for a family member, the mourner begins counting *shivah* from the time of burial of the second family member (SA YD 375:10). In other words, if a person has observed two days of mourning for a member of the family, and then a second member of the family dies and is buried on the second day, the mourner now observes seven days of *shivah*, restarting the counting of seven days with the second day of the original *shivah* counting as day one. At the conclusion of the *shivah*, the mourner need not observe any further mourning. In total the mourner has observed eight days.

Tearing a Garment (*Keriah*)

As was mentioned above, with the burial of the deceased the emphasis now changes from *kavod hamet*, honoring the dead, to *nichum avelim*, comforting the mourners. It is with this in mind that the *shivah* begins with the *keriah*, the rending of one's clothing. *keriah* is a physical expression of the mourner's anguish in a controlled, religiously sanctioned act in the presence of a rabbi and close family and friends. In the ancient near east and in some parts of the world, even today, some people cut themselves or mutilate their bodies as an act of bereavement. The Torah is in total opposition to such practices. Instead, *keriah* serves as a potent physical and emotional release of sorrow and anger at precisely the needed moment. *Keriah* also symbolizes the impermanent nature of our stay in this world and the ephemeral nature of material things.

The act of *keriah* as a sign of grief dates to biblical times. Jacob ripped his garment when he saw Joseph's coat of many colors drenched in blood. So, too, King David tore his clothes after hearing of the death of King Saul.

A rabbi or religious leader usually initiates *keriah*. The garment is first cut with a knife or blade and then the mourner takes both ends of the cut and tears the garment with his or her hands. *keriah* is done in a standing position (SA YD 340:1 based on TB *Moed Katan* 20a). A woman should be asked to assist with the *keriah* for a female mourner.

Immediately prior to the tearing of the clothes the following blessing is recited:

Barukh Attah Adonai Eloheinu Melekh Ha'olam Dayan Ha'emet.
Blessed are You, Lord our God, whose Judgement is righteous.

<small>The Hebrew can be found in Appendix 11.</small>

The complete blessing for *keriah* (as is found in the appendix) is only recited within the first three days after death. The blessing must coincide with the intense grief felt in the first three days of the loss.

Our tradition uses ritual to give form and shape to its objectives. The acts of rending a garment and reciting words that speak of divine justice allow mourners to express their inner selves in true human relatedness. In pagan cultures, the body of the mourner would be mutilated as a sign of mourning. In American Western culture, we choose to ignore the pain. Jewish tradition avoids these extremes. Instead, Jewish law asks that we rend our garments as a formal external expression of grief.

Laws of *Keriah*

- Both men and women must observe the mitzvah of *keriah*.
- Immediately following the *keriah*, women should safety-pin their cut garment for modesty reasons.
- Our sages of blessed memory sought to impress the importance of the *keriah* by stating that one who does not do *keriah* at the time of the death of a relative is worthy of death (TB *Moed Katan* 24a).
- *Keriah* is observed for the relatives that one is commanded to mourn; namely, father, mother, spouse, son, daughter, brother, half-brother, sister, and half-sister.
- A child who is old enough to understand that a family member has died, and that *keriah* is a sign of grief and mourning should be encouraged to perform *keriah* (SA YD 340:27).

> ## Appropriate Garment for *Keriah*
>
> - *Keriah* is done on the front of an outer garment that is worn indoors at normal room temperature (*Yabia Omer*, vol. 6 32:4, p. 252; also *Yalkut Yosef*, vol. 7 4:11). Therefore, one does not rend an undershirt or overcoat or other such garments for special temperatures.
> - While the initial cut may be done with a knife, the rest of the cut must be done by hand.
> - The practice of tearing a ribbon does not fulfill the mitzvah of *keriah* and should be strongly discouraged.

Keriah for a Parent

Some Sephardic communities make a distinction between the rending while one is mourning for a parent versus the rending while mourning other relatives. The communities that choose to make such a distinction will tear one's clothing on the left side next to the heart when mourning the loss of a parent. Because the heart is on the left side of the chest, most Sephardic communities today perform the *keriah* on the left side for all relatives.

For a parent, the *keriah* must be visible throughout the *shivah* period. If one is mourning the loss of a parent and must change his or her *keriah* garment during *shivah*, the second garment must also be cut. This is not the case for other relatives. Therefore, mourners who change their clothing during the *shivah* do not need to tear the new clothing. Immediately following *shivah* the rent garment can be removed (SA YD 340:14).

If *Keriah* Was Not Performed on Time

If one did not do *keriah* immediately following the burial service, it must be done sometime during the seven days of *shivah* (SA YD 340:18). If it is done before the third day of *shivah*, the appropriate blessing is recited. If it is done between the third and seventh days, the blessing is recited without including God's name (*Yabia Omer*, vol. 2 YD 23:5. page 190).

One does not perform *keriah* after the *shivah*. The reason for this is that *keriah* is only performed at a time of intense anguish. After *shivah* it is assumed that the period of intense grief is over, and therefore tearing a garment would be considered an act of wastefulness. This ruling does not apply for parents. It is assumed that the anguish for the loss of a parent warrants the tearing of a garment even after *shivah* (SA YD 396:1).

Sleepwear does not require *keriah*.

Keriah When Two Deaths Occur Simultaneously

If two family members die at the same time, *keriah* is only performed once for both deaths (SA YD 340:23). If a second family member dies after *keriah* has already been performed for a member of the family, the mourner can either extend the original tear three-and-one-half more inches or cut the same garment in a different place. The same applies if the second death occurs after *shivah* has concluded for the first family member (SA YD 340:21 based on TB *Moed Katan* 26b).

Keriah During *Chol Hamoed*

It is the accepted custom of the Sephardim that *keriah* is observed on *Chol haMoed*, the intermediate days of Pesach and Sukkot for all relatives, as long as the burial takes place at that time (*Bet Yosef*, OH 547; also YD 340:31). When this is the case, the garment is removed immediately after the *keriah* because there is no public mourning on the *moed* (*Yalkut Yosef*, vol. 7 4:17).

Lighting a Candle

It is customary to light a seven-day candle or have a candle lit for the entire *shivah* period (*Yalkut Yosef*, vol. 7 11:3) in memory of the deceased. Ideally the candle should be lit in the home of the deceased or wherever *shivah* is taking place. This is a custom that dates to the Talmudic period. The candle acts as a constant reminder of the deceased and represents the soul of the human being:

> "The soul of man is the candle of God" (Mishlei 20:27).

A candle or lighted wick is a beautiful symbol for the soul of the human being. Just like the flame on a wick, the soul is attached to the human body, giving off light and realizing the physical body's potential. The candle we light at the time of death may also represent the internal flame we all possess within ourselves, a sacred refraction of the divine light that God has shared with every one of us. The internal light equips us not only with the ability to distinguish between good and evil, compassion and cruelty, truth and falsehood, but also confers supreme value upon us, making each and every one of us special and unique, each created in the image of God.

The following declaration is made immediately prior to the lighting of the candle:

Hareni madlik ner zeh le'iluy nishmat –
avi **(father)** *imi* **(mother)** *achi* **(brother)** *achoti*
(sister) *beni* **(son)** *biti* **(daughter)**
followed by the name of the deceased.

I light this candle in loving memory of my –
father – mother – brother – sister – son – daughter.

The Meal of Consolation

Once at home the mourners sit on low chairs or on the floor and are served their first meal. This is called the *seudat havra'ah*, or meal of consolation. Our *hakhamim* stated unequivocally that the first meal must be supplied and prepared by friends, neighbors, and community members. Rambam writes as follows:

On the first day of mourning it is prohibited for the bereaved... to eat from their own food (MT *Avel* 4:9; see also SA YD 378:1).

Our sages of blessed memory cursed those who allow mourners to prepare their own *Seudat Havra'ah*:

A curse will come upon the neighbors if the mourner has to provide his own food (TY *Moed Katan* 3:1).

Preparing the mourners' food and serving them is subsumed under the mitzvah of comforting the mourners, *nichum avelim*. This mitzvah not only provides for the mourners' physical well-being, but also shows concern for their psychological needs. The *Shulchan Arukh* provides us with an interesting perspective regarding the meal of consolation. The *Shulchan Arukh* notes how the bereaved "are anxious over their loss." The mourner psychologically identifies with the deceased to the point where death becomes the only comfort. Mourners may not find the inner strength to nourish themselves, let alone prepare their own food. Being required to eat a prepared meal, however, is an affirmation of life. It is therefore the duty of the community to feed the mourners. Although they are required to sit on the floor, they must eat and affirm one of the basic acts of life's regular patterns. This is not a mere gesture of kindness but a direct means of assisting the bereaved back into society (Rabbi Emanuel Feldman).

The concept of *nichum avelim*, comforting the mourners, involves more than psychological and emotional comfort and support; it also involves taking an active role in the healing process of those in grief. While the mourners focus on their own emotional state, the community supplies their physical needs. The emphasis here is on the community and not on the individual. As individuals we have little or nothing to say to a person who has just buried a loved one. But as a community, by virtue of its very existence, we testify that death is not the end of life. Individuals live and die, whereas the community lives forever.

The meal of consolation must be the very first meal eaten by the mourners after the interment. While customs vary as to what is served, most include bread rolls for *hamotzi*, hard-boiled eggs, olives, raisins, and wine. Some vegetables or fruit may be included.

Each of the foods, over time, has developed its own folkloric and symbolic meaning. Eggs, for example, represent birth, and their shape is symbolic of the cycle of life. At a time of grief, we present the mourner with foods that remind us to affirm life. Other symbolic meanings of the egg may have to do with the fact that it is completely closed, with no mouth or opening (SA 378:8), which is symbolic of the way we want to respond to the tragedy of death. We do not question God's will; we accept it in silence, just as Aaron, the High Priest, responded when his sons died during their service in the Temple. The Torah records: *vayidom Aharon*, "Aaron remained silent" (Vayikra 10:3).

The hard-boiled egg in some communities is not served whole; it is cut in half as a symbolic act indicating that whatever bad decrees have been set upon us should be cut and severed.

The raisins also teach a beautiful lesson about life. A raisin is a dried, shriveled-up grape. From its appearance one could never believe that the finest of wines are produced from this very same fruit. So, too, human beings cannot be judged by their external appearance. Their real beauty and value, their soul, lies deep within themselves.

The wine has important significance as well. Wine is served to mark this meal as a religiously significant act. The intent, of course, is not to get drunk or be lighthearted, but to add meaning to the ritual.

Eating in the House of Mourning

Customs vary regarding the serving of food in the house of mourning to feed guests and visitors. Some Sephardi communities have the custom that visitors do not eat in the house of mourning (*Yabia Omer*, vol. 4 YD 35:4, p. 327) while other communities serve full meals.

Miscellaneous Laws About *Seudat Havra'ah*

- Jewish law is always concerned about seemingly improper acts that involve men and women. Therefore, it is proper practice at the meal of consolation that men serve men and women serve women (SA YD 378:2).

- If two mourners are sitting *shivah* together and there is no one to serve them their meal of consolation, they can serve each other as long as it is not stipulated that they are exchanging meals (SA YD 378:1).
- A mourner can refuse to eat the meal of consolation (SA YD 378:3).
- On the eve of Shabbat or Yom Tov, the meal of consolation must be served in the morning or early afternoon so that the mourner can have an appropriate appetite for Shabbat or the holy day (SA YD 378:5).
- If the burial took place more than thirty days before the mourner heard of the death, the meal of consolation is waived (SA YD 393:6).
- If two consecutive deaths occur, a meal of consolation must be served even while one is sitting *shivah* for the first death.

Birkat Hamazon (Grace After Meals)

After the *seudat havra'ah*, a special *birkat hamazon* is recited. When three or more adult males eat bread together, *birkat hamazon*, the grace after meals, is introduced by a formal invitation called *zimun*. When reciting the *zimun* in the house of mourning, the invitation is as follows:

> LEADER: He [God] will make death disappear forever, and the Lord will wipe away tears from upon every face, and He will remove the shame of His people from the entire world, for the Lord has spoken.
> Let us bless Him who comforts those who mourn, from whose [food] we have eaten.
> RESPONSE: Blessed be He who comforts those who mourn, of whose bounty we have eaten, and through whose goodness we live
>
> (Hebrew text can be found in Appendix 11.)

The regular *birkat hamazon* is recited until *bimhera beyamenu*; then the following paragraphs conclude the prayer.

> Comfort, O Lord our God, those who mourn for Zion and Jerusalem and those who are mourning in this grief. Console them in their bereavement and give them happiness after their sorrow. For it is written, 'As one whom his mother comforts, so will I comfort you, and through Jerusalem shall you be comforted.' Blessed are You, Lord who consoles those who mourn, and who will rebuild Jerusalem. May this be speedily and, in our days, Amen. Yes, in our days may Zion's city be built up and Your worship re-established in Jerusalem.
>
> Blessed are you, Lord our God, Ruler of the universe, God, our Father and Ruler, our mighty redeemer. You, Holy One of Jacob, living King, You are good, and You do that which is good.
>
> You are the God of truth, and Your decree is just. You take back our souls in Your universal rule, doing according to Your will; we are Your people and Your servants. Whatever may befall, we must acknowledge You and bless You.
>
> May He who gives strength to the bereaved, in His compassion give solace in this bereavement to us and all His people Israel. May He who creates the harmony of the spheres, in His tender love create peace for us and for all Israel, Amen.
>
> (For the entire Hebrew text of *birkat hamazon*, see Appendix II.)

On Shabbat

On Shabbat, if the mourner is saying *birkat hamazon* with no more than three men, he uses the special *zimun* (*Siddur Bet Oved*). However, with more than three people the above *zimun* is not used and the regular *birkat hamazon* for Shabbat is recited. The reason for this is because there is no public mourning on Shabbat and a group of more than three people would be considered "public."

CHAPTER 8

Laws and Customs of *Shivah*

God created ten strong things. The rock is hard, but iron crushes it. The iron is hard, but the fire softens it. The fire is strong but water quenches it. Water is strong, but the clouds carry it. The clouds are strong, but the wind scatters them. The wind is strong but the body bears it. The body is strong, but fright weakens it. Fear is powerful, but wine banishes it. Wine is strong, but sleep subdues it off. Death is stronger than all of them, but charity saves from death.
– Rabbi Yehuda HaNasi, TB *Bava Batra*

Where Is *Shivah* Observed?

Prior to the burial, the mourner is alone in his or her grief focusing on the necessary preparations for an appropriate funeral for their loved one. With the start of *shivah* the mourner is surrounded by family and friends, slowly reasserting their humanity and dignity.

Ideally there is one *shivah* observance in the home of the deceased with the entire family. If for some reason the *shivah* cannot take place in the home of the deceased, the next best situation is to observe *shivah* in the home of a close relative. The family should be together in one place for the entire seven days. The mourners should not leave the house of mourning during the *shivah* period unless there are extenuating circumstances (*Yalkut Yosef*, vol. 7 12:25) such as:

- Being needed in one's own home to care for children and/or a spouse.
- Not having enough room for everyone to sleep together in the house of mourning.
- A mourner losing, God forbid, another relative and needing to make the funeral arrangements.
- Not having a *minyan* that is able to convene in the house of mourning when the mourner must attend services to say *Kaddish*.
- If the mourner is the only mohel in a city and he is needed to perform a circumcision.

A mourner who must leave the house of *shivah* must do so inconspicuously and never be alone (*Magen Avraham* OH 239:7 based on TB *Berakhot* 54b).

Sitting on Low Chairs

The *halakhah* states that mourners do not sit on chairs; they either sit on the floor or on low stools. This tradition is first recorded in the Book of Job. The Bible tells us that Job and his friends sat on the floor during his mourning period. Rabbi Emanuel Feldman suggests that intimate contact with death has diminished the mourner's identity as a human being and therefore the mourner does not sit in the usual manner such as sitting on a chair or on a couch (p. 84). The mourner sits on a low stool as a sign of lowliness and diminution. Elderly people and those who are not fit physically able to sit on the floor or lower stools may sit in regular chairs.

Personal Grooming

During the period of *shivah* the mourner must show a disregard for personal vanity and physical comfort. The mourner experiences a temporary withdrawal from society to deal with the personal loss. At a time such as this the timeless words of King Solomon, *hevel havalim*, "Vanity of vanities, said Kohelet; Vanity of vanities, all is vanity" seem to be especially resonant. One grooms oneself to take part in society with others, to build relationships and engage in social activities. In contrast, the mourner is dealing with a relationship that has ended. Relationships are formed to plan future social events. The mourner, during *shivah*, on the other hand, is obsessed with relationships lost and with reviewing the past. Therefore, Jewish law states that during *shivah* mourners do not groom themselves for personal pleasure.

There is often confusion on the part of those who want to observe the *halakhah* but do not know how to distinguish between basic hygiene and pleasurable grooming, bathing, and showering. Jewish law forbids luxurious and self-indulgent grooming but expects mourners to maintain healthy hygiene. Based on the Talmud (TB *Moed Katan* 16b), the *Shulchan Arukh* (SA YD 381:1) and HaRambam (MT *Avel* 5:3–4) rule that one can wash parts of the body with water that is not hot during *shivah*. This may take the form of a lukewarm shower or the use of a washcloth. Most people would be very uncomfortable not washing for an entire week. The below Mishnah shares a fascinating incident suggesting that the mourning practices of grooming are not meant to disrupt basic hygiene and personal comfort.

> Rabban Gamliel bathed on the first night after the death of his wife. His disciples said to him: Master, have you not taught us that a mourner is forbidden to bathe? He replied to them: I am not like other men, I am delicate (Mishnah, *Berakhot* 2:6).

While relevant to our general topic, the above Mishnah does not represent the *halakhah*. The *halakhah* is that one should not groom oneself in a luxurious and indulgent fashion but must maintain basic cleanliness standards.

Summary of the Laws of Grooming During *Shivah*

- Bathing the entire body at one time is forbidden. Washing different body parrts in cold or lukewarm water is permitted (SA YD 381:1).

- If a mourner is excessively dirty or uncomfortable it would be permitted to be lenient in this law. The intent of the *halakhah* is to prohibit bathing for pleasure, not for necessity (SA YD 381:3).
- A sick person whose doctor recommends bathing may do so even in hot water during *shivah* (SA YD 381:3).
- Mourners may not soak or anoint their bodies with oils and cosmetics (SA YD 381:2).
- Haircutting and shaving are not permitted during *shivah* (TB *Moed Katan* 14b, SA YD 381:1). This prohibition does not include combing one's hair (SA YD 390:6). In fact, cleanliness and neatness should not be compromised during *shivah*.
- Mourners are prohibited from cutting their fingernails or toenails with an instrument (SA YD 390:7).

Extending Greetings

Mourners do not greet guests during the *shivah* period, nor do they inquire about another's welfare. If others ask about their welfare, during the first three days of *shivah* they should just respond by saying "I am a mourner" (TB *Moed Katan* 15b, SA YD 385:2). From the fourth day onward, the mourner may return greetings.

A mourner is not expected to rise in respect for any visitor, even if the guest is a renowned Hakham. A mourner who would like to show respect for a Torah scholar, however, may do so (*Yabia Omer*, vol. 3 YD 27, p. 200).

Greetings may be extended on Shabbat because not doing so would be considered a public form of mourning (SA YD 381:3).

Leather Shoes During *Shivah*

Mourners are not permitted to wear leather shoes (SA YD 375:1; 376:4; 382:1) Rabbi Yaakov Hayim Sofer (1870–1935), author of *Kaf Hachaim*, insists that one should not wear any shoes, even those that do not have any leather in them; one should only wear socks during *shivah* (*Kaf Hachaim* 554:70). The custom varies among the different Sephardic communities.

A woman within thirty days of giving birth is permitted to wear shoes during *shivah*. Similarly, a sick person, upon the recommendation of a doctor, can wear shoes (SA YD 382:2).

If a mourner must walk a long distance and not wearing shoes would be painful or dangerous, then he or she may wear shoes (SA YD 382:4).

Laundry During *Shivah*

Mourners are not permitted to wash or iron clothes during *shivah*. This prohibition includes soaking the clothes in water. Mourners are also not permitted to wear freshly laundered clothing or clothing that may have been washed by someone else during *shivah*.

Mourners are forbidden to wear new clothing even if it was bought before *shivah* (SA YD 389:1).

Under extenuating circumstances, such as two consecutive *shivah* periods, or if for some reason there are no clean clothes, a mourner can have some clothes washed without any laundering chemicals or agents (SA YD 389:1).

Children's clothing, especially soiled clothes, may be washed by people other than the mourners (SA YD 389:2).

Marital Relations During *Shivah*

A mourner is not permitted to have marital relations with their spouse during *shivah*. This law applies even on Shabbat, because, while all public practices of mourning are suspended, all private and personal demonstrations of mourning are in effect (SA YD 383:1 based on TB *Moed Katan* 15b).

A woman is not permitted to go to the *mikveh* while sitting *shivah* (SA YD 381:5).

Work and Business During *Shivah*

Jewish law states that during *shivah*, mourners are not permitted to work, manage a business, or invest any money by themselves or through the assistance of an agent. This prohibition includes non-Jewish hired employees of the mourner. These laws, however, vary so much in circumstance and case, and have so many exceptions, that one should consult a rabbi to address one's personal situation.

Expressions of Joy and Celebration

A mourner should refrain from anything that may cause him or her inappropriate laughter and unsuitable rejoicing. The Talmudic sages were concerned that such behavior will make a mockery of the *shivah* practice (TB *Moed Katan* 26b). The sages did not prohibit laughter per se, rather, they prohibited an atmosphere that would be inappropriate. Often reflecting on memories may lead to laughter, and of course that is permitted.

The Talmud introduces an example that may be prohibited for the mourner during *shivah*:

> Rav Papa said: A mourner should not place a young child on his lap because the child will bring him laughter (TB *Moed Katan* 26b).

Unlike our Ashkenaz brethren, Rabbi Yosef Karo notes that HaRambam codifies this ruling in the context of unnecessary conversation (MT *Avel* 5:20):

> If he (the mourner) is forbidden to greet a colleague during the mourning period, one can certainly infer that he is forbidden to engage in lengthy talk and frivolity, as implied by the instruction: "Be silent." He should not hold an infant in his arms so that he will not be led to laughter. And he should not enter a place of celebration and feasting.

For HaRambam and the *Shulchan Arukh* (SA YD 391:1) the prohibition of holding a child has less to do with laughter and more to do with being silent and reflective.

Some believe that children help bring solace and comfort to the mourners while other feel that a house of *shivah* is not an appropriate place for children. When deciding whether to bring children to a *shivah*, one should consider:

1. The nature of the child's relationship with the family sitting *shivah*.
2. The expressed wishes of the family.
3. The type of loss suffered by the mourners.
4. The child's behavior.
5. The child's ability to understand the meaning and significance of *shivah*.

Parents should use their best judgment and consult with others prior to bringing children to a *shivah* house.

Torah Study

In the spirit of mourners not engaging in things that bring them joy and delight, a specific kind of Torah study is prohibited during *shivah*, because it is a source of great joy and delight (*Yalkut Yosef*, vol. 7 13:2). This prohibition is limited to the Torah study that brings joy, such as the process of analysis of Talmud and *halakhah*. Examples would include the kind of study that challenges the mind, or the study of Torah texts and its exegesis that inspires the spirit. Having said this, the mourner is still obligated to fulfill the mitzvah of *Talmud Torah*, the study of Torah (*Yabia Omer*, vol. 2YD 27:2). The mourner, therefore, must fulfill the mitzvah of Talmud Torah, the daily study of Torah with the study of texts that do not inspire joy and delight. These texts may include the Book of Job, the book of Lamentations, certain parts of Jeremiah, and the laws that relate to mourning. The mourner is also permitted to study *Pirkei Avot* (Ethics of our Fathers) and other texts that focus on the development of character.

A teacher of Torah who is in mourning and has no one to replace him is permitted to teach Torah and to study in preparation for his or her classes (SA YD 384:1).

Berit Milah

The father or mother of a child to be circumcised who themselves are sitting *shivah* may attend the *berit* and may wear special clothing, newly laundered clothing, and leather shoes for the mitzvah of the *berit* and they may attend the celebratory gathering, the *seudat mitzvah*, as long as there is no music or dancing (*Mekor Chaim*, vol. 5 287:16). They attend humbly and deferentially. They should not sit at a head table nor participate in public speeches or announcements (*Yabia Omer*, vol. 7 18:12).

The father of the baby being circumcised may recite the *shehecheyanu* blessing (*Yalkut Yosef*, vol. 7 18:2).

A mourner, during *shivah* may be a *sandak*, which means that he may hold the baby during the *berit milah*, but he does not change his mourning clothing (*Mekor Chaim*, vol. 5 287:5). This leniency does not apply to any of the other traditional honors such as carrying the baby.

Some Sephardic communities have the custom of inviting family and friends to their home the night before a *berit milah* for a festive evening of prayer, study, and food. This custom is called *Berit Yitzchak* and can be observed during *shivah*. However, the focus of the evening should be the recitation of the appropriate texts and prayers, and not the festive meal (*Mekor Chaim*, vol. 5 287:15).

Pidyon Haben (Redemption of the First-Born Son)

Parents who are in mourning are permitted to participate in the redemption of the firstborn ceremony for their son. They may wear newly laundered clothing and leather shoes for the occasion. Similarly, they can partake of the festive meal if they do not sit down at a table (SA YD Rema 391:2). The father recites the *shehecheyanu* blessing at the *pidyon* of his son (*Yalkut Yosef*, vol. 7 18:2).

Weddings

A mourner who is observing the prohibitions associated with the death of a parent should not attend a wedding or any large-scale celebration for twelve months from the date of death. This rule applies for thirty days for all other relatives.

The parent of a bride or bridegroom who is in mourning may attend the wedding even during *shivah* because their absence will cause great distress to the bride and groom while their presence will bring them unique joy. The mourning parent can even partake in the festive meal, but may not sit at a table of honor, and should not participate in any dancing (*Yalkut Yosef*, vol. 7 18:8 end of footnote #9).

A mourner is not permitted to marry during *shivah* (*Yalkut Yosef*, vol. 7 18:7). After *shivah*, but within thirty days of bereavement, if the wedding had been planned the wedding may take place (SA YD 392:1). A mourner within thirty days of mourning who is scheduled to marry may get a haircut, shower, and shave in preparation for the wedding (*Mekor Chaim*, vol. 5 287:22).

Services in the House of Mourning

It is important to secure a *minyan* for services in the house of mourning during *shivah*. This practice, the Talmud tells us, is a great *zekhut*, or merit, and source of comfort for the mourners (TB *Shabbat* 154b). Ideally, services should be held in the home where the deceased lived (SA YD Rema 384:3).

The Order of Services When Held in the House of Mourning

Mirrors

It is customary to cover only the mirrors in the general area where the prayers will take place. The reason why the mirrors are covered is so that one does not pray while looking at a mirror. (*Yalkut Yosef*, vol. 7 11:7 especially note 7)

Shacharit Morning Services

The order of the prayers for *Shacharit* is the same as that of a regular morning service with a few exceptions.

- A *Sefer Torah* (Torah scroll) is brought to the home where *shivah* is taking place and read on Monday, Thursday and Shabbat (*Yalkut Yosef*, vol. 7 10:11).
- *Birkat Kohanim* (the priestly blessing) is recited during the repetition of the *amidah* (*Yalkut Yosef*, vol. 7 10:7 based on *Bet Yosef* OH 128 end).
- If the mourner is a *kohen*, he does not perform the blessing and must leave the room during the repetition of the *amidah* (Ibid.).
- On Shabbat, being that there is no public display of mourning, if the mourner is a *kohen* he performs the *Birkat Kohanim* (Ibid. and footnote 7 also *Bet Yosef*, end of 128).
- The *tachanunim*, penitent prayers, are omitted in a house of mourning (*Bet Yosef* 128, based on TB *Moed Katan* 16b and 27b).
- When prayers are held in the synagogue during *shivah*, *tachanunim* are also omitted as the *minyan* joins the mourner in his grief (*Yalkut Yosef*, vol. 7 10:9).
- Because the *tachanun* is omitted, so is Psalm 20 before *Uva LeTzion*.
- *Uva LeTzion* begins with *Attah kadosh yoshev tehillot*.
- Some communities have the custom of reciting *Kaddish Yehei Shelamah Rabbah* instead of *Kaddish Titkabal* (on the varying customs regarding this issue see *Yabia Omer*, vol. 4 YD 32:6, p. 320).
- On Rosh Chodesh, *Hallel* is recited. The mourner, however, does not participate in this part of the service (*Yalkut Yosef*, vol. 7 9:13 *Yabia Omer*, vol. 4 YD 33).
- On Hanukkah, *Hallel* is recited and the mourner participates in the *Hallel* because on Hanukkah, *Hallel* is not a custom but rather obligatory (*Yalkut Yosef*, Ibid.).
- Psalm 49 is recited in addition to the psalm of the day, after which the mourners recite *Kaddish*.
- At the conclusion of the service, *Tziduk Hadin* is recited, followed by the *Hashkavah* and *Bila Hamavet*.

Mincha

- *Tachanunim* are omitted.
- As was mentioned above, some communities have the custom of not reciting *Kaddish Titkabal*, and instead reciting *Kaddish Yehei Shelama Rabbah*.
- If *Arvit* does not immediately follow *Mincha*, then *Tziduk Hadin*, *Hashkavah*, and *Bila Hamavet* are recited at the conclusion of the *tefillah*, prayers.

Arvit

- On a weeknight the service begins with Psalm 49, followed by *Kaddish* and *Arvit*.
- In some communities *Kaddish Titkabal* is not recited, and instead *Yehei Shelamah Rabbah* is said.
- On Friday evening *Bameh Madlikin* is recited (*Yalkut Yosef*, vol. 7 10:14; see footnote on the page).
- Some communities have the custom to recite *Tziduk Hadin*, *Hashkavah*, and *Bila Hamavet* after *Arvit*.

Services in the Synagogue

When the services are not being held in the house of mourning, the mourners should be encouraged to go to a synagogue and say *Kaddish* with a *minyan*. The regular synagogue service is not changed when a mourner is present.

The following are the halakhic rules that affect the mourner in synagogue:

- Mourners do not sit in their regular seats. Many synagogues have designated seats for mourners. This *halakhah* applies for two weeks following burial (SA YD 393:2 based on TB *Moed Katan* 23a).
- When mourners are present in the synagogue *tachanunim* are omitted (*Yalkut Yosef*, vol. 7 10:9 especially footnote 9).

- At the conclusion of the service, *Tziduk Hadin, Hashkavah,* and *Bila Hamavet* are recited.

The *Kaddish* Explained

Today most people associate the recitation of the *Kaddish* with death and mourning. The reality is that this prayer has little to do with death. The content of the *Kaddish* praises God and affirms life without making any mention of the dead. There are five forms of the *Kaddish*. Two are recited during the prayer service, one after the study of Torah, and four are relevant to the mourner.

- **Chatzi Kaddish** is the first paragraph of the *Kaddish*. This is the earliest form of this prayer. It is recited in the middle of the service or before the *amidah*. In the Syrian community, it is customary for the mourner to recite this *Kaddish* along with the *shaliach tzibbur*, the leader of the prayer service.
- **Kaddish Shalem**, which includes *Titkabal*, and *Yehei Shelamah Rabbah*, and *Oseh Shalom Bimromav*, is always recited after the *amidah*.
- **Kaddish Al Israel** (also known as *Kaddish DeRabbanan*, the Rabbis' Kaddish) is recited after the study of *halakhah*, *midrash*, or *aggadah*. The mourner recites this *Kaddish* at every opportunity that arises.
- **Kaddish Yatom** is identical to the *Kaddish Shalem* except that *Titkabal* is omitted. The mourner recites this *Kaddish* throughout the year for a parent.
- **Kaddish Lehadeta** is recited immediately following the burial service at the gravesite. The text of this *Kaddish*, unlike the ones above, varies slightly from community to community.

History of the *Kaddish*

The original *Chatzi Kaddish* first appeared in the liturgy in Siddur Rav Amram Gaon, the first prayer book, compiled by Rabbi Amram ben

Sheshna Gaon, head of the Sura academy in Babylonia (856–874). *Titkabal, Yehei Shelamah Rabbah, Oseh Shalom Bimromav,* and the Rabbis' *Kaddish* are all later additions to the original *Chatzi Kaddish.*

The format of the *Kaddish* recited by the Sephardim comes from the *siddur* (prayer book) of Rabbi Saadia ben Yosef Gaon (882–942), who followed Rabbi Amram Gaon as head of the academy in Sura. This *Kaddish* went through various versions before it took on the final form that is recited today by Sephardic communities throughout the world. The earliest version that is close to the one recited by the Sephardim today is found in a classic work on liturgy by Rabbi David Abudarham (ca. 1340), a Spanish scholar from the city of Seville. *Kaddish* was a flexible liturgy that was often customized to different communities by their leaders. The early versions of the *Kaddish* were customized locally and often included the name of the rabbi and other matters specific to that community.

The earliest reference to the *Kaddish,* or more specifically a Hebrew version of a line in the *Kaddish,* is found in the Talmud. It goes as follows:

> Rabbi Yose related that once, when he entered one of the ruins of Jerusalem to pray, Elijah the prophet appeared to him and berated him for endangering his life in such a way. Elijah then asked Rabbi Yose: "What sound did you hear there?" He answered that he heard a sound like that of a dove cooing: "Alas... that I destroyed My house, burned My Temple, and exiled My children among the nations of the world!" The prophet Elijah then assured him that whenever Jews enter their synagogues or houses of Torah study and respond: *Yehei shemo hagadol mevorakh,* the Holy One, blessed be He, as it were laments: "Happy is the King who is so praised in His own house, and woe to the Father who drove His own children into exile" (TB *Berakhot* 3a).

Rabbi Hayim David HaLevy, in his book *Mekor Chaim,* points out that this allegorical Talmudic passage makes a connection between the *Kaddish* and mourning for the destruction of Jerusalem and the dispersion of the Jews (*Mekor Chaim,* vol. 1 40:1). He further notes that this passage suggests that the *Kaddish* became part of the liturgy only after the destruction of the Temple, and that part of its message is messianic in nature.

The first words of the *Kaddish*, "Exalted and sanctified be His great name" *Yitgadal Veyitkadash Shemeh Rabbah*, echo the words of Ezekiel the prophet:

> Thus, will I be exalted and sanctified, and I will make Myself known in the eyes of many nations, and they shall know that I am the Lord (*Vehitgadalti vehitkadashti*) (Yechezkel 38:23).

The above words were spoken by Ezekiel the prophet to a humiliated and disconsolate people in exile. His words boosted their morale and kindled a spark of hope for national and individual redemption. The *Kaddish*, then, is meant to be a declaration of hope and faith in our people's national purpose and personal relationship with God. It is a prayer of longing for a time when all people will accept the heavenly mission that gives meaning to life and transcends death.

The reason for its popularity may be precisely because *Kaddish* is such a powerful response to death. It involves not only the reader but also those present at the time of its recitation. "Through the *Kaddish*," writes Rabbi Joseph B. Soloveitchik, "we hurl defiance at death and its fiendish conspiracy against man." The Rav continues:

> When the mourner recites *Yeheh shemeh rabbah mevorakh*, "Glorified and sanctified be the Great name..." he declares more or less the following: No matter how powerful death is, notwithstanding the ugly end of man, however terrifying the grave is, however nonsensical and absurd everything appears, no matter how black one's despair is and how nauseating an affair life itself is, we declare and profess publicly and solemnly that we are not giving up, that we are not surrendering, that we will carry on the work of our ancestors as if nothing had happened, that we will not be satisfied with less than the full realization of the ultimate goal of the establishment of God's kingdom (*Reflection on the Rav*, Rabbi Avraham Besdin, vol. 2).

The reader not only makes this declaration himself, but he calls out to the congregation to join him. The reader begins with the words "Exalted and sanctified be His great name throughout the world that He created." The congregation then answers the reader's declaration with the following words: "Amen. May His great name be blessed forever and ever."[1] The sages of blessed memory regarded this response as the main theme of the entire *Kaddish*. They comment that the response Amen, *Yehei Shemei Rabbah Mevorakh*, is so powerful that it has the ability to inspire *teshuvah*, spiritual transformation, for those who recite it with intent (TB *Shabbat* 119a).

Responding *Amen*

The mourner should recite *Kaddish* at every service daily, beginning immediately after burial throughout the twelve-month mourning period for a parent. It is a prayer that is considered *davar shebikedushah*, a prayer of special significance, and requires a *minyan*, a quorum of ten men present to be recited. The mourner, therefore, never stands alone when reciting the *Kaddish*. The mourner is in the presence of others who respond Amen, not only as part of the prayer but also as an acknowledgment of the mourner's loss.

The response Amen is used throughout the *Tanakh*, Bible, as a means of endorsing a blessing or in some cases, even a curse (Bemidbar 5:22; Devarim 27:15 and Yirmiyahu 28:6). Its literal meaning is "So be it," or "truly." Our sages of blessed memory viewed the response of Amen as an affirmation and acceptance of faith (TB *Shevuot* 36a). A Jew is therefore obligated, according to HaRambam, to respond Amen when hearing a blessing, because his response is a testimony to the truth of the blessing and an expression of his own faith (Commentary on Mishnah, *Berakhot* 1:13; also SA OH 215). Amen is indeed so powerful a response that it is considered tantamount to having said the blessing itself. According to one opinion in the Talmud, the response Amen outweighs the recitation of the blessing itself (TB *Berakhot* 53b).

---

1. This phrase is taken almost verbatim from Daniel 2:20. The Talmud *Pesachim* 56a claims this phrase was coined by Yaakov Avinu on his deathbed.

The reason for this extraordinary statement may have to do with the root of the word Amen, which according to the Talmud is made up of three letters: *alef, mem,* and *nun,* these letters stand for *El Melekh ne'eman,* "God is a faithful King" (TB *Shabbat* 119b). While a blessing is restricted in its scope, the response Amen is all-encompassing and all-inclusive in its meaning.

Considering all this, we can now better understand the comment found in the Talmud, which states:

> One who responds Amen with the fullest devotional concentration, the gates of paradise are open [for him] (TB *Shabbat* 119).

In other words, by saying Amen in a sincere and devout fashion, one expresses total faith in God, and this indeed leads to a sense of peace and serenity that is likened to paradise.

Amen should therefore not be said in haste or mispronounced.

Kaddish as a Daily Reminder

The trajectory of the grief process is unpredictable (Keenan, Susan L. PhD, Life and Recovery). At times the sense of loss feels especially intense, while at other times it feels more resolved. The Talmud tells the story of the death of Rav, one of the great scholars and the founder of the Babylonian academy of Sura. Rav's disciples met on a riverbank shortly after his burial. Upon completing their meal, they discussed a matter of Jewish law which they were unable to resolve. One of the disciples, Rabbi Ada bar Ahava, got up and made a second tear in the garment, which he had previously rent in grief. He said: "Our teacher is dead, and we haven't even learned from him some basic laws!" Tragically, at that moment they felt the intense loss of their revered teacher differently than they had felt it before. Their teacher was gone, and his loss was especially poignant when they needed to resolve a matter of Jewish law. All mourners experience these kinds of moments. The *Kaddish* serves as a daily response to grief's surprises throughout the first year of mourning.

Laws of *Kaddish*

In Israel it is the custom among Sephardim that the mourner recites his first *Kaddish* immediately prior to burial. This is generally not the accepted custom outside Israel (*Mekor Chaim*, vol. 5 291:3).

Kaddish is recited for twelve months, beginning on the day of burial (SA OH 132:2). Some have the custom of reciting *Kaddish* for eleven months and resuming for one more month after the first *Hazkarah*, the memorial prayer (*Mekor Chaim*, vol. 5 291:15–16). Following the one-year memorial, *Kaddish* is recited annually during the week preceding the anniversary of the death.

- If one dies without children or has children who will not recite *Kaddish*, another family member or friend may recite the *Kaddish* instead (*Bet Yosef* YD 403 end).
- stepson or adopted son may choose to recite *Kaddish* for a deceased stepparent or adopted parent. Grandchildren can recite *Kaddish* if the deceased has no living children or none of the children of the deceased will be reciting Kaddish (*Kaf Hachaim* 55:28; *Mekor Chaim*, vol. 5 291:10).
- If a rabbi dies without leaving sons, *Kaddish* may be recited by one of his students (SA YD Rema 376).
- If a parent asked one or more of his children not to recite *Kaddish* after his or her death, some authorities suggest that the child not honor the parent's request (*Yabia Omer*, vol. 6 YD 31:4).
- If one only heard of the death long after the burial, *Kaddish* is recited from the moment one hears the news until the twelfth month from the time of burial (*Gesher Hachaim* 30:95).
- If one heard of the death after the twelve-month period, *Kaddish* is not recited.
- Women are permitted to recite *Kaddish* (*Aseh Lecha Rav*, vol. 5, chapter 33, pp. 230–236).[2]

---

2. Joel Wolowelsky, "Women and Kaddish." *Judaism* 44, 3 (1995).

- A child should recite *Kaddish* for a parent even if the boy is younger than age thirteen or the girl is younger than age twelve (*Mekor Chaim* 291:8).

Converts and the Laws of *Shivah*

"A *ger*, convert to Judaism, is like a newborn babe" (TB *Yevamot* 62a). The implication of this statement is that converts do not align themselves genetically with their biological parents. This principle has significant halakhic ramifications in a wide variety of areas. Two examples include the laws of inheritance, and the mitzvah of procreation. According to biblical law, a convert does not inherit from his or her father's estate (TB *Kiddushin* 17b) and does not fulfill the biblical mandate to be fruitful and multiply through the children born while still a gentile (TB *Yevamot* 62a). In other words, there is a complete genealogical break between converts and their life pre-conversion.

This genealogical break is limited, however, to matters that do not affect the honor and respect that must be shown to one's natural parents. HaRambam, in his *Mishneh Torah*, states that although halakhically and formally the convert is as a newborn child, the natural parents must continue to have and deserve a unique place in the child's life (MT *Mamrim* 5:11). *Halakhah* mandates the convert show love, honor, and respect to his or her biological parents in life and in death. Therefore, there is no doubt that converts can mourn the death of their gentile parents if they choose to do so.

Of course, the mourning practices must be Jewish rituals and not those of the convert's former religion. Rabbi Yosef Karo, in his *Bet Yosef* code, discusses this issue and suggests that converts exemplify self-respect by mourning appropriately in a way that fits their Jewish religious outlook and practices (*Bet Yosef* YD 274).

Rabbi Ovadia Yosef encourages converts to recite *Kaddish* for their biological parents (*Yabia Omer*, vol. 6 YD 36; also *Yechaveh Da'at*, vol. 6 Chapter 60). Similarly, he encourages the recitation of *Hashkavah*, the memorial prayer, at the appropriate times. "Since his parents struggled to bring him [her] into this world," writes Rabbi Yosef, "should he [she] not help them cross the threshold into the world-to-come?"

Shivah on Shabbat

All mourning observances are divided into two categories. The first are those that reflect a public mourning, and the second are those that are of a personal and private nature. On Shabbat one's mourning is diminished. Unlike the Jewish holy days that are intrinsically celebratory and communal and therefore cancel the mourning practices, Shabbat preserves all private mourning practices. On Shabbat all mourning observances that are of a public nature are suspended, but all private and personal practices are observed (TB *Moed Katan* 23a–24a also SA YD 400).

Therefore one should note the following *Halakhot* relevant to Shabbat:

- Mourners cease to observe all public mourning on Friday afternoon approximately two and a half hours before sunset in order to prepare themselves and their households for Shabbat (SA YD 396; *Mekor Chaim*, vol. 5 286:40).
- Mourners can wear leather shoes and leave the house to go to synagogue (SA YD 400:1).
- Mourners do not wear the torn garment usually worn during *shivah*; instead, freshly washed clothes may be worn in honor of Shabbat (Ibid.).
- If, however the mourner will be alone on Shabbat he may choose to continue wearing his / her torn garment.
- The private mourning practices that must be observed even on Shabbat include abstinence from marital relations and bathing because they are private practices (Ibid.).
- The study of Torah is forbidden even on Shabbat, except for study of the weekly Torah portion (Ibid.).
- In most Sephardic communities the mourners sit in their regular seats in synagogue on Shabbat (SA YD 393:4). In some *kehilot*, communities, however, the mourner sits in a designated area for mourners (*Mekor Chaim*, vol. 5 286:45 and footnote). Today the ancient custom continues in many Sephardic com-

- munities that the congregants take turns sitting behind or opposite the mourners during the service as a sign of comfort and support.

- A mourner does not get an *aliyah* to the Torah, nor is he honored with any of the *mitzvot* on Shabbat (SA YD 400:1).

- If *shivah* ends on Shabbat the mourner rises from their *shivah* before *Barukh She'amar* and gets an *Aliyah* to the Torah (*Yalkut Yosef*, vol. 7 19:6).

- A mourner who is a *kohen* can go up to the Sefer Torah for his *aliyah* if there are no other kohanim in the synagogue (*Mekor Chaim*, vol. 5 286:48).

- On Shabbat a *kohen* who is a mourner performs the *Birkat Kohanim*, Priestly Blessing, during *shivah* (Ibid.).

- A mourner who eats alone or with three or fewer people recites the mourners *birkat hamazon* after each of the Shabbat meals. If the mourner eats with more than three people, the regular *birkat hamazon* is recited (SA YD 379:4).

Motza'ei Shabbat, the Conclusion of Shabbat

When Shabbat ends, the mourner removes his or her leather shoes without touching them immediately following *Barekhu et Adonai Hamevorakh* of the *Arvit* service. If services are being held in the home of the mourner, some communities omit the verse *Vihi Noam* and begin with *Yoshev Be'seter Elyon*. If services are held in the synagogue, they proceed as usual.

Havdalah During *Shivah*

A mourner who recites the *Havdalah* does not recite the introductory verses and begins immediately with the blessing over the wine. Immediately following *Havdalah*, the mourner must change out of his Shabbat clothing and put on his or her mourner's garments.

Concluding *Shivah*

As was mentioned above, in Jewish law, part of a day is considered an entire day; therefore, on the seventh day of *shiva*, shortly following the morning services, *shiva* officially terminates. After services the *Hashkavah* is recited. Before the mourners rise from their mourning period, all those present gather around the mourners and recite the following verses:

> Thy sun shall no longer go down, nor thy moon wane. For the Lord shall be thy everlasting light and the days of thy mourning ended. As one whom his mother comforts, so will I comfort you, and through Jerusalem shall you be comforted.

(Hebrew text can be found in Appendix II.)

If the conclusion of *shiva* happens on Rosh Chodesh, the above verses should be said to the mourner immediately following the *amidah* so that the mourners can participate in the recitation of *Hallel* (*Hazon Ovadia*, vol. 2, p. 186).

Rabbi Yehudah Ashkenazi, author of the Bet Oved Siddur, describes how at the end of *shivah* those present physically lift the mourner. In other words, the comforters help to clearly distinguish the period of grief from the period of healing (post-*shivah*) by raising the mourner from the ground (*Siddur Bet Oved* p. 238). Some have the custom of taking the mourner outside the house to walk a short distance as a sign that he or she is ready to enter back into society.

Unlike our brethren the Ashkenazim who do not shower for thirty days following the burial of an immediate relative (SA YD Rema 381:1) it is the custom of the Sephardim to permit bathing of the entire body even in hot water immediately after *shivah* (MT *Avel* 6:12; SA YD 390:6; *Yabia Omer*, vol. 4 YD 34).

Various Customs Pertaining to the Concluding Service of *Shivah*

Ladino Sephardim from Turkey and Greece

On the night of the seventh day after burial, the Ladino-speaking Sephardim hold a *Meldatho*, (ladino for memorial service), at the home where *shivah* was observed. This service is called *El Corte de Siete*, meaning "the end of the seven days." Before the evening services, those present study Mishnah in memory of the deceased. At the conclusion of the study, the Mourners' Kaddish is recited, followed by the *Arvit* service; after *Arvit, Hashkavah* is recited. Those present partake in some food that is prepared by the hosts. A charity plate or container from the synagogue is passed around.

Moroccan Community

Among the Moroccan Jews the concluding service, which is called *Mish-Marah*, takes place the night before the end of *shivah*; in other words, on the night of the sixth day of mourning. The study consists of reading the Zohar, portions of Torah, and Prophets. At the *mishmarah* for a man, *Shuva Israel* (Hosea 14:2–10) is recited. At the *mishmarah* for a woman, *Vatitpalel Chana* (1 Samuel 2:1) is recited. The name of the deceased is spelled by reciting the appropriate paragraphs from Psalm 119, the *Alfa Beta*. At the conclusion of the study, *Hashkavah* and *Kaddish* are recited, and again those present are invited to partake in some food.

Syrian Community

Among the Syrians, this service is called *Arayat* and is held on the afternoon of the final day of *shivah*. The *Arayat* is held after *Mincha*. The study for this service includes Zohar and portions of the Torah. Again, food is served for those present. After the meal *Arvit* is recited, followed by *Hashkavah* and *Kaddish*.

Persian Community

The Persian community observes a memorial service on the evening before the last day of *shivah*. The service begins with *Patach Eliyahu* followed by *Mincha*. Between *Mincha* and *Arvit* words of Torah and remembrances are shared. The service concludes with *Arvit* and *Hashkavah*.

Visiting the Cemetery After *Shivah*

In some communities it is the custom to go to the cemetery after the services on the seventh day (SA YD 340:15). One does not go to the cemetery on Shabbat. If the seventh day of *shivah* is on Shabbat one may go to the cemetery on Sunday.

After leaving the graveside one should place his hand on the grave and say the following words:

> The Lord shall guide you continually, satisfy your soul in drought, and strengthen your frame. And you shall be like a watered garden, yes, like a spring of water whose waters fail not. Then shall you find delight in the Lord, and I will make you to ride on the heights of the earth and nourish you with the heritage of Jacob your father; for the mouth of the Lord has spoken it.

(Hebrew text can be found in Appendix 11.)

If *Shivah* Was Not Observed

If for some reason *shivah* was not observed immediately after burial, it should be observed within thirty days of the death (SA YD 396:1). After the thirtieth day, *shivah* is observed for an hour (*Yalkut Yosef*, vol. 7 34:1–2) and all the restrictions of *sheloshim* apply. If one begins *shivah* on the twenty-fifth day after death, it terminates on the thirtieth day.

Informing Another About a Death

If a person does not know that a family member has died, the *Shulchan Arukh* states that there is no obligation to inform him or her immediately (SA YD 402:12). If, for example, the person is going to attend a wedding ceremony, there is nothing wrong with holding the news from him or her until after the wedding. Similarly, if God forbid, there is fear that the news of the death will harm the person, it can be withheld until a more opportune time. Of course, it is forbidden to lie. If the person asks about the relative, the truth must be stated.

CHAPTER 9

Yom Tov, Chol Hamoed, and the Cycle of the Year

> I have set before you life and death, blessing and curse, therefore choose life that you and your offspring may live.
>
> – Devarim 30:19

When Holy Days Cancel Mourning

Judaism has afforded us the wisdom of a healthy response to grief and loss in which we can work through our bereavement and journey toward resolution. Jewish practice presents rituals and structure that enable mourners to develop the inner resolve necessary to return to society both emotionally and spiritually stronger. The *shivah* period enables the bereaved to acknowledge the tragedy of death in a safe and secure environment and at the same time to reaffirm their relationship with God, who is the source of both life and death. This time of adjustment has a unique dimension insofar as it mandates the members of the community to be present for the mourner, to cater to the needs of the bereaved and share in their loss. The laws and rituals of *avelut* are important aids in the expression of loss and overcoming of grief.

There are instances when *shivah* and the mourning rituals are not observed despite the benefit they afford the bereaved. This happens when *shivah* is interrupted by *Yom Tov*, a Jewish holy day. The guiding principle is as follows: "National celebration subsumes the individual" (TB *Moed Katan* 19b). Rabbi Joseph B. Soloveitchik, z"l, in an article entitled "Catharsis," deals precisely with this issue and describes the halakhic tension the individual experiences under these circumstances:

> [*Avelut*] is an inner experience of black despair, of complete existential failure, of the absurdity of being. It is a grisly experience which overwhelms man, which shatters his faith and exposes his I-awareness as a delusion. Similarly, the precept of *Simchat Yom Tov* (to rejoice on a holy day) includes, not only ceremonial actions, but a genuine experience of joy, as well. When the Torah decreed *vesamachta bechagekha*, "And thou shall rejoice in thy feast," it referred, not to merrymaking and entertaining, to artificial gaiety or some sort of shallow hilarity, but to an all-penetrating depth-experience of spiritual joy, serenity and peace of mind deriving from faith and the awareness of God s presence. Now let us visualize the following concrete situation. The mourner, who has buried a beloved wife or mother, returns home from the graveyard where he has left part of himself, where he has witnessed the mockery of human existence. He is in a mood to question the validity of our entire axiological universe. The house is empty, dreary, every piece of furniture reminds the mourner of the beloved person he has buried. Every corner is full of memories. Yet the *halakhah* addresses itself to the lonely mourner, whispering to him: "Rise from your mourning; cast the ashes from your head; change your clothes; light the festive candles; recite over a cup of wine the *Kiddush* extolling the Lord for giving us festivals of gladness and sacred seasons of joy; pronounce the blessing *shehecheyanu*: 'Blessed art thou...who has kept us in life and has preserved us and has enabled us to reach this season;' join the jubilating community and celebrate the holy day" (Soloveitchik, "Catharsis" *Tradition* 17 no. 2 [Spring 1978]).

Rabbi Soloveitchik describes what is indeed a most difficult experience, a time when Jewish law intervenes in the most intimate and personal aspects of our lives. It is an example of when the Jew is called upon to subject himself or herself in a total fashion to the divine call.

Jewish law mandates that when a festival interrupts a mourning period, it completely consumes the individual grief and cancels it. Therefore, if mourning began even one hour before dark on the eve of a Jewish holy day, the onset of the festival not only cancels the remainder of the *shivah*, but it becomes equivalent to seven full days of mourning. Therefore, with the onset of the holy day, one is only twenty-three days away from *sheloshim* (more on this later).

The following holy days interrupt and cancel the mourning of *Shivah* and *Sheloshim*:

Pesach, Sukkot, Shavuot, Rosh Hashanah, and Yom Kippur (SA YD 399:1, 6). This applies when mourning is observed before the holy day even for a short time. If, however, the mourner did not observe any form of mourning before the holy day, the *shivah* period is not cancelled and must be observed immediately after the festival.

When the holy day is going to interrupt and cancel the mourning period, the mourner is permitted to prepare after midday on the eve of the holy day. At that time, mourners can launder their clothes, but may only wear them after the holy day begins (SA YD 399:5). Bathing is permitted after midday even in hot water to prepare for the holy day. The prohibitions against getting a haircut and shaving, however, are not affected by the holy day. The mourner can get a haircut or shave only after he is reprimanded by his social peers for his unwieldy appearance after thirty days (SA YD 399:4).

If Death Occurs on *Yom Tov*

If death occurs on *Yom Tov*, during the holy day, or so close to the holy day that there is no time to make arrangements for a funeral, the body must be left untouched until after the holy day. Only under extenuating circumstances may the body be moved during a holy day. If death occurs in a hospital or nursing home on a holy day, and the hospital or nursing home does not allow the body to remain on its premises until the end of the holy day, a non-Jew should be asked to contact a funeral home that has non-Jewish employees. The body is then picked up and held until the conclusion of the holy day. The funeral service should be scheduled immediately after the holy day, even on *Chol HaMoed*, the intermediate days of the holy day.

Eulogy, *Keriah* and *Seudat Havra'ah* on Holy Days and *Chol HaMoed*

- When death occurs on *Chol HaMoed*, no eulogy is delivered even for a scholar whose body is present and not yet buried.
- *Keriah* is never performed on the holy day itself, not even in the diaspora on the second day (SA YD 340:31).
- If death and burial take place on *Chol HaMoed*, the mourners return home and *keriah* is performed. Shortly after the *keriah* the rent garment is removed, and the mourners wear regular clothing until after the holy day (Ibid.; also OH 547:6).
- A meal of consolation is served to the mourner, but it is not eaten on the floor. Rather, it is eaten at the table in the company of others (SA YD 401:4) and should not consist of eggs but of cakes and the like (*Yalkut Yosef*, 26:14).
- At the conclusion of the holy day, the mourner puts on the rent garment and observes all the restrictions of *shivah*.

Counting *Shivah* and *Sheloshim* Interrupted by *Yom Tov*

When burial takes place on *Chol HaMoed*, *shivah* begins immediately at the conclusion of the festival. In the Diaspora the last day of the holy day is counted as day one of *shivah* even though the restrictions of *shivah* are not observed until after the holy day (SA OH 548:1).

Sheloshim, however, is counted from the day of burial (ibid). Therefore, it is not necessarily twenty-three days after the *shivah*.

Comforting the Mourner on Shabbat and *Yom Tov*

Even though *shivah* does not begin until after the holy day, mourners can be visited and comforted on the holy day (*Yalkut Yosef*, vol. 7 11:1 based on SA YD 399:1). Care should be taken to make sure visits take place not only during the holy day but also throughout the seven days of *shivah*.

Laws Relating to the Calendar Cycle

Rosh Chodesh

- On Rosh Chodesh, *Hallel* is recited in the house of the mourner but the mourner/s do/does not participate in the recitation of *Hallel*. They either sit or exit the room where the *Hallel* is being recited (*Yalkut Yosef*, vol. 7 9:13). If the seventh day of *shivah* is on Rosh Chodesh the mourner is raised from their *shivah* immediately after the repetition of the *amidah* and the mourner chants *Hallel* with the worshipers.

Tishrei

- On the eve of Yom Kippur, the mourner is permitted to sit on a chair at the table and eat the *seudah hamafseket*, the last meal before the fast, joined by others (*Yalkut Yosef*, vol. 7 25:2).

- The period between Yom Kippur and the end of Sukkot is considered an especially festive time because it is the period in which King Solomon finished building the Temple in Jerusalem. Therefore, many have the custom not to fast during this period. Sephardim, however, make an exception on the anniversary date of the death of a parent. A person who has the custom of fasting on that date should continue to do so even between Yom Kippur and Sukkot (*Yalkut Yosef*, vol. 7 25:1).

- The mourner is obligated to perform the mitzvah of dwelling in the *sukkah* (SA OH 640:5). If, however, sitting in the *sukkah* is not enjoyable or is painful, the mourner is exempt.

- During *Simchat Torah* the mourner is permitted to carry a Torah scroll and encircle the *tevah* (readers' podium) but cannot participate in the dancing with the Torah (*Kaf Hachaim* OH 669:33).

Kislev

- Hanukkah does not interrupt or cancel any mourning practices and prohibitions (*Kaf Hachaim* OH 670:20).
- On Hanukkah the deceased is not eulogized (SA OH 670:1).
- Memorial services can be held during Hanukkah. Going to the cemetery, however, is not permitted.
- The mourner can light his *Hanukiah* at home with the appropriate blessings, including *shehecheyanu* on the first night. The mourner is not permitted, however, to light the *Hanukiah* in the synagogue on the first night during the twelve-month period following the death of a parent and the thirty-day period following the death of a relative (*Yalkut Yosef*, vol. 7 25:5).
- *Hallel* is recited in the home of the mourner (*Hazon Ovadia*, vol. 3, p. 37).

Adar

- Purim is like Shabbat in that any form of public mourning is prohibited, whereas personal mourning is required.
- Mourners are permitted to wear shoes, change their rent clothes, go to synagogue and listen to the reading of the *Megillah* even when mourning the death of a parent (*Yalkut Yosef*, 25:6).
- Mourners are not permitted to bathe or shave on Purim.
- Purim day is counted toward the completion of *shivah*.
- If the burial takes place on Purim day, no eulogy is delivered. *Keriah* is performed but the garment is immediately removed, and the meal of consolation is served to the mourner (*Yabia Omer*, vol. 4 YD 26; *Yalkut Yosef*, 25:6).[1]

---

1. There is an apparent contradiction in the *Shulchan Arukh* regarding how a

- The question of whether a mourner within twelve months of the death of a parent can read the *Megillah* in synagogue is disputed by the halakhic authorities, and each community must follow its own custom.
- Mourners are obligated to fulfill all the *mitzvot* of Purim, including *mishloach manot* (sending food gifts), giving charity, and partaking in a festive meal. The community, however, should not send the mourner *mishloach manot* during the year of death of a parent or within thirty days of the death of a relative (SA OH 696:6). A mourner who is within twelve months of the death of a parent may play music in honor of Purim and in order to make the Purim meal festive (*Yalkut Yosef*, vol. 7 25:11).

Nisan

- It is permitted to fast during the month of Nissan on the anniversary date of the death of a parent.
- A mourner during *shivah* who is a firstborn is not permitted to attend a *siyyum* (the festive meal celebrating the completion of a tractate of Talmud) in order to eat. A *siyyum* is traditionally observed on the eve of Pesach as a celebratory meal associated with a mitzvah.

Sivan

- Mourners are permitted to attend a *Tikun Lel Shavuot*, the midnight Torah study on Shavuot, even during *shivah* if this is something they customarily do every year (OH 559:6).

Av

- On Tisha Be'Av the mourner attends services in synagogue to participate in the *Kinot* and *Eikha* service (*Kaf Hachaim* 554:56).

---

mourner observes Purim. In OH 696:4 it states that all the laws of mourning apply on Purim and Hanukkah. In YD 401:7 it states that the public mourning practices are not observed on Purim.

- Because Tisha Be'Av is a day of national mourning for the destruction of the Bet HaMikdash, even during *shivah*, a mourner may be called up to the Torah and recite *Maftir* at the morning service on Tisha Be'Av. This does not apply at *Mincha*.

CHAPTER 10
Getting Married When in Mourning

Just as the Holy One fills the world with blessing, so does the soul fill the body. Just as the Holy One sees but cannot be seen, so does the soul see but cannot be seen. Just as the Holy One is pure so is the soul pure

– TB *Berakhot* 10a

When Death Occurs Prior to a Scheduled Wedding

If the death of an immediate relative for whom the bride or bridegroom are obligated to sit *shivah* occurs within seven days of their planned wedding, the wedding must be postponed. It can take place, however, if the scheduled date is after the conclusion of the *shivah*, even though the wedding will take place before the conclusion of the *sheloshim* (*Yalkut Yosef*, 18:7 Footnote 7).

Scheduling a Wedding

A wedding date can be scheduled any time after the *sheloshim* period even if it is to take place before the end of the twelve-month mourning period for a parent (*Mekor Chaim*, vol. 5 287:21).

When Death Occurs Immediately After a Wedding

If the death of an immediate relative of either the bride or groom takes place during the seven festive days immediately following their *chuppah,* all mourning practices are postponed until after the seven days of celebration for the bride and groom (Siddur Bet Oved; *Yabia Omer,* vol. 6 YD 34, p. 256; *Yalkut Yosef,* vol. 7 24:5).

In such a case the following *Halakhot* must be observed:

- There is no *aninut* period.
- *Keriah* is not observed even if the deceased was a parent (*Yalkut Yosef,* loc. cit.).
- The mourner recites the blessing *Dayan Ha'Emet* immediately following burial (*Yalkut Yosef,* loc. cit.).
- The bride and groom do not attend the funeral service.

Throughout the week of festive celebration following the wedding, the bride or groom who is bereaved is exempt from all the prohibitions that would normally apply to mourners. In other words, they may eat with people, be festive, launder their clothing, and even get a haircut and shave. A bereaved groom can study Torah during the entire week of festivity. The mourner is, however, prohibited from having marital relations with his or her new spouse (SA YD 383:2).

A bride or groom who is the only mourner observes an entire *shivah* period after the week of festivity. If, however, the mourner will join parents or siblings in mourning after the seven days of festive celebrations the newlywed concludes the *shivah* with the other mourners even if this means that he or she does not observe a full seven days of mourning (*Yalkut Yosef,* vol. 7 24:5). Jewish law recognizes that mourning is not a strictly private experience but also a familial experience. Therefore, the *shivah* period is dependent on the larger family or the elder of the family.

Second Marriage

The laws outlined above only apply when it is appropriate to have the *Sheva Berakhot,* the seven days of celebration for a bride and groom. The seven days of rejoicing are observed only for a first marriage for both the bride and groom. If, however, this is a second marriage for either of them, only three days of rejoicing are appropriate. In such a situation, the laws of mourning are suspended for only three days.

The seven or three days of suspended mourning do not count toward the *sheloshim*. The count of the thirty days of *sheloshim* begins with *shivah*, the mourning period (SA YD 383:2).

CHAPTER 11

Zakhor – How a Jew Remembers

Life can only be understood backwards, but it must be lived forwards.
– Soren Kierkegaard

The Obligation to Remember

Jewish law has delineated particular stages in the mourning process and has set limits for every stage of grief.

> **The first three days are for weeping, seven days for lamenting, and thirty days for abstaining from laundered garments and from cutting hair** (TB *Moed Katan*).

Post-*Shivah*

With the conclusion of *shivah*, the period of *sheloshim*, thirty-days begins. Like *shivah* the counting of the *sheloshim* begins with the burial of the deceased and concludes on the morning of the thirtieth day. HaRambam, in his code of Jewish law, the *Mishneh Torah*, writes as follows regarding the thirty-day mourning period:

> It is a rabbinical enactment that the mourner must observe certain practices of mourning for the entire thirty days. On what did the sages base the thirty-day mourning period? On the verse "She shall weep for her mother and father for a month"

(Deuteronomy 21:13). This implies that the mourner grieves for thirty days (MT *Avel* 6:1).

Throughout this period, it is appropriate to extend condolences if they were not extended during *shivah* (SA YD 380:2). The twenty-three days immediately following *shivah* are marked by the continued observance of certain restrictions. These restrictions include:

- The mourner is prohibited from getting a haircut or shaving during the *sheloshim* period (SA YD 390:1). Certain communities permit a mourner to shave after *shivah* if he can prove that the deceased parent requested that he not observe this requirement (Hakham Shaul Matlub Abadi in *Magen Ba'adi*, pp. 133–144).
- It is forbidden to cut one's fingernails and toenails with an instrument like a clipper or scissors (SA YD 390:6).
- Mourners do not wear new clothing or freshly laundered clothing during this period (SA YD 389:7).
- Mourners should not attend festive meals, parties, or celebrations (SA YD 391).
- Mourners should not attend live music performances, operas, or similar performances.
- Mourners should not listen to recorded music unless it is incidental music, such as the background music of a commercial.
- On Purim, the mourner is not given *mishloach manot* but must observe the mitzvah by sending *mishloach manot* to at least two people (see above).

Permitted Social Gatherings During *Sheloshim*

- Mourners may attend a *Kiddush* in their own synagogue.
- Mourners may partake of Shabbat meals with friends and guests.
- mourner who is a musician, photographer, or caterer and must attend a large social function for income purposes may do so.

Counting the Thirty Days of *Sheloshim*

While the word *sheloshim* means "thirty," the *sheloshim* period does not always last thirty full twenty-four-hour days. As in the case with *shivah*, the beginning of a day counts as an entire day. Therefore, *sheloshim* begins immediately after burial and that part of the day is counted as the first day and concludes in the morning of the thirtieth day. Furthermore, the *sheloshim* period can be dramatically shortened when a major festival occurs during this period. The actual duration of the *sheloshim* is subject to several variables.

- While *sheloshim* begins immediately following interment, its restrictions manifest themselves only after the *shivah* period.

- major festival (Rosh Hashanah, Yom Kippur, Sukkot, Pesach, or Shavuot) cancels the *sheloshim* period provided that the *shivah* period has been completed or was terminated by one of the major festivals. For example: (1) If *shivah* is completed even one day before Pesach, the *sheloshim is canceled*. (2) If Rosh Hashanah occurs during *shivah, sheloshim* is canceled with Yom Kippur which occurs ten days later. Similarly, if Yom Kippur cancels the *shivah*, Sukkot cancels the *sheloshim*.

- If Pesach cancels one's *shivah*, that *shivah* observance, even for one hour is considered seven days. Those seven days are added to the eight days that the festival is observed, making fifteen days completed toward the thirty days of *sheloshim*. In other words, there are now only fifteen days left of *sheloshim* restrictions.

- All the major festivals (Pesach, Shavuot, Sukkot, Shemini Atzeret) are considered to equal seven days.

- When *shivah* is terminated by Sukkot, at the end of the holy day there are only eight days toward the completion of *sheloshim*: seven days of *shivah* plus seven days of Sukkot plus seven days for Shemini Atzeret means that twenty-one days have been counted toward the thirty days of *sheloshim*.

Conclusion of *Sheloshim*

There are numerous customs as to how the conclusion of *sheloshim* is observed. Some communities hold a memorial service at the home of the mourner while others observe it privately.

Excessive Grief

Rabbi Yosef Karo, author of the *Shulchan Arukh*, states that it is forbidden to excessively mourn the death of a loved one. Indeed, left to our own intuitive devices, we might run the risk of not knowing how to limit our mourning. Because the emotional wounds incurred from the loss of a child, or the loss of a life-long companion, or the loss of a parent or sibling never fully heal, a mourner risks getting caught in a web of endless grief. Jewish law clearly marks the beginning and end of the mourning practices. On the verse in Yirmiyahu: "Weep not for the dead, neither bemoan him" (Yirmiyahu 22:10) the sages say:

> 'Weep not for the dead' excessively; 'neither bemoan him' more than required. What is the required amount? Three days for tears, seven days for tribute, thirty days to abstain from haircutting and shaving. More than this God wonders if you are more merciful than Him! (TB *Moed Katan* 27b).

In its infinite wisdom, our tradition prevents the bereaved from getting pulled into an interminable grief. There can be limits to the grief felt no matter how tragic and how painful it may be. The framework our tradition affords us prevents us from mourning too little and from mourning too long.

Haham Ovadia Yosef, *z"l*, recommends that mourners not go to the cemetery too often (*Yalkut Yosef*, vol. 7 6:16). One should be forward thinking and take joy in life and the life of one's family. Being around the cemetery and dwelling on the death of one's beloved leads to unnecessary sadness. Instead, one's energies should be placed in creating a healthy and sound future, forming positive relationships and growing emotionally and spiritually.

Twelve-Month Restrictions for Loss of a Parent

The *sheloshim* restrictions described above apply to all mourners who have lost an immediate relative. When one loses a parent, the restrictions listed above should be observed for twelve months (SA YD 391:1). Jewish law insists that one must show respect to parents while they are alive and even after their death. How so?

> The sages taught, 'Honor your father and mother' honor them during their lifetime and after their death. How? When one repeats a teaching of his or her father or mother within twelve months of their passing, one says in the name of my father my teacher or my mother my teacher, after the twelve months one says 'may their memory be a blessing' (TB *Kiddushin* 31b).

Regarding personal grooming, however, the law provides for the principle of "social reproach."[1] This means that after thirty days of mourning for a parent, if someone makes a comment to the mourner that his hair is too long or his beard is unwieldy, he is permitted to shave and get a haircut. If no one makes a comment but the mourner's hair is so long that it is quite out of character, then he can use his own judgment and get a haircut (SA YD 390:1 based on TB *Moed Katan* 22b).

Throughout the twelve-month period following the death of a parent, mourners should abstain from attending festive celebrations, parties, social gatherings, even public religious celebrations.

The exceptions to this rule are:

- It is permitted to attend the *berit milah* (circumcision) or *pidyon haben* (redemption of the firstborn) of one's own child even during *shivah*. The father of the child may dress in new clothing and partake in the *seudat mitzvah*, festive meal (*Yalkut Yosef*, vol. 7 18:12).

---

1. This expression is taken from Rabbi Maurice Lamm's book *The Jewish Way of Death and Mourning*.

- Mourners may choose to attend a *berit milah* even when the child being circumcised is not their own. They can also partake in a full formal meal if there is no music (*Gesher Hachaim* 21:8–5).
- Attending the *Bar* or *Bat Mitzvah* of one's own child is permitted if there is no music or dancing (*Yalkut Yosef*, vol. 7 18:12).
- Attending the *chuppah* (wedding ceremony) of one's own child or grandchild is permitted. One may even attend the festive meal (SA YD 402:9 *Yalkut Yosef*, vol. 7 18:8).
- After observing the *sheloshim* for a parent and within the *sheloshim* for all other relatives a mourner may attend the *chuppah* of a friend or relative if there is no musical accompaniment.
- Attending community business meetings is permitted.

Because of the complex nature of these issues and the many different situations, one should always consult a rabbi before making final decisions on these matters.

Personal Improvement

A child, our sages teach us, brings merit to a deceased parent through his or her actions, character, and good deeds (TB *Sanhedrin* 104a). A parent's influence is felt for an entire lifetime and the person one becomes is a constant reflection of the parents' influence.

Memorial Services

The memorial service for a loved one commemorates the enormous tragedy of death and is a tribute of love and honor to the deceased. It is a time set aside to reflect and remember the impact the deceased may have had in one's life. These services are referred to by different names. As previously discussed, in the Judeo-Spanish community they are called **Meldathos**, in the Syrian community they are called **Ariyat**, and the Moroccan community calls it a **Mishmarah**. These services are observed primarily for parents, spouses, children, and siblings, but can be observed for other relatives and friends.

There are various times during the first year of mourning that a memorial service is traditionally held. The various communities have different customs as to how many such services are observed.

Hazkarah

The last memorial service of the first twelve months of mourning is commonly known by its Hebrew name, *hazkarah*. The custom in some communities is to hold the first year *hazkarah* of the deceased on the date of burial; in subsequent years it is held on the date of death. In a leap year the first year *hazkarah* is observed twelve months from the date of burial. There is an alternative custom that commemorates the first year *hazkarah* and subsequent *hazkarot* on the date of death (*Yalkut Yosef*, vol. 7 22:3).

The Hebrew anniversary does not coincide with the anniversary on the Gregorian calendar in secular use. Therefore, one should consult a rabbi or synagogue for the date of the *hazkarah*. The *hazkarah* is always observed in the same month and on the same day.

Leap Years

- When death occurs in Adar 1 of a leap year, the *hazkarah* is always observed on the day of death.
- When death occurs in Adar 2 of a leap year, the *hazkarah* is observed in Adar during a regular year and Adar 2 in a leap year.
- When death occurs in Adar of a regular year, the *hazkarah* is observed in Adar 2 of a leap year (SA YD 391:2; OH 568:7).

Different Time Zones

If a death occurs on a certain date and the mourners are in another country where it is the next day, the rule is that the *hazkarah* is observed according to the date of the place where the death occurred (*Gesher Hachaim* 32:14).

Hazkarah Observances

- It is customary to begin reciting *Kaddish* with a *minyan* beginning on the Shabbat before the *hazkarah* (*Mekor Chaim*, vol. 5 291:17).

- On the day of the *hazkarah* for a parent, some have the custom to fast the entire day (SA OH 568:7).

- If the *hazkarah* falls on a holy day or Shabbat, one should not fast, as it would conflict with the joyous spirit of the day; the fast can be postponed to the next day (SA OH 568:9).

- It is appropriate to light a candle on the day of *hazkarah* either at home or in the synagogue.

- On the day of *hazkarah*, one recites psalms, studies *Mishnayot*, and has the *Hashkavah* recited.

- One should observe this day by abstaining from participating in parties or festive gatherings.

- It is customary to visit the cemetery and recite Psalm 119 (SA YD 344:20). Full text of Psalm 119 can be found in Appendix II, pp. 17–21.

- On Shabbat prior to the *hazkarah* it is customary to either be called up for *Mashlim* (the last of the seven *aliyot*) and recite *Kaddish* or be called up for the *haftarah*.

Many congregations will give priority to those observing *hazkarah* for a parent, over the *hazkarah* for a spouse, child, or sibling. On Shabbat prior to the *hazkarah*, one has the *hashkavah*, the memorial prayer, recited.

Visiting the Graves of Loved Ones

Visiting the graves of parents, loved ones, and ancestors is an ancient custom. It is a show of respect and honor to the deceased and to the cherished memories shared with the loved one. When visiting the graves of the deceased, even the graves of scholars and holy people, one should be discouraged from praying to them. The deceased are not and should never be regarded as intermediaries between God and the living.[2] Each of us has direct access to God through prayer.

The appropriate times to visit the cemetery are:

- Fast days (SA 579:10)
- On the seventh day of *shivah*
- On the thirtieth-day memorial
- On the day of the *hazkarah* each year

Some communities have the custom of visiting the cemetery before Rosh Hashanah and before the month of Nissan.

The cemetery should not be visited on Shabbat or holy days. One does not visit the cemetery during the entire month of Nissan or the entire month of Tishrei except for the visit on the *hazkarah*.

Entering the Cemetery

If one has not seen Jewish graves for thirty days, one recites the blessing before entering the cemetery (see Appendix II, p. 5). Some have the custom of placing a small pebble or stone on the headstone or grave. This is a sign of honor to the deceased and a marker that someone has visited this place.

Reciting Psalms at the Cemetery

It is most appropriate to recite psalms at the gravesite. Psalms 16, 17, 33, 72, 91, 104, and 130 are all suitable. One can recite the verses of Psalm 119 beginning with the letters that spell the name of the deceased and the word *neshamah* or soul. *Hashkavah* is said after the recitation of psalms, and if there is a *minyan*, *Kaddish Yehei Shemei Rabbah* is recited.

Leaving the Cemetery

When leaving the cemetery, it is customary to ritually wash one's hands. No blessing is said on the washing of the hands, and it is the custom not to dry them with a towel or kerchief.

---

2. For more on this subject, see the article I wrote with my son Amichai titled, "Solemn Space: Praying in a Cemetery and *Loeg LaRash*," in *Rav Shalom Banayikh*, edited by Hayyim Angel and Yitzchak Blau (Ktav Publishers, 2012).

Erecting a Monument

Erecting a monument as a marker over the grave of a loved one is an ancient tradition in Judaism. The earliest record of such a tradition can be dated back to biblical times when Jacob placed a monument on the grave of his wife Rachel (Bereshit 35:20). Our sages in Mishnah, *Shekalim* 2:5 state:

> With the remainder of the money collected for the needs of the deceased, they built a monument for his grave.

Jewish law dictates that the immediate family of the deceased is responsible for providing a monument on the grave. It is part of the mitzvah of showing honor to the deceased (*Bet Yosef* 348; MT *Avel* 4:4).

The monument has several purposes.

1. It is there to indicate that someone is buried in the ground and proper respect must be shown to that place.
2. It also serves as an indicator that *Kohanim* should avoid that place in order not to defile themselves.
3. Finally, it is a sign of honor for the deceased, so that friends and family can identify the place of burial and visit the gravesite when appropriate.

The monument is made of stone. In Hebrew the word for "stone" is *tzur*. The same word is also one of God's names describing God's ever-present nature. Just as a stone lasts forever, so too God is ever-present in our lives. Erecting a monument of stone is a way of saying that the memory of the deceased will linger forever.

Arranging for a proper monument is considered an integral part of the burial arrangements. Immediately following *shivah*, the family must begin the process of preparing the monument. Cemeteries usually have guidelines as to the maximum size for acceptable monuments. One should be cautious not to be overly ostentatious. The monument should be dignified and in good taste.

The inscription on the monument should include the full Hebrew name of the deceased and his or her mother's name as well as the full English name, the date of death, and the deceased's Jewish status (i.e., *kohen* or Levi).

Along with the above information, the inscription will include the Hebrew letters *peh nun*, פ"נ, which stand for *poh nitman*, "here rests," or *mem kof*, מ"ק, *matzevet kevurah*, "monument of burial for." Underneath the inscription the monument will also include the following Hebrew letters: *taf nun tzadik bet heh*, ת'נ'צ'ב'ה', which stand for *tehe nishmato/nishmatah tzerurah bitzror hachaim*, "May his/her soul be bound up in the bond of eternal life."

The Unveiling Service

The unveiling service is the formal dedication of the monument erected at the grave of the deceased. The ideal time to dedicate the monument is between the *sheloshim* and the beginning of the eleventh month. The unveiling should not be scheduled on *Chol HaMoed*, the intermediate days of Pesach and Sukkot, Rosh Chodesh, Hanukkah, Purim, Lag La'Omer, or during the month of Nissan. The general rule is that the unveiling should not take place on any day when the penitential *Tahanunim* prayers are not recited.

The unveiling service is centered around the recitation of Psalm 119, known as the *Alfa Beta*. The name of the deceased is spelled out with the appropriate chapters of Psalm 119 (see Appendix). If one has not been to the cemetery for thirty days, the blessing before entering the cemetery should be recited (see Appendix II, 5).

CHAPTER 12

When a Baby Dies: When Saying Hello Means Saying Goodbye

> When a baby dies, the opportunity to discover who in fact this little being was, his or her potential and characteristics dies as well. The hopes, dreams, and expectations remain unrealized. A hole is left in the fabric of the family, a lost member, a lost part of the parents' own selves.
>
> – Yamin Levy, "Confronting the Loss of a Baby"

Grieving for a Baby

Grieving the death of a baby is very different from grieving for a spouse, parent, sibling, older child, or any other loved one. There are numerous factors that affect the course of a person's grief, but the death of a baby is especially difficult to endure.

The entire experience of death and mourning in Judaism is a process that enables the bereaved to strengthen themselves, their families, and their community ties. Every stage of the grief process, from the moment one is confronted with an ailing relative and must assist the dying with the recitation of the *Viduy*, the personal confession, all the way through the first-year anniversary of the death, integrates the loss and the memory of the deceased into the life of the bereaved. All these rituals afford mourners a structure that leads to resolution and places it within a theological perspective. When a child dies in infancy, after the age of thirty days, the bereaved are afforded the same complete framework of religious observances, necessary rituals, and support to accept the death, grieve, and go on living. When the death of a baby occurs within the first thirty days of its life Jewish law does not prescribe any mourning rituals at all. The baby is named and buried.

Miscarriage and Stillbirth

When a pregnancy ends in a miscarriage or a stillbirth, or a baby dies less than thirty days after birth, from the standpoint of Jewish law one does not observe any kind of mourning ritual or grief period for this baby.

No matter how short the baby's life, the bond between parent and child cannot be denied. Research is finally being done on the effects of miscarriage, stillbirth, and infant death. As a result, health professionals and pastoral professionals are learning what parents have known all along: The sorrow and pain of losing a baby are as profound as any other loss, and in some ways even more complicated.

The need for formal religious mourning after the loss of a baby became especially clear to me after my wife and I experienced such a loss and did not have a religious structure available for grief, guidance, and support. Through our grief, I learned of the amazing power a modest ritual can have. We felt an intense need to respond spiritually and there was nothing available. We felt somewhat abandoned.

I discussed this in total candor with my rabbinical colleagues and found them to be understanding and supportive. Those who had experienced a similar loss shared my sense of abandonment and expressed a need for a change in attitude. Ever since my personal experience with the loss of a baby, I have counseled numerous couples who also expressed how they would have found comfort in a religious and spiritual response to their loss. Indeed, the loss is painful, and the silence unbearable.

During the nine-month period that I was writing my book *Confronting the Loss of a Baby: A Personal and Jewish Perspective*, I received many letters from men and women who had lost a baby and were courageous enough to share their experience. Here is one of the many letters I received from a Jewish woman describing her need for a religious response to her loss.

> Dear Rabbi Levy,
> I am very interested in the work you are doing on grief and mourning for a newborn child. As I told you over the phone our daughter was born on the way to the hospital and she was not breathing. The hospital staff could not resuscitate her. It wasn't until we left the hospital without our baby that her death became a reality. We called our rabbi who has known our family for years. He was very supportive and comforting but that was all he offered. I inquired about saying *Kaddish*, about sitting on the floor and tearing *keriah* and he said that is not done under these circumstances. "What circumstances?" I asked. He went on to explain how this kind of death is different.
> I was truly at a loss. I needed a religious anchor and there was none. We grieved silently and alone.

It is a grave misconception to view the laws and rituals of mourning as a burden on the bereaved. If anything, they are an incredible source of support and validation that ultimately pave the way to a complete healing. The mental health system is now aware of the pain of those who suffer a miscarriage or stillbirth.

And so now a new generation of social workers and rabbis grope for ways in which people can acknowledge and cope with this kind of loss. It is not enough to tell the parents that the mourning rites are not necessary, as if the rites were an onerous burden from which we are trying to spare them. The mourning rites are a therapy, not a burden, and if we excuse those who are suffering from that form of therapy, we do them no favor.

Today we recognize that holding one's baby before and after death is an opportunity to love and gather positive memories of the child. Feeling sad, angry, or lonely is a healthy reaction associated with grief.

Talking about the baby with someone who can listen is correctly viewed as therapeutic and healing. Even taking pictures and gathering mementos can become very important later. The need to arrange a religious funeral service, attend the burial, recite *Kaddish*, and recognize a mourning period with rituals that offer support and comfort to the bereaved should not be overlooked.

The bereaved who allow themselves the necessary time and afford themselves appropriate responses to grieve are more likely to be on the road to resolving their grief. Those who do not, eventually recognize that their lives are burdened by a grief they have never resolved (I.G. Leon, *When a Baby Dies: Psychotherapy for Pregnancy and Newborn Loss*, pp. 97–131).

That we can grieve and recover from a loss of this nature seems to be an amazing feat, yet human resilience is amazing. I strongly suggest that those who have lost a baby read my book *Confronting the Loss of a Baby: A Personal and Jewish Perspective* for a religious and spiritual response, in the context of Jewish Law.

> King David said… "But now he is dead, can I bring him back again? I shall go to him, but he will not come back to me" (2 Samuel 12:23).

APPENDIX I

Reflections and Meditations

I

"You protect my head on the day of kissing" (Psalm 140:8). The day when the two worlds kiss each other [is] the day a man leaves this world and enters the world-to-come.

(TY *Yevamot* 15:2)

II

Rav had a favorite saying: "The world-to-come is not like this world. In the world-to-come, there is no eating, no drinking, no procreation, no commerce, no envy, no hatred, no rivalry; the righteous sit with crowns on their heads and enjoy the radiance of the Divine Presence."

(TB *Berakhot* 17a)

III

Rabbi Joseph the son of Rabbi Joshua ben Levi became ill, and his spirit flew away. After his spirit returned to him, his father asked him, "What did you see?" He replied, "I saw a world turned upside down – the people high up here were moved down, and the lowly were moved up." Rabbi Joshua said, "My son, you saw a world in which right is made clear. But what of you and me, where were we placed?" "Just as we are esteemed here, so were we esteemed there. I also heard them say, 'Happy is he who comes with his learning in hand.' I also heard them say, 'They who were martyred by the [Roman] government, no man is allowed to stand within their compartment.'"

(TB *Pesachim* 50a)

IV

All of Israel have a portion in the world-to-come, as it is said: "Your people are all righteous. They shall inherit the world that is forever:
The branch of My planting, the work of
My hands, wherein I glory" (Isaiah 60:21).

(TB *Sanhedrin* 90a)

V

We have been taught: For twelve months the human body remains in existence while the soul ascends and descends [to join the body]. After twelve months the body ceases to exist, and the soul ascends to the treasury of souls and descends no more.

(TB *Shabbat* 152b–153a)

VI

"They are new every morning; great is Your faithfulness" (Lamentations 3:23). Rabbi Alexandri said: "Because You renew our spirits each and every morning [as we awaken], we are certain that in Your faithfulness You will restore our spirits to us at the resurrection."

(*Bereshit Rabbah* 78:1)

VII

We have been taught that Rabbi Shimon ben Eleazar said: "He who stands by a dying man at the moment of the soul's departure is obligated to rend his garment [even on Shabbat]. To what may the moment of a soul's departure be likened? To the moment when a Torah scroll is consumed by fire."

(TB *Shabbat* 105b)

VIII

Commenting on the verse in Ecclesiastes [7:1] "The day of death is better than the day of birth," Rabbi Levi explained: "This can be compared to two ocean-going ships, one leaving the harbor and the other entering. Everybody is celebrating the departing ship, but only a few are rejoicing at the ship that is arriving. A wise man seeing this said, 'I see here an irony. People should not celebrate the departing ship, since they have no way of knowing what conditions she will meet, what seas she will encounter, and what winds she will have to face. People should rejoice, rather, over the ship that is entering the harbor, because it has safely returned from its voyage.'"

(Shemot Rabbah 48:1)

IX

On the day that Rabbi Judah was dying, the rabbis declared a public fast, and offered prayers that God have mercy and spare him.... Rabbi Judah's maid went up to the roof of his house and offered this prayer: "The angels in heaven desire Rabbi Judah to join them, and the mortals on earth desire him to remain with them. May it be the will of God that the mortals overpower the angels." However, when she saw how much Rabbi Judah was suffering, she offered a second prayer: "May it be the will of God that the angels overpower the mortals." As the rabbis continued their incessant prayers, she took a jar and threw it down from the roof. It made a great noise; for a moment the rabbis ceased praying and the soul of Rabbi Judah departed."

(TB Ketuvot 104a)

X

When Rabbi Yohanan ben Zakkai's son died, his disciples came to comfort him. Rabbi Eliezer entered, sat down before him, and said to him, "Master, with your permission may I say something to you?"

"Speak," he replied.

Rabbi Eliezer said, "Adam had a son who died, yet he allowed himself to be comforted. And how do we know that he allowed himself to be comforted? For it is said: 'And Adam knew his wife again' [and they had another son] (Genesis 4:25). You too, let yourself be comforted." Said Rabbi Yohanan to him, "It is not enough that I grieve over my own son that you remind me of the grief of Adam?"

The process continued: Rabbi Joshua entered and asked him to be comforted as was Job. Rabbi Yohanan responded, "Is it not enough that I grieve over my own son, that you remind me of the grief of Job?" Rabbi Yossi reminded him that Aaron allowed himself to be comforted over the death of his two sons, and Rabbi Shimon mentioned how David was comforted when his son died.

Rabbi Elazar ben Arakh entered. As soon as Rabbi Yohanan saw him, he said to his servants, "Take my clothing and follow me to the bathhouse, for he is a great man, and I shall be unable to resist him."

Rabbi Elazar entered and sat down before him, and said to him, "I shall tell you a parable. To what may your situation be compared? To a man whom the king entrusted an object to be carefully guarded. Every day the man would weep and cry out, 'Woe is me! When shall I be freed from this trust and again be at peace? You too, master. You had a son; he studied the Torah, the Prophets, the Holy Writings, he studied Mishnah, *halakhah*, *aggadah*, and he left this world without sin. Now that you have returned that which was entrusted to you, it is appropriate for you to be comforted."

Said Rabbi Yohanan to him, "Rabbi Elazar, my son, you have comforted me the way people ought to give comfort."

(*Avot De-Rabbi Natan* 14:6)

XI

It happened that while Rabbi Meir was expounding in the house of study on a Shabbat afternoon, his two sons died. What did their mother do? She put them both on a couch and spread a sheet over them.

At the end of the Shabbat, R. Meir returned home from the house of study and asked, "Where are my two sons?" She replied, "They went to the house of study." R. Meir: "I looked for them there but did not see them." Then she gave him the cup for *Havdalah*, and he pronounced the blessing. Again, he asked, "Where are my two sons?" She replied, "They went to such-and-such a place and will be back soon." Then she brought food for him. After he had eaten, she said, "My teacher, I have a question."

> R. MEIR: "Ask your question."
> SHE: "My teacher, a while ago a man came and deposited something in my keeping. Now he has come back to claim what he left. Shall I return it to him or not?"
> R. MEIR: "My daughter, is not one who holds a deposit required to return it to its owner?"
> SHE: "Still, without your opinion, I would not have returned it."

Then what did she do? She took R. Meir by his hand, led him up to the chamber, and brought him near the couch. Then she pulled off the sheet that covered them, and he saw that both children lying on the couch were dead. He began to weep and said, "My sons, my sons, my teachers, my teachers. My sons in the way of the world, but my teachers because they illumined my eyes with their understanding of Torah."

Then she came out with: "My teacher, did you not say to me that we are required to restore to the owner what is left with us in trust? 'The Lord gave, the Lord took. May the Name of the Lord be blessed' (Job 1:21)."

(Midrash on Mishlei 31:10)

XI

Our rabbis taught: When Rabbi Yossi ben Kisma fell ill, Rabbi Hanina ben Teradion went to visit him.

Rabbi Yossi said to him: "Hanina, my brother, do you not know that heaven has ordained this [Roman] nation to reign? Even though she [Rome] has laid waste to [God's] House, burned His Temple, killed His pious ones, and caused His best ones to perish, she continues to stand! Yet what is this I hear about you? That [even though you know it is forbidden], you are gathering large crowds in public to teach them with a Torah scroll in your lap." Hanina answered, "Let the heavens have mercy."

Rabbi Yossi replied, "I speak to your words that make sense, and you say, let the heavens have mercy? I wouldn't be surprised if they burn both you and your Torah at the stake."...

It wasn't long before Rabbi Yose ben Kisma died, and the Romans eulogized him with great fanfare. When they [the Romans] returned from the funeral, they found Rabbi Hanina teaching Torah to the multitudes with a Torah scroll in his lap. They tied him together with his Torah and surrounded Hanina with kindling wood. The executioner took sponges of wool, soaked them in water, and placed them on Hanina's heart so he would not die quickly. The executioner lit the fire, and Hanina's daughter cried, "Father, is this what you deserve?" Hanina answered, "This might be difficult if I were being burned alone, but the one who would disgrace the Torah may as well disgrace me."

His students asked, "Rebbe, what do you see?" He answered, "The parchments are burning, but the letters are flying free." They replied, "You too, open your mouth and let the flames take you." Hanina answered, "Let the one who gave me life take it away and let me not harm myself."

The executioner then said to him, "Rabbi, if I raise the flame and remove the woolen sponges from over your heart, will you bring me to [your] *Olam Haba* (world-to-come)?"

"Yes," Rabbi Hanina replied.

"Swear to me." Rabbi Hanina swore to him. So, he increased the flames and removed the wool from Hanina's heart, and Hanina expired quickly. Then, suddenly, the executioner himself jumped into the flames and died.

A *bat kol* (voice from heaven) exclaimed: "Rabbi Hanina ben Teradion and the executioner have been welcomed in the world-to-come." [Upon witnessing this] Rebbe [Rabbi Judah the Prince, the leader of the Jewish community] wept and said: "There are those who earn their world-to-come in a single moment, and those for whom it takes many years."

(TB *Avodah Zarah* 18a)

XIII

I hold it true, whate'er befall;
I feel it, when I sorrow most.
'Tis better to have loved and lost
Than never to have loved at all.

(Lord Alfred Tennyson)

XIV

Rachel weeps for her children, she refuses to be comforted.

(Yirmiyahu 31:15)

XV

Moses said: "God is great, mighty, and awesome." Jeremiah said: "Gentiles are trampling in His Temple"; where is His awesomeness? He would no longer say "awesome." Daniel said: "Gentiles have enslaved His children"; where is His might? He would no longer say "mighty." They [the Men of the Great Assembly] came and said, "On the contrary! It is the culmination of His might that He represses His inclination to act and is long-suffering toward the wicked. And if He were not awesome, how could one nation [the Jews] endure among the nations of the world?"

(TB *Yoma* 69b)

XVI

Just as the Holy One fills the world with blessing, so does the soul fill the body. Just as the Holy One sees but cannot be seen, so does the soul see but cannot be seen,

Just as the Holy One is pure so is the soul pure.

(TB *Berakhot* 10a)

APPENDIX II[3]

Viduy	168
Funeral Service	172
Psalm 49	172
Psalm 16	172
Psalm 130	174
Psalm 121	174
Psalm 23	174
Tziduk Hadin	174
Psalm 91	170
The Interment	176
Psalm 91	170
Blessing Before Entering Cemetery	176
Hashkavah for Haham	176
Hashkavah for Man	180
Hashkavah for Woman	180
VeNachcha Adonai	180
Introduction to *Kaddish*	182
Mourner's *Kaddish*	182
Tearing of Garment, *Keriah*	184
Blessing for *Keriah*	184
Lighting the Memorial Candle	184
Seudat Havra'ah Meal of Consolation	184
Birkat HaMazon	184

---

3. The text in Appendix II is taken from the *Siddur Tefilat Eliyahu*, edited by Rabbi Yamin Levy in memory of Eliyahu Amirian, *z"l*.

Shivah	188
Tziduk Hadin	190
Hashkavah for Man	190
Hashkavah for Woman	192
Hashkavah for Haham	192
The Final Day of Shivah	194
Lo Yavo Od	194
Procedure for Memorial Service	194
Amar Ribi Aba	194
Mourner's *Kaddish*	198
Mourner's *Kaddish* Transliterated	211

Confession and Prayers for the Dying

רִבּוֹן Sovereign of eternity, Lord of pardon and mercy, may it be Your will, Adonai my God and God of my fathers, that the good in my life may plead where You are enthroned in glory. Behold my affliction; for "before Your rebuke there is no health in my body, and because of my wrongdoing, my frame knows no peace." And now, God of pardon, grant me now Your loving mercy, "and do not enter into judgment with Your servant." If the appointed hour is near for my passing, may my mouth not cease to declare Your unity as written in Your Torah, "Hear, Yisrael, Adonai is our God, Adonai is One." (Blessed (is His) Name, Whose glorious kingdom is forever and ever.)

מוֹדֶה I confess before You, Adonai my God, and God of my fathers, Lord, God of the spirits and all flesh, that in Your hand alone rests my healing or my death. If it be Your will, grant me a perfect healing, and may the thought of me and my prayer come before You as did the prayer of King Hezekiah in his sickness. But if now my appointed hour is near, then may my death be an atonement for all my sins and transgressions, and for all the wrong that I have committed before You in the whole of my life. Grant that my life be in the happiness of the Beyond, and that I be judged worthy of the life to come that is the destiny of the righteous. You will make known to me the path of life, the fullness of joys in Your presence, the delights that are in Your right hand for eternity. Blessed are You, Adonai, Who hears prayer.

אָנָּא Please, by the force of Your great right hand, release the bound one.

קַבֵּל Accept the prayer of Your people; strengthen us, purify us, Awesome One!

נָא Please! Mighty One, those who seek Your Unity, preserve them like the pupil (of the eye).

בָּרְכֵם Bless them, purify them, (may You) always bestow the compassion of Your benevolent righteousness upon them.

חָסִין Mighty, Holy One, in Your abundant goodness, lead Your community.

יָחִיד Unique One, Exalted, turn to Your people who are mindful of Your holiness.

שַׁוְעָתֵנוּ Accept our prayer and hear our cry, (You) Who knows hidden thoughts.

בָּרוּךְ (Softly) Blessed (is His) Name, Whose glorious kingdom is forever and ever.

ודוי שכיב מרע

ודוי שכיב מרע

רִבּוֹן הָעוֹלָמִים. בַּעַל הַסְּלִיחוֹת וְהָרַחֲמִים. יְהִי רָצוֹן מִלְּפָנֶיךָ, יְיָ אֱלֹהַי וֵאלֹהֵי אֲבוֹתַי, שֶׁיַּעֲלֶה זִכְרוֹנִי לִפְנֵי כִסֵּא כְבוֹדֶךָ לְטוֹבָה. וּרְאֵה בְעָנְיִי: כִּי אֵין מְתֹם בִּבְשָׂרִי מִפְּנֵי זַעְמֶךָ. אֵין שָׁלוֹם בַּעֲצָמַי מִפְּנֵי חַטָּאתִי: וְעַתָּה, אֱלוֹהַּ סְלִיחוֹת. הַטֵּה אֵלַי חֲסָדֶיךָ. וְאַל תָּבוֹא בְמִשְׁפָּט אֶת־עַבְדֶּךָ. וְאִם קָרְבָה עֵת פְּקֻדָּתִי לָמוּת. אַחֲדוּתְךָ לָעַד מִפִּי לֹא תָמוּשׁ. כַּכָּתוּב בְּתוֹרָתֶךָ. שְׁמַע יִשְׂרָאֵל, יְיָ אֱלֹהֵינוּ, יְיָ אֶחָד: בָּרוּךְ שֵׁם כְּבוֹד מַלְכוּתוֹ לְעוֹלָם וָעֶד.

מוֹדֶה אֲנִי לְפָנֶיךָ יְיָ אֱלֹהַי וֵאלֹהֵי אֲבוֹתַי, אֵל אֱלֹהֵי הָרוּחוֹת לְכָל־בָּשָׂר. שֶׁרְפוּאָתִי בְּיָדֶךָ. וּמִיתָתִי בְּיָדֶךָ: יְהִי רָצוֹן מִלְּפָנֶיךָ שֶׁתִּרְפָּאֵנִי רְפוּאָה שְׁלֵמָה. וְיַעֲלֶה זִכְרוֹנִי וּתְפִלָּתִי לְפָנֶיךָ כִּתְפִלַּת חִזְקִיָּה בַּחֲלוֹתוֹ. וְאִם קָרְבָה עֵת פְּקֻדָּתִי לָמוּת. תְּהֵא מִיתָתִי כַפָּרָה לְכָל־חַטֹּאתַי וּלְכָל־עֲוֹנוֹתַי וּלְכָל־פְּשָׁעָי. שֶׁחָטָאתִי וְשֶׁעָוִיתִי וְשֶׁפָּשַׁעְתִּי לְפָנֶיךָ מִיּוֹם הֱיוֹתִי: וְתֵן חֶלְקִי בְּגַן עֵדֶן. וְזַכֵּנִי לָעוֹלָם הַבָּא הַצָּפוּן לַצַּדִּיקִים, תּוֹדִיעֵנִי אֹרַח חַיִּים, שֹׂבַע שְׂמָחוֹת אֶת־פָּנֶיךָ, נְעִמוֹת בִּימִינְךָ נֶצַח: בָּרוּךְ אַתָּה, יְיָ, שׁוֹמֵעַ תְּפִלָּה:

אָנָּא בְּכֹחַ גְּדֻלַּת יְמִינְךָ, תַּתִּיר צְרוּרָה. (אב"ג ית"ץ)

קַבֵּל רִנַּת עַמְּךָ שַׂגְּבֵנוּ, טַהֲרֵנוּ נוֹרָא. (קר"ע שט"ן)

נָא גִבּוֹר דּוֹרְשֵׁי יִחוּדְךָ, כְּבָבַת שָׁמְרֵם. (נג"ד יכ"ש)

בָּרְכֵם טַהֲרֵם רַחֲמֵי צִדְקָתֶךָ, תָּמִיד גָּמְלֵם. (בט"ר צת"ג)

חֲסִין קָדוֹשׁ בְּרֹב טוּבְךָ, נַהֵל עֲדָתֶךָ. (חק"ב טנ"ע)

יָחִיד גֵּאֶה לְעַמְּךָ פְּנֵה, זוֹכְרֵי קְדֻשָּׁתֶךָ. (יג"ל פז"ק)

שַׁוְעָתֵנוּ קַבֵּל וּשְׁמַע צַעֲקָתֵנוּ, יוֹדֵעַ תַּעֲלֻמוֹת. (שק"ו צי"ת)

בָּרוּךְ שֵׁם כְּבוֹד מַלְכוּתוֹ לְעוֹלָם וָעֶד. **(Softly)**

Confession and Prayers for the Dying

וִיהִי   May the pleasantness of Adonai, our God, be upon us, and the work of our hands established for us, and the work of our hands—establish it.

Psalm 91

יֹשֵׁב He who dwells in the shelter of the Supreme One, will abide under the protection of Shaddai. I say of Adonai, (He is) my refuge and my stronghold, my God in Whom I trust. For He will save you from the snare-trap, from destructive pestilence. With His wings He will cover you and beneath His wings, you will find refuge; His truth is a shield, a full shield. You will not fear the terror of night, nor the arrow that flies by day; the pestilence that prowls in darkness, nor the deadly plague that ravages at noon. A thousand will fall at your (left) side, and ten thousand at your (right) side but it shall not come near you. Only with your eyes will you behold and see the punishment of the wicked. For you (have proclaimed): "Adonai is my refuge," the Supreme One you have made your dwelling. No evil shall befall you, and no plague shall come near your tent. For His angels He will command on your behalf—to guard you in all your ways. They will carry you upon their hands, lest you hurt your foot on a rock. You will tread upon lion and snake; you will trample young lion and serpent. Because he clings to Me with desire, I will save him; I will strengthen him, for he knows My Name. When he calls upon Me, I will answer him; I am with him in distress, I will free him and honor him. I will satiate him with longevity, and will let him see My deliverance. I will satiate him with longevity, and will let him see My deliverance.

וַיְהִי It happened in the thirtieth year, in the fourth (month), on the fifth of the month, as I was among the exiles by the river Kevar; the heavens opened and I saw visions of God.

בִּשְׁנַת In the year of King Uzziah's death, I saw my Master sitting upon a high and lofty throne, and its legs filled the Temple. *Seraphim* were standing above, at His service. Each one had six wings; with two it would cover its face, with two it would cover its legs, and with two it would fly. And (the angels) call one to another and said: "Holy, holy, holy is Adonai of Hosts: the fullness of all the earth is His glory."

שְׁמַע	Hear, Yisrael: Adonai is our God, Adonai is One.
יְיָ	Adonai, He is God Adonai, He is God.
יְיָ	Adonai is King, Adonai was King, Adonai will be King forever and ever.
מֹשֶׁה	Moshe is true, and his Torah is true.
לִישׁוּעָתְךָ	For Your salvation I hope, Adonai.
שַׂמֵּחַ	Gladden the soul of Your servant, for to You, my Master, I lift up my soul.
בְּיָדְךָ	In Your hand, I entrust my spirit; You redeemed me Adonai, God of truth.
שְׁמַע	Hear, Yisrael: Adonai is our God, Adonai is One.

ודוי שכיב מרע

וִיהִי נֹעַם אֲדֹנָי אֱלֹהֵינוּ עָלֵינוּ, וּמַעֲשֵׂה יָדֵינוּ כּוֹנְנָה עָלֵינוּ, וּמַעֲשֵׂה יָדֵינוּ כּוֹנְנֵהוּ.
תהלים צא

יֹשֵׁב בְּסֵתֶר עֶלְיוֹן, בְּצֵל שַׁדַּי יִתְלוֹנָן: אֹמַר לַייָ מַחְסִי וּמְצוּדָתִי, אֱלֹהַי אֶבְטַח־בּוֹ: כִּי הוּא יַצִּילְךָ מִפַּח יָקוּשׁ מִדֶּבֶר הַוּוֹת: בְּאֶבְרָתוֹ יָסֶךְ לָךְ, וְתַחַת־כְּנָפָיו תֶּחְסֶה, צִנָּה וְסֹחֵרָה אֲמִתּוֹ: לֹא־תִירָא מִפַּחַד לָיְלָה, מֵחֵץ יָעוּף יוֹמָם: מִדֶּבֶר בָּאֹפֶל יַהֲלֹךְ מִקֶּטֶב יָשׁוּד צָהֳרָיִם: יִפֹּל מִצִּדְּךָ אֶלֶף וּרְבָבָה מִימִינֶךָ אֵלֶיךָ לֹא יִגָּשׁ: רַק בְּעֵינֶיךָ תַבִּיט, וְשִׁלֻּמַת רְשָׁעִים תִּרְאֶה: כִּי־אַתָּה יְיָ מַחְסִי, עֶלְיוֹן שַׂמְתָּ מְעוֹנֶךָ: לֹא־תְאֻנֶּה אֵלֶיךָ רָעָה, וְנֶגַע לֹא־יִקְרַב בְּאָהֳלֶךָ: כִּי מַלְאָכָיו יְצַוֶּה־לָּךְ, לִשְׁמָרְךָ בְּכָל־דְּרָכֶיךָ: עַל־כַּפַּיִם יִשָּׂאוּנְךָ פֶּן־תִּגֹּף בָּאֶבֶן רַגְלֶךָ: עַל־שַׁחַל וָפֶתֶן תִּדְרֹךְ תִּרְמֹס כְּפִיר וְתַנִּין: כִּי בִי חָשַׁק וַאֲפַלְּטֵהוּ אֲשַׂגְּבֵהוּ כִּי־יָדַע שְׁמִי: יִקְרָאֵנִי וְאֶעֱנֵהוּ, עִמּוֹ־אָנֹכִי בְצָרָה, אֲחַלְּצֵהוּ וַאֲכַבְּדֵהוּ: אֹרֶךְ יָמִים אַשְׂבִּיעֵהוּ, וְאַרְאֵהוּ בִּישׁוּעָתִי: אֹרֶךְ יָמִים אַשְׂבִּיעֵהוּ, וְאַרְאֵהוּ בִּישׁוּעָתִי:

וַיְהִי בִּשְׁלֹשִׁים שָׁנָה בָּרְבִיעִי בַּחֲמִשָּׁה לַחֹדֶשׁ וַאֲנִי בְתוֹךְ־הַגּוֹלָה עַל־נְהַר־כְּבָר נִפְתְּחוּ הַשָּׁמַיִם וָאֶרְאֶה מַרְאוֹת אֱלֹהִים:
ישעיה ו׳ א־ג

בִּשְׁנַת־מוֹת הַמֶּלֶךְ עֻזִּיָּהוּ וָאֶרְאֶה אֶת־אֲדֹנָי יֹשֵׁב עַל־כִּסֵּא רָם וְנִשָּׂא וְשׁוּלָיו מְלֵאִים אֶת־הַהֵיכָל: שְׂרָפִים עֹמְדִים מִמַּעַל לוֹ שֵׁשׁ כְּנָפַיִם שֵׁשׁ כְּנָפַיִם לְאֶחָד, בִּשְׁתַּיִם יְכַסֶּה פָנָיו, וּבִשְׁתַּיִם יְכַסֶּה רַגְלָיו, וּבִשְׁתַּיִם יְעוֹפֵף: וְקָרָא זֶה אֶל־זֶה וְאָמַר קָדוֹשׁ | קָדוֹשׁ קָדוֹשׁ יְהֹוָה צְבָאוֹת מְלֹא כָל־הָאָרֶץ כְּבוֹדוֹ:

שְׁמַע יִשְׂרָאֵל, יְיָ אֱלֹהֵינוּ, יְיָ אֶחָד:

יְיָ הוּא הָאֱלֹהִים יְיָ הוּא הָאֱלֹהִים:

יְיָ מֶלֶךְ יְיָ מָלָךְ יְיָ יִמְלֹךְ לְעֹלָם וָעֶד:

אָנָּא יְיָ הוֹשִׁיעָה נָּא: (2)

אָנָּא יְיָ הַצְלִיחָה נָּא: (2)

שַׂמֵּחַ נֶפֶשׁ עַבְדֶּךָ, כִּי אֵלֶיךָ אֲדֹנָי נַפְשִׁי אֶשָּׂא:

בְּיָדְךָ אַפְקִיד רוּחִי פָּדִיתָה אוֹתִי יְהֹוָה אֵל אֱמֶת:

שְׁמַע יִשְׂרָאֵל, יְיָ אֱלֹהֵינוּ, יְיָ אֶחָד:

The Order of Mourning

Chapel/Cemetery Service

Psalm 49

לַמְנַצֵּחַ To Him Who grants victory, a psalm of the sons of Koraḥ. Hear this all peoples, listen all inhabitants of the decaying world! Sons of Adam and sons of men, rich and poor together. My mouth shall speak wisdom, and the meditation of my heart shall be of understanding. I will incline my ear to a parable, I will begin to solve my riddle to the accompaniment of a harp. Why should I fear in the days of evil when the iniquity I trod upon surrounds me? (There are) those who trust in their wealth and take pride in their great riches. A man will not redeem his brother, neither can he give to God his ransom. The redemption of their soul is too costly and it shall cease to be forever. Should he then live forever, would he never see the grave? For he sees that wise men die, the fools and senseless perish equally and leave their wealth to others. Their inner thoughts are that their houses (will last) forever, their homes for generation after generation; (for) they have proclaimed their names throughout the lands. But man does not endure in his splendor, he is likened to the beasts that perish. This is their way—their folly remains with them, and (yet), their descendants take pleasure in their speech, *Selah*. Like sheep—they are destined for the grave; death shall be their shepherd, and the upright shall dominate them at morning, their form will be consumed in the grave; (it will not remain) their dwelling-place. But God will redeem my soul from the (grasp of) the grave, for He will take me (to Himself) *Selah*. Fear not when a man grows rich, when the glory of his house is increased. For when he dies, he shall carry nothing away, his glory will not descend after him. Because while he lived, he blessed his soul. (saying): they will praise you because you have done well for yourself. He will join the generation of his fathers, they shall not see light, for all eternity. Man, with (all) his splendor, (but) without understanding, is likened to the beasts that perish.

Psalm 16

מִכְתָּם A Miḥtam of David. Preserve me, Almighty, for I have taken refuge in You. You said to Adonai, "You are my Master, I have no good without You." As for the holy ones on earth, and to the noble, they are my delight. Let the sorrow of those who follow other gods increase; I will not pour their libations of blood nor carry their names upon my lips. Adonai, You are the portion of my inheritance and of my cup; You guide my destiny. My lot has fallen in pleasant places; a beautiful inheritance is mine. I will bless Adonai Who has given me counsel, even for the nights in which my mind instructed me. I set Adonai before me always, because He is always at my right, so that I should not falter. Therefore, my heart rejoiced and my soul exulted, even my flesh will dwell in safety. For You will not abandon my soul to the grave nor will you allow Your pious one to see the pit. You will make known to me the path of life, the fullness of joys in Your presence, the delights that are in Your right hand for eternity.

סדר אבלות

סדר אבלות

Chapel/Cemetery Service

תהלים מט

לַ**מְנַצֵּחַ** לִבְנֵי־קֹרַח מִזְמוֹר שִׁמְעוּ־זֹאת כָּל־הָעַמִּים, הַאֲזִינוּ כָּל־יֹשְׁבֵי חָלֶד גַּם־בְּנֵי אָדָם, גַּם־בְּנֵי־אִישׁ, יַחַד עָשִׁיר וְאֶבְיוֹן פִּי יְדַבֵּר חָכְמוֹת, וְהָגוּת לִבִּי תְבוּנוֹת אַטֶּה לְמָשָׁל אָזְנִי, אֶפְתַּח בְּכִנּוֹר חִידָתִי לָמָּה אִירָא בִּימֵי רָע, עֲוֹן עֲקֵבַי יְסֻבֵּנִי הַבֹּטְחִים עַל־חֵילָם, וּבְרֹב עָשְׁרָם יִתְהַלָּלוּ אָח לֹא־פָדֹה יִפְדֶּה אִישׁ, לֹא־יִתֵּן לֵאלֹהִים כָּפְרוֹ וְיֵקַר פִּדְיוֹן נַפְשָׁם, וְחָדַל לְעוֹלָם וִיחִי־עוֹד לָנֶצַח, לֹא יִרְאֶה הַשָּׁחַת כִּי יִרְאֶה חֲכָמִים יָמוּתוּ, יַחַד כְּסִיל וָבַעַר יֹאבֵדוּ, וְעָזְבוּ לַאֲחֵרִים חֵילָם קִרְבָּם בָּתֵּימוֹ לְעוֹלָם, מִשְׁכְּנֹתָם לְדֹר וָדֹר, קָרְאוּ בִשְׁמוֹתָם עֲלֵי אֲדָמוֹת וְאָדָם בִּיקָר בַּל־יָלִין, נִמְשַׁל כַּבְּהֵמוֹת נִדְמוּ זֶה דַרְכָּם כֵּסֶל לָמוֹ, וְאַחֲרֵיהֶם בְּפִיהֶם יִרְצוּ, סֶלָה כַּצֹּאן לִשְׁאוֹל שַׁתּוּ מָוֶת יִרְעֵם, וַיִּרְדּוּ בָם יְשָׁרִים לַבֹּקֶר, וְצוּרָם לְבַלּוֹת שְׁאוֹל מִזְּבֻל לוֹ אַךְ־אֱלֹהִים יִפְדֶּה נַפְשִׁי מִיַּד־שְׁאוֹל, כִּי יִקָּחֵנִי, סֶלָה אַל־תִּירָא כִּי־יַעֲשִׁר אִישׁ, כִּי־יִרְבֶּה כְּבוֹד בֵּיתוֹ כִּי לֹא בְמוֹתוֹ יִקַּח הַכֹּל, לֹא־יֵרֵד אַחֲרָיו כְּבוֹדוֹ כִּי־נַפְשׁוֹ בְּחַיָּיו יְבָרֵךְ, וְיוֹדֻךָ כִּי־תֵיטִיב לָךְ תָּבוֹא עַד־דּוֹר אֲבוֹתָיו, עַד־נֵצַח לֹא יִרְאוּ־אוֹר אָדָם בִּיקָר וְלֹא יָבִין, נִמְשַׁל כַּבְּהֵמוֹת נִדְמוּ

תהלים טז

מִכְתָּם לְדָוִד, שָׁמְרֵנִי אֵל כִּי־חָסִיתִי בָךְ: אָמַרְתְּ לַיהוָה אֲדֹנָי אָתָּה, טוֹבָתִי בַּל־עָלֶיךָ: לִקְדוֹשִׁים אֲשֶׁר־בָּאָרֶץ הֵמָּה, וְאַדִּירֵי כָּל־חֶפְצִי־בָם: יִרְבּוּ עַצְּבוֹתָם אַחֵר מָהָרוּ, בַּל־אַסִּיךְ נִסְכֵּיהֶם מִדָּם, וּבַל־אֶשָּׂא אֶת־שְׁמוֹתָם עַל־שְׂפָתָי: יְהוָה מְנָת־חֶלְקִי וְכוֹסִי, אַתָּה תּוֹמִיךְ גּוֹרָלִי: חֲבָלִים נָפְלוּ־לִי בַּנְּעִמִים, אַף־נַחֲלָת שָׁפְרָה עָלָי: אֲבָרֵךְ אֶת־יְהוָה אֲשֶׁר יְעָצָנִי, אַף־לֵילוֹת יִסְּרוּנִי כִלְיוֹתָי: שִׁוִּיתִי יְהוָה לְנֶגְדִּי תָמִיד, כִּי מִימִינִי בַּל־אֶמּוֹט: לָכֵן | שָׂמַח לִבִּי וַיָּגֶל כְּבוֹדִי, אַף־בְּשָׂרִי יִשְׁכֹּן לָבֶטַח: כִּי | לֹא־תַעֲזֹב נַפְשִׁי לִשְׁאוֹל, לֹא־תִתֵּן חֲסִידְךָ לִרְאוֹת שָׁחַת: תּוֹדִיעֵנִי אֹרַח חַיִּים, שֹׂבַע שְׂמָחוֹת אֶת־פָּנֶיךָ, נְעִמוֹת בִּימִינְךָ נֶצַח:

The Order of Mourning

Psalm 130

שִׁיר A Song of Ascents. Out of the depths I have called to You, Adonai. My Master, hear my voice; let Your ears be attentive to the voice of my supplications. If You, God, should take account of iniquities, my Master, who could survive? For with You is forgiveness, in order that You be feared. I hope for Adonai, my soul hopes; and for His word, I wait. My soul (waits) for my Master more than the watchman (waits) for the morning, (more than) the watchman (waits) for the morning. Wait, Yisrael, upon Adonai, for with Adonai there is loving-kindness, and with Him there is much redemption. And He will redeem Yisrael from all its iniquities.

Psalm 121

שִׁיר A Song of Ascents. I will lift my eyes to the mountains: from where will my help come? My help comes from Adonai, Maker of heaven and earth. He will not let your foot slip, may He who guards you not slumber. Behold, the Guardian of Yisrael does not slumber nor sleep. Adonai is your Guardian, Adonai is your shelter at your right hand. By day the sun will not smite you, nor the moon at night. Adonai will guard you from all evil; He will preserve your soul. Adonai will guard your going and coming, from now and forever.

Psalm 23

מִזְמוֹר A psalm of David: Adonai is my shepherd, I shall lack nothing. He makes me lie in lush pastures, He leads me beside tranquil waters. He restores my soul, He directs me in the path of righteousness for the sake of His Name. Though I walk in the valley of the shadow of death, I will fear no evil for You are with me, Your rod and Your staff comfort me. You will prepare a table for me in the full presence of my enemies, You anointed my head with oil, my cup overflows. (May) only good and kindness pursue me all the days of my life, and I shall dwell in the House of Adonai for length of days.

The eulogy is now delivered.

After the eulogy, everyone is asked to please rise.

(On days we say 'Penitential Prayers')

צַדִּיק You are righteous, Adonai, and Your judgments are just. Adonai is righteous in all His ways and merciful in all His acts. The judgments of Adonai are true, they are altogether right. In that the word of the King is supreme, who could say to Him, "What are You doing?" He is One, and who could possibly answer Him back? That which His spirit wills, He does. He is the Rock, His work is perfect. for all His ways are just. The God of faith in whom there is no imperfection, just and upright is He. He is the true Judge, He judges with righteousness and truth. Blessed is the Judge of truth, for all His judgments are righteous and true.

סדר אבלות

תהלים קל

שִׁיר הַמַּעֲלוֹת, מִמַּעֲמַקִּים קְרָאתִיךָ יְיָ אֲדֹנָי, שִׁמְעָה בְקוֹלִי, תִּהְיֶינָה אָזְנֶיךָ קַשֻּׁבוֹת, לְקוֹל תַּחֲנוּנָי אִם־עֲוֹנוֹת תִּשְׁמָר־יָהּ, אֲדֹנָי מִי יַעֲמֹד כִּי־עִמְּךָ הַסְּלִיחָה, לְמַעַן תִּוָּרֵא קִוִּיתִי יְיָ קִוְּתָה נַפְשִׁי, וְלִדְבָרוֹ הוֹחָלְתִּי נַפְשִׁי לַאדֹנָי, מִשֹּׁמְרִים לַבֹּקֶר, שֹׁמְרִים לַבֹּקֶר יַחֵל יִשְׂרָאֵל אֶל־יְיָ, כִּי־עִם־יְיָ הַחֶסֶד, וְהַרְבֵּה עִמּוֹ פְדוּת וְהוּא יִפְדֶּה אֶת־יִשְׂרָאֵל, מִכֹּל עֲוֹנוֹתָיו

תהלים קכא

שִׁיר לַמַּעֲלוֹת, אֶשָּׂא עֵינַי אֶל־הֶהָרִים, מֵאַיִן יָבֹא עֶזְרִי: עֶזְרִי מֵעִם יְיָ, עֹשֵׂה שָׁמַיִם וָאָרֶץ: אַל־יִתֵּן לַמּוֹט רַגְלֶךָ, אַל־יָנוּם שֹׁמְרֶךָ: הִנֵּה לֹא־יָנוּם וְלֹא יִישָׁן, שׁוֹמֵר יִשְׂרָאֵל: יְיָ שֹׁמְרֶךָ, יְיָ צִלְּךָ עַל־יַד יְמִינֶךָ: יוֹמָם הַשֶּׁמֶשׁ לֹא־יַכֶּכָּה, וְיָרֵחַ בַּלָּיְלָה: יְיָ יִשְׁמָרְךָ מִכָּל־רָע, יִשְׁמֹר אֶת־נַפְשֶׁךָ: יְיָ יִשְׁמָר־צֵאתְךָ וּבוֹאֶךָ, מֵעַתָּה וְעַד־עוֹלָם:

תהלים כג

מִזְמוֹר לְדָוִד, יְהֹוָה רֹעִי לֹא אֶחְסָר: בִּנְאוֹת דֶּשֶׁא יַרְבִּיצֵנִי, עַל־מֵי מְנֻחוֹת יְנַהֲלֵנִי: נַפְשִׁי יְשׁוֹבֵב, יַנְחֵנִי בְמַעְגְּלֵי־צֶדֶק לְמַעַן שְׁמוֹ: גַּם כִּי־אֵלֵךְ בְּגֵיא צַלְמָוֶת לֹא־אִירָא רָע, כִּי־אַתָּה עִמָּדִי, שִׁבְטְךָ וּמִשְׁעַנְתֶּךָ הֵמָּה יְנַחֲמֻנִי: תַּעֲרֹךְ לְפָנַי שֻׁלְחָן נֶגֶד צֹרְרָי, דִּשַּׁנְתָּ בַשֶּׁמֶן רֹאשִׁי, כּוֹסִי רְוָיָה: אַךְ טוֹב וָחֶסֶד יִרְדְּפוּנִי כָּל־יְמֵי חַיָּי, וְשַׁבְתִּי בְּבֵית־יְהֹוָה לְאֹרֶךְ יָמִים:

The eulogy is now delivered.

After the eulogy, everyone is asked to please rise.

(On days we say tahanunim)

צַדִּיק אַתָּה יְיָ, וְיָשָׁר מִשְׁפָּטֶיךָ צַדִּיק יְיָ בְּכָל־דְּרָכָיו, וְחָסִיד בְּכָל־מַעֲשָׂיו צִדְקָתְךָ צֶדֶק לְעוֹלָם, וְתוֹרָתְךָ אֱמֶת מִשְׁפְּטֵי־יְיָ אֱמֶת, צָדְקוּ יַחְדָּיו בַּאֲשֶׁר דְּבַר־מֶלֶךְ שִׁלְטוֹן, וּמִי יֹאמַר־לוֹ מַה־תַּעֲשֶׂה וְהוּא בְאֶחָד וּמִי יְשִׁיבֶנּוּ, וְנַפְשׁוֹ אִוְּתָה וַיָּעַשׂ הַצּוּר תָּמִים פָּעֳלוֹ, כִּי כָּל־דְּרָכָיו מִשְׁפָּט אֵל אֱמוּנָה וְאֵין עָוֶל, צַדִּיק וְיָשָׁר הוּא דַּיַּן אֱמֶת שׁוֹפֵט צֶדֶק וֶאֱמֶת, בָּרוּךְ דַּיַּן הָאֱמֶת כִּי כָּל־מִשְׁפָּטָיו צֶדֶק וֶאֱמֶת.

175

The Order of Mourning

Before entering the cemetery

בָּרוּךְ Blessed are You, Adonai our God, King of the Universe, Who formed you with justice, and Who has given us life with justice, and Who has sustained us with justice, and Who knows the number of all of you with justice. And He, in the hereafter, will raise us to new life with justice. Blessed are You, Adonai, Who revives the dead.

On entering the cemetery

סוֹף In the final analysis, all is heard, so fear God and heed His commandments, for that is the lot of all humankind.

וְהוּא And He, the merciful One, atones iniquity and does not destroy; He frequently withdraws His anger and does not arouse all His rage.

On lowering into the grave just before covering with dirt, the following is said: "If we have offended you during your lifetime, at this time we ask 'Meḥila', forgiveness".

וְהוּא And He, the merciful One, atones iniquity and does not destroy; He frequently withdraws His anger and does not arouse all His rage. (3)

כִּי For you are dust, and to dust, you shall return. (3)

After covering the coffin with dirt, the Memorial Prayer is recited.

For Rabbis and other distinguished religious leaders of the community

וְהַחָכְמָה Where is wisdom to be found and where is the place of understanding? Fortunate is the person who has found wisdom, and the person who evokes understanding. How great is the goodness that You have stored away for those who fear You; much have You performed for those who seek refuge in You in the presence of people. How precious is Your kindness, O God, that only those men who find refuge in the shade of Your wings will be satisfied from the affluence of Your house, and from the stream of Your delights You will give them to drink. A good name is better than good oil and the day of one's death is better than the day of his birth. God, full of mercy, He Who is filled with great compassion over the essence, spirit and soul of he who has passed on with a good name, (**NAME son of NAME OF FATHER**), may the spirit of God place him in the Garden of Eden. May the King, in His mercy, have compassion on him.

סדר אבלות

Before entering the cemetery

בָּרוּךְ אַתָּה, יְיָ, אֱלֹהֵינוּ מֶלֶךְ הָעוֹלָם, אֲשֶׁר־יָצַר אֶתְכֶם בַּדִּין, וְהֶחֱיָה אֶתְכֶם בַּדִּין, וְזָן אֶתְכֶם בַּדִּין, וְיוֹדֵעַ מִסְפַּר כֻּלְּכֶם בַּדִּין. וְהוּא עָתִיד לְהַחֲיוֹתְכֶם וְלַהֲקִימְכֶם בַּדִּין. בָּרוּךְ אַתָּה, יְיָ, מְחַיֵּה הַמֵּתִים.

On entering the cemetery

סוֹף דָּבָר הַכֹּל נִשְׁמָע אֶת־הָאֱלֹהִים יְרָא, וְאֶת־מִצְוֹתָיו שְׁמוֹר, כִּי זֶה כָּל־הָאָדָם.

וְהוּא רַחוּם, יְכַפֵּר עָוֹן, וְלֹא־יַשְׁחִית, וְהִרְבָּה לְהָשִׁיב אַפּוֹ, וְלֹא־יָעִיר כָּל־חֲמָתוֹ: (3)

On lowering into the grave just before covering with dirt, the following is said: "If we have offended you during your lifetime, at this time we ask 'Meḥila', forgiveness".

וְהוּא רַחוּם, יְכַפֵּר עָוֹן, וְלֹא־יַשְׁחִית, וְהִרְבָּה לְהָשִׁיב אַפּוֹ, וְלֹא־יָעִיר כָּל־חֲמָתוֹ: (3)

כִּי עָפָר אַתָּה, וְאֶל עָפָר תָּשׁוּב: (3)

After covering the coffin with dirt, the השכבה (Hashkava) is recited.

For Rabbis and other distinguished religious leaders of the community

וְהַחָכְמָה מֵאַיִן תִּמָּצֵא, וְאֵי זֶה מְקוֹם בִּינָה. אַשְׁרֵי אָדָם מָצָא חָכְמָה, וְאָדָם יָפִיק תְּבוּנָה. מָה רַב־טוּבְךָ אֲשֶׁר־צָפַנְתָּ לִּירֵאֶיךָ, פָּעַלְתָּ לַחוֹסִים בָּךְ נֶגֶד בְּנֵי אָדָם. מַה־יָּקָר חַסְדְּךָ אֱלֹהִים, וּבְנֵי אָדָם בְּצֵל כְּנָפֶיךָ יֶחֱסָיוּן. יִרְוְיֻן מִדֶּשֶׁן בֵּיתֶךָ, וְנַחַל עֲדָנֶיךָ תַשְׁקֵם. טוֹב שֵׁם מִשֶּׁמֶן טוֹב, וְיוֹם הַמָּוֶת מִיּוֹם הִוָּלְדוֹ. אֵל מָלֵא רַחֲמִים הוּא יִתְמַלֵּא בְּרַחֲמָיו הַמְרוּבִּים, עַל נֶפֶשׁ רוּחַ וּנְשָׁמָה שֶׁל הַנִּפְטָר בְּשֵׁם טוֹב מִן הָעוֹלָם ((NAME son of NAME OF FATHER)) וְרוּחַ יְיָ תְּנִיחֶנּוּ בְּגַן עֵדֶן הַמֶּלֶךְ בְּרַחֲמָיו יְרַחֵם עָלָיו.

The Order of Mourning

(On days we do NOT say' Penitential Prayers')

יְיָ מָה־אָדָם Adonai, what is man, that you should take knowledge of him, or the son of man, that you should make account of him? Man is like a breath; his days are like a passing shadow, *Selah*. The small and great are there; and the servant is free from his master. Behold, he puts no trust in his servants; and he charges his angels with folly. How much less man, who is a worm? And the son of man, who is a maggot? The end of the matter is, all has been heard. Fear God, and keep His commandments; for this is the whole duty of man.

The pallbearers at the chapel and at the cemetery are announced, as well as the time and location of services.

On taking the coffin out, say

Psalm 91

יֹשֵׁב He who dwells in the shelter of the Supreme One, will abide under the protection of Shaddai. I say of Adonai, (He is) my refuge and my stronghold, my God in Whom I trust. For He will save you from the snare-trap, from destructive pestilence. With His wings, He will cover you and beneath His wings, you will find refuge; His truth is a shield, a full shield. You will not fear the terror of night, nor the arrow that flies by day; the pestilence that prowls in darkness, nor the deadly plague that ravages at noon. A thousand will fall at your (left) side, and ten thousand at your (right) side but it shall not come near you. Only with your eyes will you behold and see the punishment of the wicked. For you (have proclaimed): "Adonai is my refuge," the Supreme One you have made your dwelling. No evil shall befall you, and no plague shall come near your tent.

כִּי For His angels He will command on your behalf—to guard you in all your ways. (3)

If the chapel and cemetery are in two separate locations, the hands are washed when leaving the chapel.

At the Interment

The following is recited while accompanying the coffin to the edge of the cemetery

Psalm 91

יֹשֵׁב He who dwells in the shelter of the Supreme One, will abide under the protection of Shaddai. I say of Adonai, (He is) my refuge and my stronghold, my God in Whom I trust. For He will save you from the snare-trap, from destructive pestilence. With His wings, He will cover you and beneath His wings, you will find refuge; His truth is a shield, a full shield. You will not fear the terror of night, nor the arrow that flies by day; the pestilence that prowls in darkness, nor the deadly plague that ravages at noon. A thousand will fall at your (left) side, and ten thousand at your (right) side but it shall not come near you. Only with your eyes will you behold and see the punishment of the wicked. For you (have proclaimed): "Adonai is my refuge," the Supreme One you have made your dwelling. No evil shall befall you, and no plague shall come near your tent.

כִּי For His angels He will command on your behalf—to guard you in all your ways. (3)

סדר אבלות

(On days we do NOT say taḥanunim)

יְיָ, מָה־אָדָם וַתֵּדָעֵהוּ, בֶּן־אֱנוֹשׁ וַתְּחַשְּׁבֵהוּ, אָדָם לַהֶבֶל דָּמָה, יָמָיו כְּצֵל עוֹבֵר מִי גֶבֶר יִחְיֶה וְלֹא יִרְאֶה־מָּוֶת, יְמַלֵּט נַפְשׁוֹ מִיַּד־שְׁאוֹל, סֶלָה קָטֹן וְגָדוֹל שָׁם הוּא, וְעֶבֶד חָפְשִׁי מֵאֲדֹנָיו הֵן בַּעֲבָדָיו לֹא יַאֲמִין, וּבְמַלְאָכָיו יָשִׂים תָּהֳלָה אַף כִּי־אֱנוֹשׁ רִמָּה, וּבֶן־אָדָם תּוֹלֵעָה

The pallbearers at the chapel and at the cemetery are announced, as well as the time and location of services.

On taking the coffin out, say

תהלים צא

יֹשֵׁב בְּסֵתֶר עֶלְיוֹן, בְּצֵל שַׁדַּי יִתְלוֹנָן: אֹמַר לַיְיָ מַחְסִי וּמְצוּדָתִי, אֱלֹהַי אֶבְטַח־בּוֹ: כִּי הוּא יַצִּילְךָ מִפַּח יָקוּשׁ, מִדֶּבֶר הַוּוֹת: בְּאֶבְרָתוֹ יָסֶךְ לָךְ, וְתַחַת־כְּנָפָיו תֶּחְסֶה, צִנָּה וְסֹחֵרָה אֲמִתּוֹ: לֹא־תִירָא מִפַּחַד לָיְלָה, מֵחֵץ יָעוּף יוֹמָם: מִדֶּבֶר בָּאֹפֶל יַהֲלֹךְ, מִקֶּטֶב יָשׁוּד צָהֳרָיִם: יִפֹּל מִצִּדְּךָ אֶלֶף, וּרְבָבָה מִימִינֶךָ אֵלֶיךָ לֹא יִגָּשׁ: רַק בְּעֵינֶיךָ תַבִּיט, וְשִׁלֻּמַת רְשָׁעִים תִּרְאֶה: כִּי־אַתָּה יְיָ מַחְסִי, עֶלְיוֹן שַׂמְתָּ מְעוֹנֶךָ: לֹא תְאֻנֶּה אֵלֶיךָ רָעָה, וְנֶגַע לֹא יִקְרַב בְּאָהֳלֶךָ:

כִּי מַלְאָכָיו יְצַוֶּה־לָּךְ, לִשְׁמָרְךָ בְּכָל־דְּרָכֶיךָ: (3)

If the chapel and cemetery are in two separate locations, the hands are washed when leaving the chapel.

At the Interment

The following is recited while accompanying the coffin to the edge of the cemetery

תהלים צא

יֹשֵׁב בְּסֵתֶר עֶלְיוֹן, בְּצֵל שַׁדַּי יִתְלוֹנָן: אֹמַר לַיְיָ מַחְסִי וּמְצוּדָתִי, אֱלֹהַי אֶבְטַח־בּוֹ: כִּי הוּא יַצִּילְךָ מִפַּח יָקוּשׁ, מִדֶּבֶר הַוּוֹת: בְּאֶבְרָתוֹ יָסֶךְ לָךְ, וְתַחַת כְּנָפָיו תֶּחְסֶה, צִנָּה וְסֹחֵרָה אֲמִתּוֹ: לֹא תִירָא מִפַּחַד לָיְלָה, מֵחֵץ יָעוּף יוֹמָם: מִדֶּבֶר בָּאֹפֶל יַהֲלֹךְ, מִקֶּטֶב יָשׁוּד צָהֳרָיִם: יִפֹּל מִצִּדְּךָ אֶלֶף, וּרְבָבָה מִימִינֶךָ אֵלֶיךָ לֹא יִגָּשׁ: רַק בְּעֵינֶיךָ תַבִּיט, וְשִׁלֻּמַת רְשָׁעִים תִּרְאֶה: כִּי־אַתָּה יְיָ מַחְסִי, עֶלְיוֹן שַׂמְתָּ מְעוֹנֶךָ: לֹא תְאֻנֶּה אֵלֶיךָ רָעָה, וְנֶגַע לֹא יִקְרַב בְּאָהֳלֶךָ:

כִּי מַלְאָכָיו יְצַוֶּה־לָּךְ, לִשְׁמָרְךָ בְּכָל־דְּרָכֶיךָ: (3)

The Order of Mourning

For a man

אַשְׁרֵי אִישׁ Happy is the man who fears Adonai, who delights greatly in his commandments. A good name is better than good oil and the day of one's death is better than the day of his birth. God, full of mercy, He Who is filled with great compassion over the essence, spirit and soul of he who has passed on with a good name (**NAME son of NAME OF FATHER**), may the spirit of God place him in the Garden of Eden. May the King, in His mercy, have compassion on him.

For a woman

אֵשֶׁת־חַיִל **A** woman of valor, who can find? Far beyond the most precious stones is her value. False is grace and vain is beauty; a God-fearing woman is the one deserving of praise. Give to her from the fruit of her hands; her deeds will praise her at the gates. The Merciful One, to Whom all mercy belongs, and by Whose word, worlds were created - This World and the World to Come, and Who stored therein righteous and pious women who do His will - according to His edict and His glory and His might. He shall decree that there ascend before Him the remembrance of the soul of the woman (**NAME daughter of NAME OF FATHER**) May the spirit of God place her in the Garden of Eden. May the King, in His mercy, have compassion on her.

After the Memorial Prayer, bend down, and with the left hand touching the grave, say the following three times

Yeshaya 58:11

וְנָחֲךָ And the Lord shall guide you continually, and satisfy your soul in drought, and make strong your bones; and you shall be like a watered garden, and like a spring of water, whose waters fail not.

Kaddish is said at this point. Depending on the weather, it may be said at graveside or back at the cemetery chapel. The hands are washed when leaving the cemetery.

סדר אבלות

For a man

אַשְׁרֵי אִישׁ יָרֵא אֶת־יְיָ, בְּמִצְוֺתָיו חָפֵץ מְאֹד. אַשְׁרֵי תְמִימֵי־דָרֶךְ, הַהוֹלְכִים בְּתוֹרַת יְיָ. טוֹב שֵׁם מִשֶּׁמֶן טוֹב, וְיוֹם הַמָּוֶת מִיּוֹם הִוָּלְדוֹ. אֵל מָלֵא רַחֲמִים הוּא יִתְמַלֵּא בְּרַחֲמָיו הַמְרוּבִּים עַל נֶפֶשׁ רוּחַ וּנְשָׁמָה שֶׁל הַנִּפְטָר בְּשֵׁם טוֹב מִן הָעוֹלָם (NAME son of NAME OF FATHER) רוּחַ יְיָ תְּנִיחֶנּוּ בְּגַן עֵדֶן הַמֶּלֶךְ בְּרַחֲמָיו יְרַחֵם עָלָיו.

For a woman

אֵשֶׁת־חַיִל מִי יִמְצָא, וְרָחוֹק מִפְּנִינִים מִכְרָהּ. שֶׁקֶר הַחֵן וְהֶבֶל הַיֹּפִי, אִשָּׁה יִרְאַת יְיָ הִיא תִתְהַלָּל. תְּנוּ־לָהּ מִפְּרִי יָדֶיהָ, וִיהַלְלוּהָ בַשְּׁעָרִים מַעֲשֶׂיהָ. רַחֲמָנָא דְרַחֲמָנוּתָא דִי לֵיהּ הִיא. וּבְמֵימְרֵהּ אִתְבְּרִיאוּ עָלְמַיָּא עָלְמָא הָדֵין וְעָלְמָא דְאָתֵי. וּגְנַז בֵּיהּ צִדְקָנִיּוֹת וְחַסְדָּנִיּוֹת דְּעָבְדָן רְעוּתֵיהּ. וּבְמֵימְרֵהּ וּבִיקָרֵיהּ וּבְתָקְפֵּיהּ יֹאמַר לְמֵעַל קַדְמוֹהִי. דְּכַרְן נֶפֶשׁ הָאִשָּׁה הַכְּבוּדָה וְהַצְּנוּעָה וְהַנִּכְבֶּדֶת מָרַת (NAME son of NAME OF FATHER) רוּחַ יְיָ תְּנִיחֶנָּה בְּגַן עֵדֶן הַמֶּלֶךְ בְּרַחֲמָיו יְרַחֵם עָלֶיהָ.

After the השכבה, bend down, and with the left hand touching the grave, say the following three times

ישעיה נח: יא

וְנָחֲךָ יְיָ תָּמִיד וְהִשְׂבִּיעַ בְּצַחְצָחוֹת נַפְשֶׁךָ. וְעַצְמוֹתֶיךָ יַחֲלִיץ. וְהָיִיתָ כְּגַן רָוֶה. וּכְמוֹצָא מַיִם אֲשֶׁר לֹא יְכַזְּבוּ מֵימָיו: (3)

Kaddish is said at this point. Depending on the weather, it may be said at graveside or back at the cemetery chapel. The hands are washed when leaving the cemetery.

The Order of Mourning

Introduction to the Kaddish

אָמַר Rabba, son of Bar Hana, said in the name of Rabbi Yohanan, that in the time to come, the pious will be called by the name of the Holy One, blessed be He, as it is said (Isaiah 43:7) "Everyone that is called by My name and whom I have created for My glory, I have formed him, and indeed, I have made him. Rabbi Eliezer taught that in the time to come, the word "holy" will be applied to the pious as it is applied to the Holy One, blessed be He, as it is said (Isaiah 4:3) "And it shall come to pass that he that is left in Zion, and he that remains in Jerusalem, shall be called holy, even everyone that is written among the living in Jerusalem." Therefore, as the Psalmist declares, (Psalms 5:12) "Let all those who put their trust in You rejoice; let them always shout for joy, because You defend them; and let those who love Your name be joyful in You."

רִבִּי Rabbi Hananya son of Akashya says: The Holy One, blessed is He, wished to give merit to Yisrael. He therefore gave them the Torah and the commandments in such abundance, as it is said: "For the sake of His righteousness, Adonai made the Torah so great and glorious."

Mourner's Kaddish - Kaddish Al Yisrael
(A transliteration of the Kaddish can be found on page 487)

יִתְגַּדַּל Exalted and sanctified be His great Name, (Amen) in the world which He created according to His will, and may He rule His kingdom and may He bring forth His redemption and hasten the coming of His Mashiah (Amen). In your lifetime and in your days, and in the lifetime of the entire House of Yisrael, speedily and in the near future—and say Amen.

יְהֵא (Amen) May His great Name be blessed forever and for all eternity. Blessed and praised, glorified, and exalted and uplifted, honored and elevated and extolled be the Name of the Holy One, blessed is He (Amen); above all the blessings and hymns, praises and consolations which we utter in the world—and say Amen. (Amen)

עַל Upon Yisrael, and upon our Sages, and upon their disciples, and upon all the disciples of their disciples, and upon all those who engage in the study of the Holy Torah in this land and in every land, may there be for us, for you, and for them, favor, kindness, compassion, from the Master of heaven and earth and say Amen. (Amen)

יְהֵא May there be abundant peace from heaven, life, plenty, salvation, consolation, deliverance, healing, redemption, forgiveness, atonement, relief, and rescue for us and for all His people Yisrael and say Amen. (Amen) He Who makes peace in His high heavens, may He, in His mercy, make peace for us and for all His people Yisrael and say Amen. (Amen)

The hands are washed after leaving the cemetery.

סדר אבלות

Introduction to the Kaddish

אָמַר רַבָּה בַּר בַּר חָנָה אָמַר רִבִּי יוֹחָנָן. עֲתִידִים צַדִּיקִים שֶׁיִּקָּרְאוּ עַל שְׁמוֹ שֶׁל הַקָּדוֹשׁ בָּרוּךְ הוּא. שֶׁנֶּאֱמַר, כֹּל הַנִּקְרָא בִשְׁמִי וְלִכְבוֹדִי בְּרָאתִיו, יְצַרְתִּיו אַף־עֲשִׂיתִיו. אָמַר רִבִּי אֱלִיעֶזֶר, עֲתִידִים צַדִּיקִים שֶׁיֹּאמְרוּ לִפְנֵיהֶם קָדוֹשׁ, כְּדֶרֶךְ שֶׁאוֹמְרִים לִפְנֵי הַקָּדוֹשׁ בָּרוּךְ הוּא. שֶׁנֶּאֱמַר וְהָיָה הַנִּשְׁאָר בְּצִיּוֹן וְהַנּוֹתָר בִּירוּשָׁלַיִם. קָדוֹשׁ יֵאָמֶר לוֹ. כָּל־הַכָּתוּב לַחַיִּים בִּירוּשָׁלָיִם. וְנֶאֱמַר וְיִשְׂמְחוּ כָל־חוֹסֵי בָךְ לְעוֹלָם יְרַנֵּנוּ, וְתָסֵךְ עָלֵימוֹ וְיַעְלְצוּ בְךָ אֹהֲבֵי שְׁמֶךָ.

רִבִּי חֲנַנְיָה בֶּן־עֲקַשְׁיָא אוֹמֵר, רָצָה הַקָּדוֹשׁ בָּרוּךְ הוּא לְזַכּוֹת אֶת־יִשְׂרָאֵל, לְפִיכָךְ הִרְבָּה לָהֶם תּוֹרָה וּמִצְוֹת, שֶׁנֶּאֱמַר, יְיָ חָפֵץ לְמַעַן צִדְקוֹ יַגְדִּיל תּוֹרָה וְיַאְדִּיר:

Mourner's Kaddish - קַדִּישׁ עַל יִשְׂרָאֵל
(A transliteration of the Kaddish can be found on page 487)

יִתְגַּדַּל וְיִתְקַדַּשׁ שְׁמֵהּ רַבָּא. (Amen) בְּעָלְמָא דִּי־בְרָא כִרְעוּתֵיהּ, וְיַמְלִיךְ מַלְכוּתֵיהּ, וְיַצְמַח פּוּרְקָנֵיהּ, וִיקָרֵב מְשִׁיחֵיהּ. (Amen) בְּחַיֵּיכוֹן וּבְיוֹמֵיכוֹן וּבְחַיֵּי דְכָל־בֵּית יִשְׂרָאֵל, בַּעֲגָלָא וּבִזְמַן קָרִיב וְאִמְרוּ אָמֵן:

(Amen) **יְהֵא שְׁמֵהּ רַבָּא מְבָרַךְ לְעָלַם (וּ)לְעָלְמֵי עָלְמַיָּא יִתְבָּרַךְ, וְיִשְׁתַּבַּח, וְיִתְפָּאַר, וְיִתְרוֹמַם, וְיִתְנַשֵּׂא, וְיִתְהַדָּר, וְיִתְעַלֶּה, וְיִתְהַלָּל שְׁמֵהּ דְּקֻדְשָׁא בְּרִיךְ הוּא:** (Amen) לְעֵלָּא מִן כָּל בִּרְכָתָא, שִׁירָתָא, תֻּשְׁבְּחָתָא, וְנֶחָמָתָא, דַּאֲמִירָן בְּעָלְמָא, וְאִמְרוּ אָמֵן: (Amen)

עַל יִשְׂרָאֵל, וְעַל רַבָּנָן, וְעַל תַּלְמִידֵיהוֹן, וְעַל כָּל תַּלְמִידֵי תַלְמִידֵיהוֹן, דְּעָסְקִין בְּאוֹרַיְתָא קַדִּשְׁתָּא, דִּי בְאַתְרָא הָדֵין וְדִי בְכָל אֲתַר וַאֲתַר. יְהֵא לָנָא וּלְהוֹן וּלְכוֹן, חִנָּא וְחִסְדָּא וְרַחֲמֵי, מִן קֳדָם מָארֵי שְׁמַיָּא וְאַרְעָא וְאִמְרוּ אָמֵן:
(Amen)

יְהֵא שְׁלָמָא רַבָּא מִן שְׁמַיָּא, חַיִּים וְשָׂבָע וִישׁוּעָה וְנֶחָמָה וְשֵׁיזָבָא וּרְפוּאָה וּגְאֻלָּה וּסְלִיחָה וְכַפָּרָה וְרֶוַח וְהַצָּלָה, לָנוּ וּלְכָל־עַמּוֹ יִשְׂרָאֵל, וְאִמְרוּ אָמֵן:
(Amen) [1]עֹשֶׂה שָׁלוֹם בִּמְרוֹמָיו, הוּא בְּרַחֲמָיו יַעֲשֶׂה שָׁלוֹם עָלֵינוּ, וְעַל כָּל־עַמּוֹ יִשְׂרָאֵל, וְאִמְרוּ אָמֵן:
(Amen)

---

1. Take 3 steps back, bow to the left and say עֹשֶׂה שָׁלוֹם בִּמְרוֹמָיו, bow to the right and say הוּא בְּרַחֲמָיו יַעֲשֶׂה שָׁלוֹם, straighten and say עָלֵינוּ, וְעַל כָּל־עַמּוֹ יִשְׂרָאֵל וְאִמְרוּ אָמֵן.

The Order of Mourning

Tearing of the Garment

Generally, the Rending of the Garment and the Meal of Consolation are performed at the home of one of the mourners. Occasionally, because of circumstances, this procedure may be performed at the cemetery chapel.

Blessing Before Tearing the Garment

This blessing is said individually, by each mourner, while standing.

בָּרוּךְ Blessed are You, Adonai, our God, King of the universe, Judge of Truth.

Lighting of the Candle

A seven day candle is lit at this point. All the mourners gather together, while the eldest among them lights the candle. They all say together:

I / We light this candle in loving memory of my / our dear husband / wife / father / mother / brother / sister / son / daughter, **(NAME son of / daughter of (NAME OF DECEASED'S FATHER)** may his/ her resting place be in the Garden of Eden.

The Meal of Consolation

The Meal of Consolation is eaten while sitting on the floor or low stools. It usually consists of rolls, hard-boiled eggs (which have been peeled but left whole), greek olives, raisins and wine. A tablecloth is spread before the mourners, and those able to sit on the floor to join the mourners in the meal should do so. Paper plates, cups, napkins and a knife to cut the eggs are provided. Water for the washing of hands is brought to pour over the hands of the mourners utilizing a pitcher and deep bowl to catch the water. Others may wash in the kitchen. The blessing for the washing of hands is said. The individual leading the service then makes the Amotzi blessing on the rolls, prefixing the blessing with the words 'Blessed be the One who judger Truth and Justice". He then cuts the eggs with the knife, and distributes a roll, a piece of egg and a few olives to the mourners and anyone else joining in the meal. The meal is followed by the Grace After Meals for Mourners (below).

Grace After Meals for Mourners

For the Meal of Consolation only, the Avelim cannot be counted toward the 'zimun', i.e. for a zimun of three, there must at least three who participate in the meal, not counting the Avelim; for a zimun of ten, there must be at least ten who participate in the meal, not counting Avelim. This Grace After Meals is said during the entire week of Mourning (Shiva) except on Shabbat.

בִּלַּע He (God) will make death disappear forever, and Adonai will wipe away tears from every face, and He will remove the shame of His people from the entire world, because Adonai has spoken. May those who died for you live again; say, O God, "Let my corpses arise, awaken and sing, you who are asleep in the earth", for Your dew is a dew of lights and the land shall spew out the dead. And He, the merciful One, will forgive iniquity, and not destroy man; He will frequently turn aside His anger and not arouse all His wrath at once.

The Leader: Let us bless Him (our God) Who consoles mourners.

Those present: Blessed is He (our God) Who consoles mourners, from Whose bounty we have eaten and through Whose great goodness we have lived.

The Leader: Blessed is He (our God) Who consoles mourners, from Whose bounty we have eaten and through Whose great goodness we have lived.

סדר אבלות

Tearing of the Garment

Generally, the Tearing of the garment and the Meal of Consolation are performed at the home of one of the mourners. Occasionally, because of circumstances, this procedure may be performed at the cemetery chapel.

Blessing Before Tearing the Garment
This blessing is said individually, by each mourner, while standing.

בָּרוּךְ אַתָּה, יְיָ, אֱלֹהֵינוּ מֶלֶךְ הָעוֹלָם, דַּיַּן הָאֱמֶת.

Lighting of the Candle

A seven day candle is lit at this point. All the mourners gather together, while the eldest among them lights the candle. They all say together:

לְעִילּוּי נִשְׁמַת מֹר/מָרַת בַּעֲלִי /אִשְׁתִּי /אָבִי /אִמִּי /אָחִי /אֲחוֹתִי /בְּנִי /בִּתִּי (פ"ב"פ) שֶׁתְּהֵא מְנוּחָתוֹ/מְנוּחָתָהּ בְּגַן עֵדֶן.

סעודת הבראה

The Meal of Consolation is eaten while sitting on the floor or low stools. It usually consists of rolls, hard-boiled eggs (which have been peeled but left whole), greek olives, raisins and wine. A tablecloth is spread before the mourners, and those able to sit on the floor to join the mourners in the meal should do so. Paper plates, cups, napkins and a knife to cut the eggs are provided. Water for the washing of hands is brought to pour over the hands of the mourners utilizing a pitcher and deep bowl to catch the water. Others may wash in the kitchen. The blessing for the washing of hands is said. The individual leading the service then makes the Hamotzi blessing on the rolls, prefixing the blessing with the words בָּרוּךְ דַּיַּן הָאֱמֶת וְהַצֶּדֶק. He then cuts the eggs with the knife, and distributes a roll, a piece of egg and a few olives to the mourners and anyone else joining in the meal. The meal is followed by the Grace After Meals for Mourners (below).

ברכת המזון לאבלים

For the Meal of Consolation only, the Avelim cannot be counted toward the 'zimun', i.e. for a zimun of three, there must at least three who participate in the meal, not counting the Avelim; for a zimun of ten, there must be at least ten who participate in the meal, not counting Avelim. This Grace After Meals is said during the entire week of Mourning (Shiva) except on Shabbat.

בִּלַּע הַמָּוֶת לָנֶצַח, וּמָחָה אֲדֹנָי אֱלֹהִים דִּמְעָה מֵעַל כָּל־פָּנִים. וְחֶרְפַּת עַמּוֹ יָסִיר מֵעַל כָּל־הָאָרֶץ, כִּי יְיָ דִּבֵּר: יִחְיוּ מֵתֶיךָ נְבֵלָתִי יְקוּמוּן, הָקִיצוּ וְרַנְּנוּ שֹׁכְנֵי עָפָר, כִּי טַל אוֹרֹת טַלֶּךָ, וָאָרֶץ רְפָאִים תַּפִּיל: וְהוּא רַחוּם יְכַפֵּר עָוֹן וְלֹא־יַשְׁחִית, וְהִרְבָּה לְהָשִׁיב אַפּוֹ, וְלֹא־יָעִיר כָּל־חֲמָתוֹ:

The Leader	<div dir="rtl">נְבָרֵךְ (בעשרה אֱלֹהֵינוּ) מְנַחֵם אֲבֵלִים:</div>
Those present	<div dir="rtl">בָּרוּךְ (בעשרה אֱלֹהֵינוּ) מְנַחֵם אֲבֵלִים שֶׁאָכַלְנוּ מִשֶּׁלּוֹ וּבְטוּבוֹ הַגָּדוֹל חָיִינוּ.</div>
The Leader	<div dir="rtl">בָּרוּךְ (בעשרה אֱלֹהֵינוּ) מְנַחֵם אֲבֵלִים שֶׁאָכַלְנוּ מִשֶּׁלּוֹ וּבְטוּבוֹ הַגָּדוֹל חָיִינוּ.</div>

The Order of Mourning

בָּרוּךְ Blessed are You, Adonai our God, King of the Universe, Who nourishes us and the entire world with His goodness, with favor, with kindness, and with mercy. He provides food for all flesh, for His kindness endures forever. And through His great goodness, we have never lacked and we will not lack food always, forever and ever. For He is Almighty Who nourishes and maintains all, and His table is set for all, and prepared sustenance and nourishment for all His creatures which He has created with kindness and compassion. As it is said: "Open Your hand and satisfy the desire of every living being." Blessed are You, Adonai, Who nourishes all in His mercy.

נוֹדֶה We thank You, Adonai, our God, for Your parceling out as a heritage to our fathers, a land which is desirable, good, and spacious; a covenant and Torah; life and sustenance. For Your bringing us out of the land of Egypt, and redeeming us from the house of bondage; for Your covenant which You sealed in our flesh; for Your Torah which You taught us; for the statutes of Your will which You made known to us; for life and sustenance with which You nourish and maintain us.

(On Hanukkah and Purim, include '(We thank You) for the miracles', page 227)

וְעַל For everything Adonai, our God, We thank You and bless Your Name, as it is said: "When You have eaten and are satisfied, You will bless Adonai, your God, for the good land which He has given to you." Blessed are You, Adonai, for the land and for the food.

רַחֵם Have compassion, Adonai, our God, on us, and on Yisrael, Your people, and on Yerushalayim, Your city, and on Mount Tsiyyon, the dwelling place of Your glory, and on Your sanctuary, and on Your temple, and on Your Holy of Holies, and on the great and holy House upon which Your Name is called. Our Father, tend us, nourish us, maintain us, sustain us, relieve us and grant us relief speedily from all our troubles. Adonai, our God may we never be in need of the gifts of men nor of their loans, (for their giving is limited and their shame is great) but only of Your hand which is full and expansive, generous and open, so that we may not be shamed in this world, nor humiliated in the World to Come. And may You restore the kingdom of the house of David Your anointed, quickly, in our lifetime.

(On Rosh Hodesh, include 'may there ascend, and come', top of page 229)

נַחֵם Console, Adonai, our God, the mourners of Tsiyyon and the mourner of Yerushalayim, as well as the mourners who are mourning in this grief. Console them in their bereavement, and give them happiness after their sorrow. For it is written, "As one whom his mother comforts, so will I comfort you, and through Yerushalayim shall you be comforted."

סדר אבלות

בָּרוּךְ אַתָּה, יְיָ, אֱלֹהֵינוּ מֶלֶךְ הָעוֹלָם, הַזָּן אֶת־הָעוֹלָם כֻּלּוֹ בְּטוּבוֹ בְּחֵן בְּחֶסֶד וּבְרַחֲמִים הוּא נוֹתֵן לֶחֶם לְכָל־בָּשָׂר כִּי לְעוֹלָם חַסְדּוֹ. וּבְטוּבוֹ הַגָּדוֹל תָּמִיד לֹא חָסַר־לָנוּ, וְאַל יֶחְסַר־לָנוּ מָזוֹן תָּמִיד לְעוֹלָם וָעֶד. כִּי הוּא אֵל זָן וּמְפַרְנֵס לַכֹּל. וְשֻׁלְחָנוֹ עָרוּךְ לַכֹּל, וְהִתְקִין מִחְיָה וּמָזוֹן לְכָל־בְּרִיּוֹתָיו אֲשֶׁר בָּרָא בְּרַחֲמָיו וּבְרוֹב חֲסָדָיו כָּאָמוּר, [2]פּוֹתֵחַ אֶת־יָדֶךָ, וּמַשְׂבִּיעַ לְכָל־חַי רָצוֹן. בָּרוּךְ אַתָּה, יְיָ, הַזָּן בְּרַחֲמָיו אֶת־הַכֹּל.

נוֹדֶה לְךָ יְיָ אֱלֹהֵינוּ עַל שֶׁהִנְחַלְתָּ לַאֲבוֹתֵינוּ, אֶרֶץ חֶמְדָּה טוֹבָה וּרְחָבָה, בְּרִית וְתוֹרָה, חַיִּים וּמָזוֹן, עַל שֶׁהוֹצֵאתָנוּ מֵאֶרֶץ מִצְרַיִם, וּפְדִיתָנוּ מִבֵּית עֲבָדִים, וְעַל בְּרִיתְךָ שֶׁחָתַמְתָּ בִּבְשָׂרֵנוּ, וְעַל תּוֹרָתְךָ שֶׁלִּמַּדְתָּנוּ, וְעַל חֻקֵּי רְצוֹנְךָ שֶׁהוֹדַעְתָּנוּ וְעַל חַיִּים וּמָזוֹן שֶׁאַתָּה זָן וּמְפַרְנֵס אוֹתָנוּ.

(On Ḥanukkah and Purim, include עַל הַנִּסִּים page 227)

וְעַל הַכֹּל יְיָ אֱלֹהֵינוּ אֲנוּ מוֹדִים לָךְ, וּמְבָרְכִים אֶת־שְׁמֶךָ, כָּאָמוּר וְאָכַלְתָּ וְשָׂבָעְתָּ וּבֵרַכְתָּ אֶת־יְיָ אֱלֹהֶיךָ עַל הָאָרֶץ הַטֹּבָה אֲשֶׁר נָתַן לָךְ. בָּרוּךְ אַתָּה, יְיָ, עַל הָאָרֶץ וְעַל הַמָּזוֹן.

רַחֵם יְיָ אֱלֹהֵינוּ, עָלֵינוּ וְעַל יִשְׂרָאֵל עַמֶּךָ, וְעַל יְרוּשָׁלַיִם עִירֶךָ, וְעַל הַר צִיּוֹן מִשְׁכַּן כְּבוֹדֶךָ, וְעַל הֵיכָלֶךָ, וְעַל מְעוֹנֶךָ, וְעַל דְּבִירֶךָ, וְעַל הַבַּיִת הַגָּדוֹל וְהַקָּדוֹשׁ שֶׁנִּקְרָא שִׁמְךָ עָלָיו. אָבִינוּ, רְעֵנוּ, זוּנֵנוּ, פַּרְנְסֵנוּ, כַּלְכְּלֵנוּ, הַרְוִיחֵנוּ, הַרְוַח־לָנוּ מְהֵרָה מִכָּל־צָרוֹתֵינוּ, וְאַל־תַּצְרִיכֵנוּ יְיָ אֱלֹהֵינוּ, לִידֵי מַתְּנוֹת בָּשָׂר וָדָם, וְלֹא לִידֵי הַלְוָאָתָם. (שֶׁמַּתְּנָתָם מְעוּטָה וְחֶרְפָּתָם מְרֻבָּה) אֶלָּא לְיָדְךָ הַמְּלֵאָה, וְהָרְחָבָה, הָעֲשִׁירָה וְהַפְּתוּחָה, יְהִי רָצוֹן, שֶׁלֹּא נֵבוֹשׁ בָּעוֹלָם הַזֶּה וְלֹא נִכָּלֵם לָעוֹלָם הַבָּא וּמַלְכוּת בֵּית דָּוִד מְשִׁיחֶךָ תַּחֲזִירֶנָּה לִמְקוֹמָהּ בִּמְהֵרָה בְּיָמֵינוּ.

(On Rosh Ḥodesh, include יַעֲלֶה וְיָבֹא page 229)

נַחֵם יְיָ אֱלֹהֵינוּ אֶת־אֲבֵלֵי צִיּוֹן וְאֶת־אֲבֵלֵי יְרוּשָׁלַיִם וְאֶת־הָאֲבֵלִים הַמִּתְאַבְּלִים בָּאֵבֶל הַזֶּה, נַחֲמֵם מֵאֶבְלָם, וְשַׂמְּחֵם מִיגוֹנָם, כָּאָמוּר כְּאִישׁ אֲשֶׁר אִמּוֹ תְּנַחֲמֶנּוּ, כֵּן אָנֹכִי אֲנַחֶמְכֶם, וּבִירוּשָׁלַיִם תְּנֻחָמוּ.

---

2. Spread both hands upward, palms up, when reciting this sentence, as an expression of our dependence on Hashem for our livelihood.

The Order of Mourning

בָּרוּךְ Blessed are You, Adonai, who consoles those who mourn, and who will rebuild Yerushalayim.

בְּחַיֵּינוּ In our lifetime may You rebuild the city of Tsiyyon and reestablish the (Temple) service in Yerushalayim.

בָּרוּךְ Blessed are You, Adonai, our God, King of the universe, God, our Father, our King, our Mighty One, our Redeemer, our Holy One, the Holy One of Yaakov, Living God, Who is good and beneficent, God of truth, Who judges with righteousness, Who takes back souls, Who reigns over His world, (so as) to do His will; and we are His people and His servants. For all this we are obligated to give thanks to Him and bless Him. He Who closes breaches, may He close this breach for us and for all His people Yisrael, with compassion.

עוֹשֶׂה He Who makes peace in His high heavens, may He, in His mercy, make peace for us and for all His people Yisrael and say Amen.

At this point, for the Meal of Consolation only, wine is given to those who participated in the meal, followed by the after-blessing for wine, which can be found on page 232. Raisins are then distributed to everyone present.

The Shiva

(The Seven Day Mourning Period)

The family now enters a seven day period of mourning. If it is not too early in the afternoon, Minha (the afternoon prayer) may be said at this time. Evening services should take place at the time announced at the funeral. Because of space constraints, some families may elect to have the services held at the synagogue. Whether in the home or in the synagogue, a floor-mounted candle is lit before the Morning (Shaharit) services and the Arvit (Evening) services. Services are held every evening during the week except on Shabbat (Friday night and Saturday night). They are held on Saturday night only at the **'Korte De Syete'** (the end of the seven day mourning period. This occurs when the funeral took place on Sunday). There is no **'Korte De Syete'** service if it is interrupted by a Holiday (no Meldado, no Mishnayot read, not even the final **'Your sun shall no more go down'**) (see page 448). All meals for the mourners are provided by family and friends.

After each morning and evening service, the **'You are righteous, Adonai,'** (on days we say supplications), or the **'Adonai, what is man,'** (on days we do not), is recited followed by the Hashkava (Memorial Prayer). After the Hashkava, it is proper to say, 'and/or **'Min Ashamayim Tenuhamu'**.

סדר אבלות

בָּרוּךְ אַתָּה, יְיָ, מְנַחֵם אֲבֵלִים וּבוֹנֵה יְרוּשָׁלַיִם בִּמְהֵרָה בְיָמֵינוּ, אָמֵן.

בְּחַיֵּינוּ וּבְחַיֵּי כָּל־קְהַל בֵּית יִשְׂרָאֵל תִּבָּנֶה עִיר צִיּוֹן וְתִכּוֹן הָעֲבוֹדָה בִּירוּשָׁלָיִם.

בָּרוּךְ אַתָּה, יְיָ, אֱלֹהֵינוּ מֶלֶךְ הָעוֹלָם, לָעַד הָאֵל, אָבִינוּ, מַלְכֵּנוּ, אַדִּירֵנוּ, בּוֹרְאֵנוּ, גּוֹאֲלֵנוּ, קְדוֹשֵׁנוּ, קְדוֹשׁ יַעֲקֹב, הַמֶּלֶךְ הַחַי, הַטּוֹב וְהַמֵּטִיב, אֵל אֱמֶת, דַּיַּן אֱמֶת, שׁוֹפֵט בְּצֶדֶק, לוֹקֵחַ נְפָשׁוֹת, שַׁלִּיט בְּעוֹלָמוֹ, לַעֲשׂוֹת כִּרְצוֹנוֹ, וַאֲנַחְנוּ עַמּוֹ וַעֲבָדָיו, וְעַל הַכֹּל אֲנַחְנוּ חַיָּבִים לְהוֹדוֹת לוֹ וּלְבָרְכוֹ. גּוֹדֵר פְּרָצוֹת הוּא יִגְדּוֹר אֶת־הַפִּרְצָה הַזֹּאת מֵעָלֵינוּ וּמֵעַל כָּל־עַמּוֹ יִשְׂרָאֵל בְּרַחֲמִים: עֹשֶׂה שָׁלוֹם בִּמְרוֹמָיו הוּא בְרַחֲמָיו יַעֲשֶׂה שָׁלוֹם עָלֵינוּ וְעַל כָּל־עַמּוֹ יִשְׂרָאֵל, וְאִמְרוּ אָמֵן.

At this point, for the Meal of Consolation only, wine is given to those who participated in the meal, followed by the after-blessing for wine, which can be found on page 232. Raisins are then distributed to everyone present.

השבעה

(The Seven Day Mourning Period)

The family now enters a seven day period of mourning. If it is not too early in the afternoon, Minḥa (the afternoon prayer) may be said at this time. Evening services should take place at the time announced at the funeral. Because of space constraints, some families may elect to have the services held at the synagogue, but it is preferable to have them in the home. Whether in the home or in the synagogue, a floor-mounted candle is lit before the Morning (Shaḥarit) services and the Arvit (Evening) services. Services are held every evening during the week except on Shabbat (Friday night and Saturday night). They are held on Saturday night only at the end of the seven day mourning period. This occurs when the funeral took place on Sunday). There is no **Shiva Memorial Service** if it is interrupted by a Holiday (no Mishnayot read, not even the final לֹא־יָבוֹא עוֹד שִׁמְשֵׁךְ) (see page 448). All meals for the mourners are provided by family and friends.

After each morning and evening service, the צִדּוּק הַדִּין (on days we say taḥanunim), or the ה' מָה־אָדָם וַתֵּדָעֵהוּ (on days we do not), is recited followed by the Hashkava (Memorial Prayer). After the Hashkava, it is proper to say, '**Min Hashamayim Tenuḥamu**'.

Justification of the Divine Decree

(On days we say 'supplications')

צַדִּיק You are righteous, Adonai, and Your judgments are just. Adonai is righteous in all His ways and merciful in all His acts. The judgments of Adonai are true, they are altogether right. In that the word of the King is supreme, who could say to Him, "What are You doing?" He is One, and who could possibly answer Him back? That which His spirit wills, He does. He is the Rock, His work is perfect. for all His ways are just. The God of faith in whom there is no imperfection, just and upright is He. He is the true Judge, He judges with righteousness and truth. Blessed is the Judge of truth, for all His judgments are righteous and true. In the final analysis, all is heard, so fear God and heed His commandments, for that is the lot of all humankind.

(On days we do NOT say 'supplications')

יְיָ מָה־אָדָם Adonai, what is man, that you should take knowledge of him, or the son of man, that you should make account of him? Man is like a breath; his days are like a passing shadow, *Selah*. The small and great are there; and the servant is free from his master. Behold, he puts no trust in his servants; and he charges his angels with folly. How much less man, who is a worm? And the son of man, which is a maggot? The end of the matter, all has been heard. Fear God, and keep his commandments; for this is the whole duty of man.

The Hashkavot- Memorial Prayers

For a man

אַשְׁרֵי אִישׁ Happy is the man who fears Adonai, who delights greatly in his commandments. Blessed are they whose way is perfect; who walk in the Torah of Adonai. A good name is better than good oil and the day of one's death is better than the day of his birth. May the Almighty, Who is full of mercy, confer his abundant mercy upon the soul, spirit, and being of the one who departed this world with a good name, (NAME son of NAME OF FATHER), may the spirit of God place him in the Garden of Eden. May the King, in His mercy, have compassion on him.

סדר אבלות

צדוק הדין

(On days we say taḥanunim)

צַדִּיק אַתָּה יְיָ, וְיָשָׁר מִשְׁפָּטֶיךָ. צַדִּיק יְיָ בְּכָל־דְּרָכָיו, וְחָסִיד בְּכָל־מַעֲשָׂיו. צִדְקָתְךָ צֶדֶק לְעוֹלָם, וְתוֹרָתְךָ אֱמֶת. מִשְׁפְּטֵי־יְיָ אֱמֶת, צָדְקוּ יַחְדָּו. בַּאֲשֶׁר דְּבַר־מֶלֶךְ שִׁלְטוֹן, וּמִי יֹאמַר־לוֹ מַה־תַּעֲשֶׂה. וְהוּא בְאֶחָד וּמִי יְשִׁיבֶנּוּ, וְנַפְשׁוֹ אִוְּתָה וַיָּעַשׂ. הַצּוּר תָּמִים פָּעֳלוֹ, כִּי כָל־דְּרָכָיו מִשְׁפָּט. אֵל אֱמוּנָה וְאֵין עָוֶל, צַדִּיק וְיָשָׁר הוּא. דַּיָּן אֱמֶת שׁוֹפֵט צֶדֶק וֶאֱמֶת, בָּרוּךְ דַּיַּן הָאֱמֶת כִּי כָל־מִשְׁפָּטָיו צֶדֶק וֶאֱמֶת. סוֹף דָּבָר הַכֹּל נִשְׁמָע, אֶת־הָאֱלֹהִים יְרָא, וְאֶת־מִצְוֹתָיו שְׁמוֹר כִּי זֶה כָּל־הָאָדָם.

(On days we do NOT say taḥanunim)

יְיָ מָה־אָדָם וַתֵּדָעֵהוּ, בֶּן־אֱנוֹשׁ וַתְּחַשְּׁבֵהוּ, אָדָם לַהֶבֶל דָּמָה, יָמָיו כְּצֵל עוֹבֵר. מִי גֶבֶר יִחְיֶה וְלֹא יִרְאֶה־מָּוֶת, יְמַלֵּט נַפְשׁוֹ מִיַּד־שְׁאוֹל, סֶלָה. קָטֹן וְגָדוֹל שָׁם הוּא, וְעֶבֶד חָפְשִׁי מֵאֲדֹנָיו. הֵן בַּעֲבָדָיו לֹא יַאֲמִין, וּבְמַלְאָכָיו יָשִׂים תָּהֳלָה. אַף כִּי־אֱנוֹשׁ רִמָּה, וּבֶן־אָדָם תּוֹלֵעָה. סוֹף דָּבָר הַכֹּל נִשְׁמָע, אֶת־הָאֱלֹהִים יְרָא, וְאֶת־מִצְוֹתָיו שְׁמוֹר, כִּי זֶה כָּל־הָאָדָם.

השכבות

For a man

אַשְׁרֵי אִישׁ יָרֵא אֶת־יְיָ, בְּמִצְוֹתָיו חָפֵץ מְאֹד. אַשְׁרֵי תְמִימֵי־דָרֶךְ, הַהֹלְכִים בְּתוֹרַת יְיָ. טוֹב שֵׁם מִשֶּׁמֶן טוֹב, וְיוֹם הַמָּוֶת מִיּוֹם הִוָּלְדוֹ. אֵל מָלֵא רַחֲמִים הוּא יִתְמַלֵּא בְּרַחֲמָיו הַמְרוּבִּים עַל נֶפֶשׁ רוּחַ וְנִשְׁמָה שֶׁל הַנִּפְטָר (NAME son of NAME OF FATHER)) בְּשֵׁם טוֹב מִן הָעוֹלָם רוּחַ יְיָ תְּנִיחֶנּוּ בְּגַן עֵדֶן הַמֶּלֶךְ בְּרַחֲמָיו יְרַחֵם עָלָיו.

The Order of Mourning - Memorial Prayers

For a woman

אֵשֶׁת־חַיִל A woman of valor, who can find? Far beyond the most precious stones is her value. False is grace and vain is beauty; a God-fearing woman is the one deserving of praise. Give to her from the fruit of her hands; her deeds will praise her at the gates. The Merciful One, to Whom all mercy belongs, and by Whose word, worlds were created - This World and the World to Come, and Who stored therein righteous and pious women who do His will - according to His edict and His glory and His might. He shall decree that there ascend before Him the remembrance of the soul of the woman (NAME daughter of NAME OF FATHER) May the spirit of God place her in the Garden of Eden. May the King, in His mercy, have compassion on her.

For Rabbis and other distinguished religious leaders of the community

וְהַחָכְמָה Where is wisdom to be found and where is the place of understanding? Fortunate is the person who has found wisdom, and the person who evokes understanding. How great is the goodness that You have stored away for those who fear You; much have You performed for those who seek refuge in You in the presence of people. How precious is Your kindness, O God, that only those men who find refuge in the shade of Your wings will be satisfied from the affluence of Your house, and from the stream of Your delights You will give them to drink. A good name is better than good oil and the day of one's death is better than the day of his birth. May the Almighty, Who is full of mercy, confer His abundant mercy upon the soul, spirit, and being of the one who departed this world with a good name, (NAME son of NAME OF FATHER), may the spirit of God place him in the Garden of Eden. May the King, in His mercy, have compassion on him.

After each Memorial Prayer, the following is recited to conclude the service.

בִּלַּע He will make death disappear forever, and Adonai will wipe away tears from upon every face, and He will remove the shame of His people from the entire world, for Adonai has spoken. May those who died for you live again. say, O God, "Let my corpses arise, awaken and sing, you who are asleep in the earth," for Your dew is a dew of lights and the land shall spew out the dead. And He, the merciful One, atones iniquity, and does not destroy; He frequently withdraws His anger, and does not arouse all His rage.

On leaving the presence of the mourners, they should be approached with the following words of comfort: 'May (he) (she) be comforted from Heaven.'

סדר אבלות - השכבות

For a woman

אֵשֶׁת־חַיִל מִי יִמְצָא, וְרָחוֹק מִפְּנִינִים מִכְרָהּ. שֶׁקֶר הַחֵן וְהֶבֶל הַיּוֹפִי, אִשָּׁה יִרְאַת יְיָ הִיא תִתְהַלָּל. תְּנוּ־לָהּ מִפְּרִי יָדֶיהָ, וִיהַלְלוּהָ בַשְּׁעָרִים מַעֲשֶׂיהָ. רַחֲמָנָא דְרַחֲמָנוּתָא דִי לֵיהּ הִיא. וּבְמֵימְרֵהּ אִתְבְּרִיאוּ עָלְמַיָּא, עָלְמָא הָדֵין וְעָלְמָא דְאָתֵי. וּגְנַז בֵּיהּ צַדְקָנִיּוֹת וְחַסְדָּנִיּוֹת דְּעָבְדָן רְעוּתֵיהּ. וּבְמֵימְרֵיהּ וּבִיקָרֵיהּ וּבְתָקְפֵּיהּ יֹאמַר לְמֵיעַל קֳדָמוֹהִי. דִּכְרַן נֶפֶשׁ הָאִשָּׁה הַכְּבוּדָה וְהַצְּנוּעָה וְהַנִּכְבֶּדֶת מָרַת (NAME son of NAME OF FATHER) רוּחַ יְיָ תְּנִיחֶנָּה בְּגַן עֵדֶן, הַמֶּלֶךְ בְּרַחֲמָיו יְרַחֵם עָלֶיהָ.

For Rabbis and other distinguished religious leaders of the community

וְהַחָכְמָה מֵאַיִן תִּמָּצֵא, וְאֵי זֶה מְקוֹם בִּינָה. אַשְׁרֵי אָדָם מָצָא חָכְמָה, וְאָדָם יָפִיק תְּבוּנָה. מָה רַב־טוּבְךָ אֲשֶׁר־צָפַנְתָּ לִּירֵאֶיךָ, פָּעַלְתָּ לַחוֹסִים בָּךְ נֶגֶד בְּנֵי אָדָם. מַה־יָּקָר חַסְדְּךָ אֱלֹהִים, וּבְנֵי אָדָם בְּצֵל כְּנָפֶיךָ יֶחֱסָיוּן. יִרְוְיֻן מִדֶּשֶׁן בֵּיתֶךָ, וְנַחַל עֲדָנֶיךָ תַשְׁקֵם. טוֹב שֵׁם מִשֶּׁמֶן טוֹב, וְיוֹם הַמָּוֶת מִיּוֹם הִוָּלְדוֹ. אֵל מָלֵא רַחֲמִים, הוּא יִתְמַלֵּא בְּרַחֲמָיו הַמְּרוּבִּים עַל נֶפֶשׁ רוּחַ וּנְשָׁמָה שֶׁל הַנִּפְטָר בְּשֵׁם טוֹב מִן הָעוֹלָם (NAME son of NAME OF FATHER) רוּחַ יְיָ תְּנִיחֶנּוּ בְּגַן עֵדֶן הַמֶּלֶךְ בְּרַחֲמָיו יְרַחֵם עָלָיו.

After each Hashkava, the following is recited to conclude the service.

בִּלַּע הַמָּוֶת לָנֶצַח, וּמָחָה אֲדֹנָי אֱלֹהִים דִּמְעָה מֵעַל כָּל־פָּנִים. וְחֶרְפַּת עַמּוֹ יָסִיר מֵעַל כָּל־הָאָרֶץ, כִּי יְיָ דִּבֵּר: יִחְיוּ מֵתֶיךָ נְבֵלָתִי יְקוּמוּן, הָקִיצוּ וְרַנְּנוּ שֹׁכְנֵי עָפָר, כִּי טַל אוֹרוֹת טַלֶּךָ, וָאָרֶץ רְפָאִים תַּפִּיל: וְהוּא רַחוּם יְכַפֵּר עָוֹן וְלֹא־יַשְׁחִית, וְהִרְבָּה לְהָשִׁיב אַפּוֹ, וְלֹא־יָעִיר כָּל־חֲמָתוֹ:

On leaving the presence of the mourners, they should be approached with the following words of comfort: מִן הַשָּׁמַיִם תְּנֻחֲמוּ or תְּנֻחֲמוּ מִן הַשָּׁמַיִם

The Order of Mourning - Memorial Prayers

The Final Day of the Shiva
On the morning of the final day of the Shiva, the mourners are released from their deepest mourning by others saying the following verses. If the last day of Shiva occurs on Shabbat, and the mourners are in the synagogue, it is said just prior to taking out the Sefer Torah.

Yeshaya 60:20 and 66:13
לֹא־יָבוֹא Your sun shall no more go down; nor shall your moon withdraw itself; for the Lord shall be your everlasting light, and the days of your mourning shall be ended. And, it is written: As one whom his mother comforts, so will I comfort you; and you shall be comforted in Jerusalem.

The Memorial Service
The Memorial Service is held during the first year at the following times: the night after the 30th day, and the 7th, 9th, 11th and 12th month based on the Jewish date of burial. During the first year, mourners are considered to be within the year. Thereafter, Memorial Services are held annually based on the Jewish date of death.

Procedure for a regular Memorial Service

The one leading the service asks everyone to rise and says the following:

כָּל All Yisrael have a share in the World to Come, as it is said: "And all Your people will be righteous—they will inherit the land forever; they are My plants, the work of My hands, wherein I glory." We are reading for the elevation of the soul of **(NAME** son of / daughter of **NAME OF FATHER)** may his/her soul be bound in the bond of life. Amen. May it be Your will.

> Mishnayot are now read in memory of the departed. They are selected based on those that begin with the letters making up the name of the deceased. For example, for an individual whose name was Yitshak ben Rivka, Mishnayot beginning with the letters י, צ, ח, ק, ב, נ, ר, ב, ק, ה would be selected. Four additional Mishnayot are read; one from אבות, one from מדות and one from תמיד spelling the word אמת (truth). Another Mishna beginning נפל לתוכו יין which spells out the word נשמה (soul) is also read. After the reading of the Mishnayot, the one leading the service continues as follows:

(The following passage describes the passing of the Holy Sage Ribbi Shimon bar Yohai.)

דכתיב **As it is written:** "For there Ashem has commanded the blessing. May there be life forever!"

אָמַר Ribbi Aba said: The Holy Torch[1] did not cease to say *(the word)* 'life'[2] before his words became still. And I was writing, and I thought to continue writing, and I did not hear[3]. And I did not lift up my head, and I was unable to gaze. Meanwhile we trembled, we heard a voice that was calling and saying "*(for they add to you)* length of days and years of life *(and peace)*". Afterwards I heard another voice *(saying)* " Life he requested of You, *(You gave it to him; length of days forever and ever)*".

---
1. Referring to Ribbi Shimon bar Yohai
2. In the verse quoted immediately above
3. Probable meaning: and I was not able to hear

סדר אבלות

The Final Day of the Shiva
On the morning of the final day of the Shiva, the mourners are released from their deepest mourning by others saying the following verses. If the last day of Shiva occurs on Shabbat, and the mourners are in the synagogue, it is said just prior to taking out the Sefer Torah.

ישעיה ס: כ, סו: יג

לֹא־יָבוֹא עוֹד שִׁמְשֵׁךְ וִירֵחֵךְ לֹא יֵאָסֵף, כִּי יְהֹוָה יִהְיֶה־לָּךְ לְאוֹר עוֹלָם וְשָׁלְמוּ יְמֵי אֶבְלֵךְ: וּכְתִיב. כְּאִישׁ אֲשֶׁר אִמּוֹ תְּנַחֲמֶנּוּ, כֵּן אָנֹכִי אֲנַחֶמְכֶם וּבִירוּשָׁלַיִם תְּנֻחָמוּ:

The Memorial Service
The Memorial Service is held during the first year at the following times: the night after the 30th day, and the 7th, 9th, 11th and 12th month based on the Jewish date of burial. During the first year, mourners are considered to be within the year. Thereafter, Memorial Services are held annually based on the Jewish date of death.

Procedure for a regular Memorial Service

The one leading the service asks everyone to rise and says the following:

כָּל־יִשְׂרָאֵל יֵשׁ לָהֶם חֵלֶק לָעוֹלָם הַבָּא, שֶׁנֶּאֱמַר, וְעַמֵּךְ כֻּלָּם צַדִּיקִים לְעוֹלָם יִירְשׁוּ אָרֶץ, נֵצֶר מַטָּעַי מַעֲשֵׂה יָדַי לְהִתְפָּאֵר: הֲרֵי אֲנַחְנוּ קוֹרְאִים לְעִלּוּי נִשְׁמַת פב"פ שֶׁתְּהֵא נִשְׁמָתוֹ (נִשְׁמָתָהּ) צְרוּרָה בִּצְרוֹר הַחַיִּים אָמֵן, כֵּן יְהִי רָצוֹן:

Mishnayot are now read in memory of the departed. They are selected based on those that begin with the letters making up the name of the deceased. For example, for an individual whose name was Yitshak ben Ribka, Mishnayot beginning with the letters י, צ, ח, ק, ב, נ, ר, ב, ק, ה would be selected. Four additional Mishnayot are read; one from אבות, one from מדות and one from תמיד spelling the word אמת (truth). Another Mishna beginning נפל לתוכו יין which spells out the word נשמה (soul) is also read. After the reading of the Mishnayot, the one leading the service continues as follows:

דִּכְתִיב, כִּי שָׁם צִוָּה יְהֹוָה אֶת־הַבְּרָכָה חַיִּים עַד־הָעוֹלָם:

אָמַר רִבִּי אַבָּא לָא סַיֵּים בּוֹצִינָא קַדִּישָׁא לְמֵימַר חַיִּים עַד דְּאִשְׁתְּכוּ מְלוֹי. וַאֲנָא כָּתַבְנָא, סָבַרְנָא לְמִכְתַּב טָפֵי. וְלָא שָׁמַעְנָא וְלָא זָקִיפְנָא רֵישָׁאי. דִּנְהוֹרָא הֲוָה סַגִּי וְלָא הֲוָה יָכִילְנָא לְאִסְתַּכְּלָא. אַדְּהָכִי אִזְדַּעְזַעְנָא. שָׁמַעְנָא קָלָא דְקָארֵי וְאָמַר 'אֹרֶךְ יָמִים וּשְׁנוֹת חַיִּים וְשָׁלוֹם יוֹסִיפוּ לָךְ': שָׁמַעְנָא קָלָא אַחֲרָא, חַיִּים שָׁאַל מִמְּךָ נָתַתָּ לּוֹ אֹרֶךְ יָמִים

The Order of Mourning - Memorial Prayers

כָּל הַהוּא יוֹמָא Throughout that day, the fire never ceased in the house, and there was nobody that came near him, for they were unable to, because the light and the fire surrounded him. That whole day I fell on the ground and cried. After the fire had left, I saw the Holy Torch, Holy of Holies[4], that had left this world, wrapped (*in a garment*) and laying on his right (*side*), and his face was smiling.

קָם רִבִּי אֶלְעָזָר His son Ribbi Elazar stood up and took his hands and kissed them. And I licked the dust beneath his feet. The colleagues wanted to cry and they could not speak. The colleagues began weeping, and his son Ribbi Elazar fell three times and could not open his mouth. Afterwards he started and said "Father, Father, there were three (*of us*)[5], they returned (*to remain only*) one[6]. Now the wild animals will wander, and the birds of the sky will sink into the holes[7] of the Great Sea[8] and the colleagues will drink blood[9]."

קָם רִבִּי חִיָּיא Ribbi Hiyya stood up on his feet and said, "Until now the Holy Torch[10] looked after us. Now is not the time except to occupy ourselves with his honor." Ribbi Elazar and Ribbi Aba got up and took him (*from his place*) on a bed that was fashioned like a ladder (*in order to put him on his bed*). Who saw the confusion of the colleagues! Beautiful smells were coming up from the entire house. They raised him up unto his bed. Only Ribbi Elazar and Ribbi Aba occupied themselves with him.

אָתוּ טְרִיקִין Hitters[11] and shield-bearers came from the village of Tzippori[12], and the people of Meron chased them away, and their multitudes shouted at them, for they wanted that he should not be buried there (*but rather in their village instead*). After the bier had left (*the house*), he rose up in the air, and a fire was blazing before him. They heard a voice (*saying*) "Enter, come, and gather to the celebration of Ribbi Shimon." "He will come in peace; they will rest on their resting places."

כַּד עָאל לִמְעָרְתָּא When he entered into the (*burial*) cave[13], they heard a voice within the cave. "This is the man who shakes the earth, trembles kingdoms", how many prosecutors in the heavens are stilled today because of you, this is Ribbi Shimon bar Yohai whose Master is praised through you daily[14]. Fortunate is his portion above and below. How many of the highest treasures are kept for him, on him it is said 'As for you, go to (*your*) end; you will rest – then arise for your portion at the End of Days".

בָּרוּךְ Blessed is Adonai forever, Amen and Amen.

בָּרוּךְ Blessed is our God who created us for his glory, separated us from those who stray, gave us the Torah of truth, and implanted eternal life within us. The Merciful One, may He open our heart through his Torah and imbue our heart with love and awe of Him, that we may do his will and serve Him wholeheartedly, so that we do not struggle in vain nor produce for futility. May it be Your will, Adonai, our God and the God of our forefathers, that we observe Your decrees and commandments in This World, and merit

---

4. Referring to Ribbi Shimon bar Yohai
5. There were three great Sages: Ribbi Elazar, his father Ribbi Shimon bar Yohai and grandfather Ribbi Pinhas ben Yair
6. When Ribbi Pinhas ben Yair and Ribbi Shimon bar Yohai passed away only one was left, Ribbi Elazar
7. i.e. the depths
8. Usually referring to the Mediterranean
9. This "Great Tree," (i.e. Ribbi Shimon bar Yohai) sheltered the animals and birds and provided nourishment for everyone. Now that he has left the animals will wander, the birds will sink in the sea, and the colleagues, bereft of nourishment, will (figuratively) drink blood
10. Referring to Ribbi Shimon bar Yohai
11. Possibly warriors
12. They wanted Ribbi Shimon bar Yohai to be buried in their village and came to take him by force
13. The custom was to bury the dead in caves
14. i.e. Ashem is praised that He has such an outstanding servant

סדר אבלות

עוֹלָם וָעֶד. **כָּל הַהוּא יוֹמָא** לָא אַפְסִיק אֶשָּׁא מִן בֵּיתָא וְלָא הֲוָה מָאן דְּמָטֵי לְגַבֵּיהּ דְּלָא יָכִיל. דִּנְהוֹרָא וְאֶשָּׁא הֲוָה בְּסוֹחֲרָנֵיהּ כָּל הַהוּא יוֹמָא. נָפֵילְנָא עַל אַרְעָא וְגָעֵינָא. בָּתַר דְּאָזִיל אֶשָּׁא חָמֵינָא לְבוֹצִינָא קַדִּישָׁא קֹדֶשׁ הַקֳּדָשִׁים דְּאִסְתַּלַּק מִן עָלְמָא אִתְעַטָּף שָׁכִיב עַל יְמִינֵיהּ וְאַנְפּוֹי חַיְיכִין. **קָם רַבִּי אֶלְעָזָר** בְּרֵיהּ נָטִיל יְדוֹי וְנָשִׁיק לוֹן. וַאֲנָא לְחִיכְנָא עַפְרָא דִּתְחוֹת רַגְלוֹי. בָּעוֹ חַבְרַיָּיא לְמִבְכֵּי וְלָא יָכִילוּ לְמַלְּלָא. שָׁארוּ חַבְרַיָּיא בִּבְכִיָּה. וְרַבִּי אֶלְעָזָר בְּרֵיהּ נָפַל תְּלַת זִמְנִין וְלָא יָכִיל לְמִפְתַּח פּוּמֵיהּ. לְבָתַר פָּתַח וְאָמַר אַבָּא אַבָּא. תְּלַת הֲווֹ. חַד אִתְחֲזָרוּ הַשִּׁתָּא תְּנוּד חֵיוָתָא. צִפֳּרָן טָאסִין מִשְׁתַּקְעָן בְּנוּקְבָא דְּיַמָּא רַבָּא. וְחַבְרַיָּיא כֻּלְּהוּ שְׁתִיָן דָּמָא. **קָם רַבִּי חִיָּיא** עַל רַגְלוֹי וְאָמַר. עַד הַשְּׁתָּא בּוֹצִינָא קַדִּישָׁא מִסְתַּכַּל עֲלָן. הַשְׁתָּא לָאו הוּא עִדָּן אֶלָּא לְאִשְׁתַּדְּלָא בִּיקָרֵיהּ. קָם רַבִּי אֶלְעָזָר וְרַבִּי אַבָּא. נַטְלוּ לֵיהּ בְּטִקְרָא דְּסַקְלָא מָאן חָמָא עִרְבּוּבְיָא דְּחַבְרַיָּיא וְכָל בֵּיתָא הֲוָה סָלִיק רֵיחִין. סָלִיקוּ בֵּיהּ בְּפוּרְיֵיהּ. וְלָא אִשְׁתַּמַּשׁ בֵּיהּ אֶלָּא רַבִּי אֶלְעָזָר וְרַבִּי אַבָּא. **אָתוּ טְרִיקִין** וּמָארֵי תְּרִיסִין דִּכְפַר צִפּוֹרִי וְטָרְדֵי בְהוֹ וַהֲווֹ בְּנֵי מְרוֹנְיָא צָוְחִין בִּקְטִירִין דַּחֲשִׁיבוּ דְּלָא יִתְקְבַר תַּמָּן. בָּתַר דְּנָפַק פּוּרְיָא הֲוָה סָלִיק בַּאֲוִירָא וְאֶשָּׁא הֲוָה לָהִיט קַמֵּיהּ. שָׁמְעוּ קָלָא עוּלוּ וְאָתוּ וְאִתְכַּנְּשׁוּ לְהִלּוּלָא דְּרַבִּי שִׁמְעוֹן, 'יָבוֹא שָׁלוֹם יָנוּחוּ עַל מִשְׁכְּבוֹתָם'. **כַּד עָאל** לִמְעַרְתָּא שָׁמְעוּ קָלָא בִּמְעָרְתָא. 'זֶה הָאִישׁ מַרְעִישׁ הָאָרֶץ מַרְגִּיז מַמְלָכוֹת'. כַּמָּה פִּטְרִין בִּרְקִיעָא מִשְׁתַּכְּכִין בְּיוֹמָא דֵין בְּגִינָךְ. דְּנָא רַבִּי שִׁמְעוֹן בֶּן יוֹחַאי דְּמָארֵיהּ מִשְׁתַּבַּח בֵּיהּ בְּכָל יוֹמָא. זַכָּאָה חוּלָקֵיהּ לְעֵילָא וְתַתָּא. כַּמָּה גְּנִיזִין עִלָּאִין מִסְתַּמְּרָן לֵיהּ. עֲלֵיהּ אִתְּמַר. וְאַתָּה לֵךְ לַקֵּץ וְתָנוּחַ וְתַעֲמֹד לְגוֹרָלְךָ לְקֵץ הַיָּמִין:

בָּרוּךְ יְיָ לְעוֹלָם אָמֵן וְאָמֵן:

בָּרוּךְ אֱלֹהֵינוּ, שֶׁבְּרָאָנוּ לִכְבוֹדוֹ, וְהִבְדִּילָנוּ מִן־הַתּוֹעִים, וְנָתַן לָנוּ תּוֹרַת אֱמֶת, וְחַיֵּי עוֹלָם נָטַע בְּתוֹכֵנוּ. הָרַחֲמָן הוּא יִפְתַּח לִבֵּנוּ בְּתוֹרָתוֹ וְיָשֵׂם בְּלִבֵּנוּ אַהֲבָתוֹ וְיִרְאָתוֹ, לַעֲשׂוֹת רְצוֹנוֹ וּלְעָבְדוֹ בְּלֵבָב שָׁלֵם. לְמַעַן לֹא נִיגַע לָרִיק, וְלֹא נֵלֵד לַבֶּהָלָה: יְהִי רָצוֹן מִלְּפָנֶיךָ, יְיָ אֱלֹהֵינוּ וֵאלֹהֵי אֲבוֹתֵינוּ, שֶׁנִּשְׁמֹר חֻקֶּיךָ וּמִצְוֹתֶיךָ

The Meldado

that we live and inherit goodness and blessing for the life of the World to Come. So that my soul might sing to You and not be stilled. Adonai, my God, forever will I thank You. Adonai desired, for the sake of its righteousness, that the Torah be made great and glorious. And those knowing Your Name will trust in You, and You forsake not those who seek You, Adonai. Adonai, our Master, how mighty is Your Name throughout the earth. Be strong, and let your hearts take courage, all who wait longingly for Adonai.

רִבִּי חֲנַנְיָה Rabbi Hananya son of Akashya says: The Holy One, blessed is He, wished to give merit to Yisrael. He therefore gave them the Torah and the commandments in such abundance, as it is said: "For the sake of His righteousness, Adonai made the Torah so great and glorious."

Mourner's Kaddish - Kaddish Al Yisrael

יִתְגַּדַּל Exalted and sanctified be His great Name, (Amen) in the world which He created according to His will, and may He rule His kingdom and may He bring forth His redemption and hasten the coming of His Mashiah (Amen). In your lifetime and in your days, and in the lifetime of the entire House of Yisrael, speedily and in the near future—and say Amen.

יְהֵא (Amen) May His great Name be blessed forever and for all eternity. Blessed and praised, glorified, and exalted and uplifted, honored and elevated and extolled be the Name of the Holy One, blessed is He (Amen); above all the blessings and hymns, praises and consolations which we utter in the world—and say Amen. (Amen)

עַל Upon Yisrael, and upon our Sages, and upon their disciples, and upon all the disciples of their disciples, and upon all those who engage in the study of the Holy Torah in this land and in every land, may there be for us, for you, and for them, favor, kindness, compassion, from the Master of heaven and earth and say Amen. (Amen)

יְהֵא May there be abundant peace from heaven, life, plenty, salvation, consolation, deliverance, healing, redemption, forgiveness, atonement, relief, and rescue for us and for all His people Yisrael and say Amen. (Amen) He Who makes peace in His high heavens, may He, in His mercy, make peace for us and for all His people Yisrael and say Amen. (Amen)

The Memorial Prayer is then said.

After the Memorial Prayer, it is proper to say 'Menuhato (for a male)/ Menuhata (for a female) Be'gan Eden' ('May his/her rest be in the Garden of Eden in Paradise')

סדר אבלות

בָּעוֹלָם הַזֶּה, וְנִזְכֶּה וְנִחְיֶה וְנִפְרֶה וְנִירַשׁ טוֹבָה וּבְרָכָה, לְחַיֵּי הָעוֹלָם הַבָּא: לְמַעַן יְזַמֶּרְךָ כָבוֹד וְלֹא יִדֹּם, יְיָ אֱלֹהַי לְעוֹלָם אוֹדֶךָּ: יְיָ חָפֵץ לְמַעַן צִדְקוֹ, יַגְדִּיל תּוֹרָה וְיַאְדִּיר. וְיִבְטְחוּ בְךָ יוֹדְעֵי שְׁמֶךָ, כִּי לֹא־עָזַבְתָּ דּוֹרְשֶׁיךָ יְיָ: יְיָ אֲדֹנֵינוּ מָה־אַדִּיר שִׁמְךָ בְּכָל־הָאָרֶץ: חִזְקוּ וְיַאֲמֵץ לְבַבְכֶם כָּל־הַמְיַחֲלִים לַיְיָ:

רַבִּי חֲנַנְיָה בֶּן־עֲקַשְׁיָא אוֹמֵר, רָצָה הַקָּדוֹשׁ בָּרוּךְ הוּא לְזַכּוֹת אֶת־יִשְׂרָאֵל, לְפִיכָךְ הִרְבָּה לָהֶם תּוֹרָה וּמִצְוֹת, שֶׁנֶּאֱמַר, יְיָ חָפֵץ לְמַעַן צִדְקוֹ יַגְדִּיל תּוֹרָה וְיַאְדִּיר:

קַדִּישׁ עַל יִשְׂרָאֵל - Mourner's Kaddish

יִתְגַּדַּל וְיִתְקַדַּשׁ שְׁמֵהּ רַבָּא. (Amen) בְּעָלְמָא דִּי־בְרָא כִרְעוּתֵיהּ, וְיַמְלִיךְ מַלְכוּתֵיהּ, וְיַצְמַח פּוּרְקָנֵיהּ, וִיקָרֵב מְשִׁיחֵיהּ. (Amen) בְּחַיֵּיכוֹן וּבְיוֹמֵיכוֹן וּבְחַיֵּי דְכָל־בֵּית יִשְׂרָאֵל, בַּעֲגָלָא וּבִזְמַן קָרִיב וְאִמְרוּ אָמֵן:

(Amen) **יְהֵא** שְׁמֵהּ רַבָּא מְבָרַךְ לְעָלַם (וּ)לְעָלְמֵי עָלְמַיָּא יִתְבָּרַךְ, וְיִשְׁתַּבַּח, וְיִתְפָּאַר, וְיִתְרוֹמַם, וְיִתְנַשֵּׂא, וְיִתְהַדָּר, וְיִתְעַלֶּה, וְיִתְהַלָּל שְׁמֵהּ דְּקֻדְשָׁא בְּרִיךְ הוּא: (Amen) לְעֵלָּא מִן כָּל בִּרְכָתָא, שִׁירָתָא, תֻּשְׁבְּחָתָא, וְנֶחָמָתָא, דַּאֲמִירָן בְּעָלְמָא, וְאִמְרוּ אָמֵן:

עַל יִשְׂרָאֵל, וְעַל רַבָּנָן, וְעַל תַּלְמִידֵיהוֹן, וְעַל כָּל תַּלְמִידֵי תַלְמִידֵיהוֹן, דְּעָסְקִין בְּאוֹרַיְתָא קַדִּשְׁתָּא, דִּי בְאַתְרָא הָדֵין וְדִי בְכָל אֲתַר וַאֲתַר. יְהֵא לָנָא וּלְהוֹן וּלְכוֹן, חִנָּא וְחִסְדָּא וְרַחֲמֵי, מִן קֳדָם מָארֵי שְׁמַיָּא וְאַרְעָא וְאִמְרוּ אָמֵן: (Amen)

יְהֵא שְׁלָמָא רַבָּא מִן שְׁמַיָּא, חַיִּים וְשָׂבָע וִישׁוּעָה וְנֶחָמָה וְשֵׁיזָבָא וּרְפוּאָה וּגְאֻלָּה וּסְלִיחָה וְכַפָּרָה וְרֶוַח וְהַצָּלָה, לָנוּ וּלְכָל־עַמּוֹ יִשְׂרָאֵל, וְאִמְרוּ אָמֵן: (Amen) [4]עֹשֶׂה שָׁלוֹם בִּמְרוֹמָיו, הוּא בְרַחֲמָיו יַעֲשֶׂה שָׁלוֹם עָלֵינוּ, וְעַל כָּל־עַמּוֹ יִשְׂרָאֵל, וְאִמְרוּ אָמֵן: (Amen)

The השכבה (Hashkava) is then said.

After the Hashkava, it is proper to say 'Menuḥato (for a male)/ Menuḥata (for a female)

---

3. Hakham Yedidya Shofet would add this word.
4. Take 3 steps back, bow to the left and say עֹשֶׂה שָׁלוֹם בִּמְרוֹמָיו, bow to the right and say הוּא בְרַחֲמָיו יַעֲשֶׂה שָׁלוֹם, עָלֵינוּ, straighten and say וְעַל כָּל־עַמּוֹ יִשְׂרָאֵל וְאִמְרוּ אָמֵן

The Order of Mourning

Alpha Beta
Psalm 119

א אַשְׁרֵי Blessed are they whose way is perfect; who walk in the Torah of Adonai. Blessed are they who keep His testimonies, and seek Him with their whole heart. They also do no iniquity, but they walk in His ways. You have commanded us to keep Your precepts diligently. O that my paths were directed to keep Your statutes; then I would not be ashamed, while I have respect for all Your commandments. I will praise You with an upright heart, when I shall have learned Your righteous judgements. I will keep Your statutes; do not utterly forsake me.

ב בַּמֶּה With what shall a youth purify his way? Surely, by observing Your decrees. I have sought You with my whole heart; let me not wander from Your precepts. I have treasured up Your word in my heart; that I might not sin against You. Blessed are You, Adonai, teach me Your statutes. With my lips, I have declared all the judgements of Your mouth. I have rejoiced in the way of Your testimonies, as much as in all riches. I will speak of Your precepts, and have respect unto Your ways. I will delight myself in Your statutes; I will not forget Your word.

ג גְּמֹל Deal bountifully with Your servant, that I may live and keep Your word. Open my eyes, that I may behold the wonders of Your law. I am a sojourner on the earth; do not hide Your commandments from me. My soul breaks for longing for Your judgements at all times. You have rebuked the proud who are accursed, who stray from Your commandments. Remove reproach and contempt from me, for I have kept Your testimonies. Princes also did sit and speak against me, but Your servant meditated in Your statutes. Your testimonies also are my delight, they are my counselors.

ד דָּבְקָה My soul cleaves to the dust; revive me according to Your word. I have declared my ways and You have answered me; teach me Your statutes. Make me understand the way of Your precepts, and I will talk of Your wondrous works. My soul faints from heaviness; strengthen me according to Your word. Remove from me the path of falsehood, and grant me Your law graciously. I have chosen the path of truth; I have set Your judgements before me. I have adhered to Your testimonies; Adonai, do not shame me. I run in the way of Your commandments, when You shall enlarge my heart.

ה הוֹרֵנִי Teach me, Adonai, the way of Your statutes, and I will keep it to the end. Give me understanding that I may keep Your law, and I will observe it with my whole heart. Lead me in the path of Your commandments, for I delight in it. Incline my heart to Your testimonies, and not to covetousness. Avert my eyes from beholding vanity; revive me in Your ways. Confirm Your word to Your servant, that leads to veneration for You. Remove from me the reproach I dread, for Your judgements are good. I have longed for Your precepts; revive me with Your righteousness.

אלפא ביתא

תהלים קיט

אַשְׁרֵי תְמִימֵי־דָרֶךְ, הַהֹלְכִים בְּתוֹרַת יְהוָה: אַשְׁרֵי נֹצְרֵי עֵדֹתָיו, בְּכָל־לֵב יִדְרְשׁוּהוּ: אַף לֹא־פָעֲלוּ עַוְלָה, בִּדְרָכָיו הָלָכוּ: אַתָּה צִוִּיתָה פִקֻּדֶיךָ, לִשְׁמֹר מְאֹד: אַחֲלַי יִכֹּנוּ דְרָכָי, לִשְׁמֹר חֻקֶּיךָ: אָז לֹא־אֵבוֹשׁ, בְּהַבִּיטִי אֶל־כָּל־מִצְוֹתֶיךָ: אוֹדְךָ בְּיֹשֶׁר לֵבָב, בְּלָמְדִי מִשְׁפְּטֵי צִדְקֶךָ: אֶת־חֻקֶּיךָ אֶשְׁמֹר, אַל־תַּעַזְבֵנִי עַד־מְאֹד:

בַּמֶּה יְזַכֶּה־נַּעַר אֶת־אָרְחוֹ, לִשְׁמֹר כִּדְבָרֶךָ: בְּכָל־לִבִּי דְרַשְׁתִּיךָ, אַל־תַּשְׁגֵּנִי מִמִּצְוֹתֶיךָ: בְּלִבִּי צָפַנְתִּי אִמְרָתֶךָ, לְמַעַן לֹא אֶחֱטָא־לָךְ: בָּרוּךְ אַתָּה, יְהוָה, לַמְּדֵנִי חֻקֶּיךָ: בִּשְׂפָתַי סִפַּרְתִּי, כֹּל מִשְׁפְּטֵי־פִיךָ: בְּדֶרֶךְ עֵדְוֹתֶיךָ שַׂשְׂתִּי, כְּעַל כָּל־הוֹן: בְּפִקֻּדֶיךָ אָשִׂיחָה, וְאַבִּיטָה אֹרְחֹתֶיךָ: בְּחֻקֹּתֶיךָ אֶשְׁתַּעֲשָׁע, לֹא אֶשְׁכַּח דְּבָרֶךָ:

גְּמֹל עַל־עַבְדְּךָ אֶחְיֶה, וְאֶשְׁמְרָה דְבָרֶךָ: גַּל־עֵינַי וְאַבִּיטָה, נִפְלָאוֹת מִתּוֹרָתֶךָ: גֵּר אָנֹכִי בָאָרֶץ, אַל־תַּסְתֵּר מִמֶּנִּי מִצְוֹתֶיךָ: גָּרְסָה נַפְשִׁי לְתַאֲבָה, אֶל־מִשְׁפָּטֶיךָ בְכָל־עֵת: גָּעַרְתָּ זֵדִים אֲרוּרִים, הַשֹּׁגִים מִמִּצְוֹתֶיךָ: גַּל מֵעָלַי חֶרְפָּה וָבוּז, כִּי עֵדֹתֶיךָ נָצָרְתִּי: גַּם יָשְׁבוּ שָׂרִים בִּי נִדְבָּרוּ, עַבְדְּךָ יָשִׂיחַ בְּחֻקֶּיךָ: גַּם־עֵדֹתֶיךָ שַׁעֲשֻׁעָי, אַנְשֵׁי עֲצָתִי:

דָּבְקָה לֶעָפָר נַפְשִׁי, חַיֵּנִי כִּדְבָרֶךָ: דְּרָכַי סִפַּרְתִּי וַתַּעֲנֵנִי, לַמְּדֵנִי חֻקֶּיךָ: דֶּרֶךְ־פִּקּוּדֶיךָ הֲבִינֵנִי, וְאָשִׂיחָה בְּנִפְלְאוֹתֶיךָ: דָּלְפָה נַפְשִׁי מִתּוּגָה, קַיְּמֵנִי כִּדְבָרֶךָ: דֶּרֶךְ־שֶׁקֶר הָסֵר מִמֶּנִּי, וְתוֹרָתְךָ חָנֵּנִי: דֶּרֶךְ־אֱמוּנָה בָחָרְתִּי, מִשְׁפָּטֶיךָ שִׁוִּיתִי: דָּבַקְתִּי בְעֵדְוֹתֶיךָ, יְהוָה אַל־תְּבִישֵׁנִי: דֶּרֶךְ־מִצְוֹתֶיךָ אָרוּץ, כִּי תַרְחִיב לִבִּי:

הוֹרֵנִי יְהוָה דֶּרֶךְ חֻקֶּיךָ, וְאֶצְּרֶנָּה עֵקֶב: הֲבִינֵנִי וְאֶצְּרָה תוֹרָתֶךָ, וְאֶשְׁמְרֶנָּה בְכָל־לֵב: הַדְרִיכֵנִי בִּנְתִיב מִצְוֹתֶיךָ, כִּי־בוֹ חָפָצְתִּי: הַט־לִבִּי אֶל־עֵדְוֹתֶיךָ, וְאַל אֶל־בָּצַע: הַעֲבֵר עֵינַי מֵרְאוֹת שָׁוְא, בִּדְרָכֶךָ חַיֵּנִי: הָקֵם לְעַבְדְּךָ אִמְרָתֶךָ, אֲשֶׁר לְיִרְאָתֶךָ: הַעֲבֵר חֶרְפָּתִי אֲשֶׁר יָגֹרְתִּי, כִּי מִשְׁפָּטֶיךָ טוֹבִים: הִנֵּה תָּאַבְתִּי לְפִקֻּדֶיךָ, בְּצִדְקָתְךָ חַיֵּנִי:

The Order of Mourning

|ו| **וִיבֹאֻנִי** Let Your mercies also come to me, Adonai; Your salvation, according to Your word. Then I shall have a word to answer him who reproaches me, for I have trusted in Your word. Do not take the word of truth entirely out of my mouth, for I have hope for Your judgements. And I will keep Your law continually; for ever and ever. And walk freely, for I seek Your precepts. And I will speak of Your testimonies in the presence of kings, and will not be ashamed. And I will delight myself in Your commandments which I have loved. I will also lift up my hand to Your commandments which I have loved, and meditate on Your statutes.

|ז| **זְכֹר** Remember the word to Your servant in which You gave me hope. This was my comfort in my affliction; Your word has revived me. The arrogant have derided me exceedingly, yet I have not swerved from Your Torah. I remembered Your judgments of old, Adonai, and with them I comforted myself. Horror has seized me, because of the wicked who forsake Your Torah. Your statutes have been my song in the house of my pilgrimage. Adonai, I have remembered Your name at night, and have kept Your Torah. This was mine because I kept your precepts.

|ח| **חֶלְקִי** I have said it is my portion, Adonai, to keep Your words. I have entreated You with my whole heart; be merciful to me according to Your word. I considered my ways and turned my feet to Your testimonies. I hurried and did not tarry to keep Your commandments. The bands of the wicked have oppressed me, yet, I have not forgotten Your Torah. At midnight I rise to give thanks to You, for Your righteous judgments. I am a companion of all who revere You, and keep Your precepts. The earth, Adonai, is full of Your kindness, teach me Your statutes.

|ט| **טוֹב** You have dealt kindly with Your servant, Adonai, according to Your word. Teach me good judgment and knowledge, for I believe in Your commandments. Before I was afflicted, I went astray, but now I have kept Your word. You are good and You do good; teach me Your statutes. The proud have forged lies against me, but I will keep Your precepts with my whole heart. Their heart is gross like fat, but I delight in Your Torah. It is good for me that I have been afflicted, that I might learn Your statutes. The Torah of Your mouth is better to me than thousands of gold and silver.

|י| **יָדֶיךָ** Your hands have made and fashioned me; give me understanding that I may learn Your commandments. May they who revere You see me and rejoice, because I hope in Your word. I know, Adonai, that Your judgments are right, and that in faithfulness, You have afflicted me. Let Your kindness, I beg You, come to comfort me, according to Your word to Your servant. Let Your mercies come unto me that I may live; for Your Torah is my delight. Let the arrogant be shamed, for they have dealt perversely and falsely with me, but I will meditate on Your precepts. Let those who revere You, and know Your testimonies, turn to me. Let my heart be perfect in Your statutes, that I may not be ashamed.

אלפא ביתא

וִיבֹאֻנִי חֲסָדֶיךָ יְהוָה, תְּשׁוּעָתְךָ כְּאִמְרָתֶךָ: וְאֶעֱנֶה חֹרְפִי דָבָר, כִּי־בָטַחְתִּי בִּדְבָרֶךָ: וְאַל־תַּצֵּל מִפִּי דְבַר־אֱמֶת עַד־מְאֹד, כִּי לְמִשְׁפָּטֶךָ יִחָלְתִּי: וְאֶשְׁמְרָה תוֹרָתְךָ תָמִיד, לְעוֹלָם וָעֶד: וְאֶתְהַלְּכָה בָרְחָבָה, כִּי פִקֻּדֶיךָ דָרָשְׁתִּי: וַאֲדַבְּרָה בְעֵדֹתֶיךָ נֶגֶד מְלָכִים, וְלֹא אֵבוֹשׁ: וְאֶשְׁתַּעֲשַׁע בְּמִצְוֹתֶיךָ, אֲשֶׁר אָהָבְתִּי: וְאֶשָּׂא־כַפַּי אֶל־מִצְוֹתֶיךָ אֲשֶׁר אָהָבְתִּי, וְאָשִׂיחָה בְחֻקֶּיךָ:

זְכָר־דָּבָר לְעַבְדֶּךָ, עַל אֲשֶׁר יִחַלְתָּנִי: זֹאת נֶחָמָתִי בְעָנְיִי, כִּי אִמְרָתְךָ חִיָּתְנִי: זֵדִים הֱלִיצֻנִי עַד־מְאֹד, מִתּוֹרָתְךָ לֹא נָטִיתִי: זָכַרְתִּי מִשְׁפָּטֶיךָ מֵעוֹלָם | יְהוָה וָאֶתְנֶחָם: זַלְעָפָה אֲחָזַתְנִי מֵרְשָׁעִים, עֹזְבֵי תּוֹרָתֶךָ: זְמִרוֹת הָיוּ־לִי חֻקֶּיךָ, בְּבֵית מְגוּרָי: זָכַרְתִּי בַלַּיְלָה שִׁמְךָ יְהוָה, וָאֶשְׁמְרָה תּוֹרָתֶךָ: זֹאת הָיְתָה־לִּי, כִּי פִקֻּדֶיךָ נָצָרְתִּי:

חֶלְקִי יְהוָה אָמַרְתִּי, לִשְׁמֹר דְּבָרֶיךָ: חִלִּיתִי פָנֶיךָ בְכָל־לֵב, חָנֵּנִי כְּאִמְרָתֶךָ: חִשַּׁבְתִּי דְרָכָי, וָאָשִׁיבָה רַגְלַי אֶל־עֵדֹתֶיךָ: חַשְׁתִּי וְלֹא הִתְמַהְמָהְתִּי, לִשְׁמֹר מִצְוֹתֶיךָ: חֶבְלֵי רְשָׁעִים עִוְּדֻנִי, תּוֹרָתְךָ לֹא שָׁכָחְתִּי: חֲצוֹת־לַיְלָה אָקוּם לְהוֹדוֹת לָךְ, עַל מִשְׁפְּטֵי צִדְקֶךָ: חָבֵר אָנִי לְכָל־אֲשֶׁר יְרֵאוּךָ, וּלְשֹׁמְרֵי פִּקּוּדֶיךָ: חַסְדְּךָ יְהוָה מָלְאָה הָאָרֶץ, חֻקֶּיךָ לַמְּדֵנִי:

טוֹב עָשִׂיתָ עִם־עַבְדְּךָ, יְהוָה כִּדְבָרֶךָ: טוּב טַעַם וָדַעַת לַמְּדֵנִי, כִּי בְמִצְוֹתֶיךָ הֶאֱמָנְתִּי: טֶרֶם אֶעֱנֶה אֲנִי שֹׁגֵג, וְעַתָּה אִמְרָתְךָ שָׁמָרְתִּי: טוֹב־אַתָּה וּמֵטִיב, לַמְּדֵנִי חֻקֶּיךָ: טָפְלוּ עָלַי שֶׁקֶר זֵדִים, אֲנִי בְּכָל־לֵב אֶצֹּר פִּקּוּדֶיךָ: טָפַשׁ כַּחֵלֶב לִבָּם, אֲנִי תּוֹרָתְךָ שִׁעֲשָׁעְתִּי: טוֹב־לִי כִי־עֻנֵּיתִי, לְמַעַן אֶלְמַד חֻקֶּיךָ: טוֹב־לִי תוֹרַת־פִּיךָ, מֵאַלְפֵי זָהָב וָכָסֶף:

יָדֶיךָ עָשׂוּנִי וַיְכוֹנְנוּנִי, הֲבִינֵנִי וְאֶלְמְדָה מִצְוֹתֶיךָ: יְרֵאֶיךָ יִרְאוּנִי וְיִשְׂמָחוּ, כִּי לִדְבָרְךָ יִחָלְתִּי: יָדַעְתִּי יְהוָה כִּי־צֶדֶק מִשְׁפָּטֶיךָ, וֶאֱמוּנָה עִנִּיתָנִי: יְהִי־נָא חַסְדְּךָ לְנַחֲמֵנִי, כְּאִמְרָתְךָ לְעַבְדֶּךָ: יְבֹאוּנִי רַחֲמֶיךָ וְאֶחְיֶה, כִּי־תוֹרָתְךָ שַׁעֲשֻׁעָי: יֵבֹשׁוּ זֵדִים כִּי־שֶׁקֶר עִוְּתוּנִי, אֲנִי אָשִׂיחַ בְּפִקּוּדֶיךָ: יָשׁוּבוּ לִי יְרֵאֶיךָ, וְיֹדְעֵי עֵדֹתֶיךָ: יְהִי־לִבִּי תָמִים בְּחֻקֶּיךָ, לְמַעַן לֹא אֵבוֹשׁ:

The Order of Mourning

כ | כָּלְתָה My soul longs for Your salvation; I hope in Your word. My eyes long for Your word, as I say "When will You comfort me?" Though I was like a leather skin in the smoke; yet, I did not forget Your statutes. How many are the days of Your servant; when will You judge those who pursue me? The proud have dug pits for me, which is not according to Your law. All Your commandments are faithful; they persecute me wrongfully; O help me. They had almost consumed me on earth, but I did not forsake Your precepts. Revive me according to Your lovingkindness, and I will keep the testimony of Your mouth.

ל | לְעוֹלָם Your word, Adonai, is established in heaven forever. Your faithfulness is from generation to generation; You have established the earth and it stands firm. According to Your ordinances, all things stand this day, for they are all Your servants. Were Your Torah not my delight, I would have perished in my affliction. I never will forget Your precepts, for with them, You have revived me. I am Yours, save me, for I have sought Your precepts. Though wicked men wait for me to destroy me, I consider Your testimonies. I have traced the limits of all perfection, but Your commandment is immeasurable.

מ | מָה How I love Your Torah; it is my meditation all day. You have made me wiser than my enemies with Your commandments, for they are always with me. I gained understanding from all my teachers, because Your testimonies are my meditation. From the ancients I gained understanding because I kept Your precepts. I have restrained my feet from every evil way, so that I might keep Your word. I have not departed from Your judgments, for You have taught me. How sweet are Your words to my palate; yes, sweeter than honey to my mouth. Through Your precepts I obtained understanding; I therefore hate every false way.

נ | נֵר Your word is a lamp unto my feet, and a light to my path. I have sworn, and I will perform it, that I will keep Your righteous judgments. I am sorely afflicted; revive me, Adonai, according to Your word. Adonai, accept, please, the freewill-offerings of my mouth, and teach me Your judgments. Though my soul is continually in my hand, yet I have not forgotten Your Torah. The wicked have laid a trap for me, yet I have not strayed from Your precepts. I have taken Your testimonies as my inheritance forever, for they are the joy of my heart. I have always inclined my heart to keep Your statutes, forever, with every step.

ס | סֵעֲפִים I hate those who have vain thoughts, but Your Torah I love. You are my shelter and my shield; I hope in Your word. Depart from me, evildoers, so that I may keep the commandments of my God. Uphold me according to Your word that I may live, and let me not be ashamed of my hope. Sustain me, and I shall be safe; and I will always delight myself with Your statutes. You have spurned all those who err from Your statutes, for their deceit is false. You have removed all the wicked of the earth like dross; therefore, I love Your statutes. My flesh trembles in awe of You, and I revere Your judgments.

אלפא ביתא

כָּלְתָה לִתְשׁוּעָתְךָ נַפְשִׁי, לִדְבָרְךָ יִחָלְתִּי: כָּלוּ עֵינַי לְאִמְרָתֶךָ, לֵאמֹר מָתַי תְּנַחֲמֵנִי: כִּי־הָיִיתִי כְּנֹאד בְּקִיטוֹר, חֻקֶּיךָ לֹא שָׁכָחְתִּי: כַּמָּה יְמֵי־עַבְדֶּךָ, מָתַי תַּעֲשֶׂה בְרֹדְפַי מִשְׁפָּט: כָּרוּ־לִי זֵדִים שִׁיחוֹת, אֲשֶׁר לֹא כְתוֹרָתֶךָ: כָּל־מִצְוֹתֶיךָ אֱמוּנָה, שֶׁקֶר רְדָפוּנִי עָזְרֵנִי: כִּמְעַט כִּלּוּנִי בָאָרֶץ, וַאֲנִי לֹא־עָזַבְתִּי פִקֻּדֶיךָ: כְּחַסְדְּךָ חַיֵּנִי, וְאֶשְׁמְרָה עֵדוּת פִּיךָ:

לְעוֹלָם יְהוָה, דְּבָרְךָ נִצָּב בַּשָּׁמָיִם: לְדֹר וָדֹר אֱמוּנָתֶךָ, כּוֹנַנְתָּ אֶרֶץ וַתַּעֲמֹד: לְמִשְׁפָּטֶיךָ עָמְדוּ הַיּוֹם, כִּי הַכֹּל עֲבָדֶיךָ: לוּלֵי תוֹרָתְךָ שַׁעֲשֻׁעָי, אָז אָבַדְתִּי בְעָנְיִי: לְעוֹלָם לֹא־אֶשְׁכַּח פִּקּוּדֶיךָ, כִּי־בָם חִיִּיתָנִי: לְךָ־אֲנִי הוֹשִׁיעֵנִי, כִּי פִקּוּדֶיךָ דָרָשְׁתִּי: לִי קִוּוּ רְשָׁעִים לְאַבְּדֵנִי, עֵדֹתֶיךָ אֶתְבּוֹנָן: לְכָל־תִּכְלָה רָאִיתִי קֵץ, רְחָבָה מִצְוָתְךָ מְאֹד:

מָה־אָהַבְתִּי תוֹרָתֶךָ, כָּל־הַיּוֹם הִיא שִׂיחָתִי: מֵאֹיְבַי תְּחַכְּמֵנִי מִצְוֹתֶךָ, כִּי לְעוֹלָם הִיא־לִי: מִכָּל־מְלַמְּדַי הִשְׂכַּלְתִּי, כִּי עֵדְוֹתֶיךָ שִׂיחָה לִי: מִזְּקֵנִים אֶתְבּוֹנָן, כִּי פִקּוּדֶיךָ נָצָרְתִּי: מִכָּל־אֹרַח רָע כָּלִאתִי רַגְלָי, לְמַעַן אֶשְׁמֹר דְּבָרֶךָ: מִמִּשְׁפָּטֶיךָ לֹא־סָרְתִּי, כִּי־אַתָּה הוֹרֵתָנִי: מַה־נִּמְלְצוּ לְחִכִּי אִמְרָתֶךָ, מִדְּבַשׁ לְפִי: מִפִּקּוּדֶיךָ אֶתְבּוֹנָן, עַל־כֵּן שָׂנֵאתִי ׀ כָּל־אֹרַח שָׁקֶר:

נֵר־לְרַגְלִי דְבָרֶךָ, וְאוֹר לִנְתִיבָתִי: נִשְׁבַּעְתִּי וָאֲקַיֵּמָה, לִשְׁמֹר מִשְׁפְּטֵי צִדְקֶךָ: נַעֲנֵיתִי עַד־מְאֹד, יְהוָה חַיֵּנִי כִדְבָרֶךָ: נִדְבוֹת פִּי רְצֵה־נָא יְהוָה, וּמִשְׁפָּטֶיךָ לַמְּדֵנִי: נַפְשִׁי בְכַפִּי תָמִיד, וְתוֹרָתְךָ לֹא שָׁכָחְתִּי: נָתְנוּ רְשָׁעִים פַּח לִי, וּמִפִּקּוּדֶיךָ לֹא תָעִיתִי: נָחַלְתִּי עֵדְוֹתֶיךָ לְעוֹלָם, כִּי־שְׂשׂוֹן לִבִּי הֵמָּה: נָטִיתִי לִבִּי לַעֲשׂוֹת חֻקֶּיךָ, לְעוֹלָם עֵקֶב:

סֵעֲפִים שָׂנֵאתִי, וְתוֹרָתְךָ אָהָבְתִּי: סִתְרִי וּמָגִנִּי אָתָּה, לִדְבָרְךָ יִחָלְתִּי: סוּרוּ־מִמֶּנִּי מְרֵעִים, וְאֶצְּרָה מִצְוֹת אֱלֹהָי: סָמְכֵנִי כְאִמְרָתְךָ וְאֶחְיֶה, וְאַל־תְּבִישֵׁנִי מִשִּׂבְרִי: סְעָדֵנִי וְאִוָּשֵׁעָה, וְאֶשְׁעָה בְחֻקֶּיךָ תָמִיד: סָלִיתָ כָּל־שׁוֹגִים מֵחֻקֶּיךָ, כִּי־שֶׁקֶר תַּרְמִיתָם: סִגִים הִשְׁבַּתָּ כָל־רִשְׁעֵי־אָרֶץ, לָכֵן אָהַבְתִּי עֵדֹתֶיךָ: סָמַר מִפַּחְדְּךָ בְשָׂרִי, וּמִמִּשְׁפָּטֶיךָ יָרֵאתִי:

The Order of Mourning

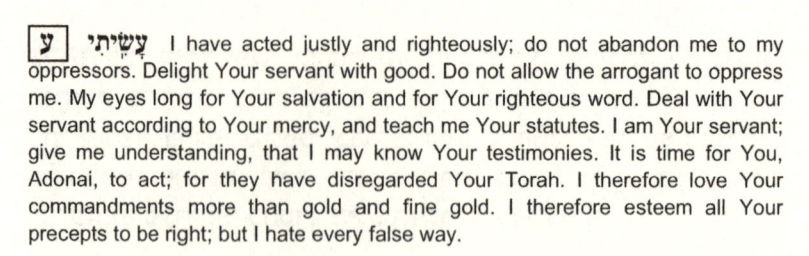

ע עָשִׂיתִי I have acted justly and righteously; do not abandon me to my oppressors. Delight Your servant with good. Do not allow the arrogant to oppress me. My eyes long for Your salvation and for Your righteous word. Deal with Your servant according to Your mercy, and teach me Your statutes. I am Your servant; give me understanding, that I may know Your testimonies. It is time for You, Adonai, to act; for they have disregarded Your Torah. I therefore love Your commandments more than gold and fine gold. I therefore esteem all Your precepts to be right; but I hate every false way.

פ פְּלָאוֹת Your testimonies are wonderful; my soul therefore keeps them. The opening up of Your words enlightens; it gives understanding to the simple. I opened my mouth and panted; for I longed for Your commandments. Turn to me and be merciful to me, as You are used to doing with those who love Your name. Establish my steps in Your word, and let not any iniquity have dominion over me. Deliver me from the oppression of man, that I may keep Your precepts. Cause Your face to shine upon Your servant, and teach me Your statutes. Streams of water flow from my eyes, because they do not keep Your law.

צ צַדִּיק You are righteous, Adonai, and Your judgments are upright. Your testimonies, which You have commanded us, are righteous and exceedingly faithful. My zeal has consumed me, because my enemies have forgotten Your words. Your word is exceedingly pure; and Your servant loves it. I am little and despised, yet I have not forgotten Your precepts. Your righteousness is everlasting righteousness, and Your law is truth. Trouble and distress have seized me, but Your commandments are my delight. The righteousness of Your testimonies is everlasting, make me understand them, that I may live.

ק קָרָאתִי I called with my whole heart, answer me, Adonai, that I may keep Your statutes. I cried to You, "Save me", that I may keep Your testimonies. I rose before dawn and prayed; I hoped in Your word. My eyes watched before the break of day, to meditate on Your word. Hear my voice according to Your lovingkindness; Adonai, revive me according to Your judgment. They who pursue mischief come close; they are far from Your Torah. Your are near, Adonai, and all Your commandments are truth. Heretofore I have known of Your testimonies, that You laid their foundation forever.

ר רְאֵה Behold my affliction and save me; I have not forgotten Your Torah. Plead my cause and deliver me; revive me according to Your word. Salvation is far from the wicked; they do not seek Your statutes. Your tender mercies are abundant, Adonai, revive me according to Your judgment. My persecutors and enemies are many, yet I do not swerve from Your testimonies. I look on sinners and feel loathing, because they did not keep Your word. Behold, that I love Your precepts; revive me, Adonai, according to Your word. Your word is true from the beginning, and all Your righteous judgments endure forever.

אלפא ביתא

עָשִׂיתִי מִשְׁפָּט וָצֶדֶק, בַּל־תַּנִּיחֵנִי לְעֹשְׁקָי: עֲרֹב עַבְדְּךָ לְטוֹב, אַל־יַעַשְׁקֻנִי זֵדִים: עֵינַי כָּלוּ לִישׁוּעָתֶךָ, וּלְאִמְרַת צִדְקֶךָ: עֲשֵׂה עִם־עַבְדְּךָ כְחַסְדֶּךָ, וְחֻקֶּיךָ לַמְּדֵנִי: עַבְדְּךָ־אָנִי הֲבִינֵנִי, וְאֵדְעָה עֵדֹתֶיךָ: עֵת לַעֲשׂוֹת לַיהוָה, הֵפֵרוּ תּוֹרָתֶךָ: עַל־כֵּן אָהַבְתִּי מִצְוֹתֶיךָ, מִזָּהָב וּמִפָּז: עַל־כֵּן | כָּל־פִּקּוּדֵי כֹל יִשָּׁרְתִּי, כָּל־אֹרַח שֶׁקֶר שָׂנֵאתִי:

פְּלָאוֹת עֵדְוֹתֶיךָ, עַל־כֵּן נְצָרָתַם נַפְשִׁי: פֵּתַח־דְּבָרֶיךָ יָאִיר, מֵבִין פְּתָיִים: פִּי־פָעַרְתִּי וָאֶשְׁאָפָה, כִּי לְמִצְוֹתֶיךָ יָאָבְתִּי: פְּנֵה־אֵלַי וְחָנֵּנִי, כְּמִשְׁפָּט לְאֹהֲבֵי שְׁמֶךָ: פְּעָמַי הָכֵן בְּאִמְרָתֶךָ, וְאַל־תַּשְׁלֶט־בִּי כָל־אָוֶן: פְּדֵנִי מֵעֹשֶׁק אָדָם, וְאֶשְׁמְרָה פִּקּוּדֶיךָ: פָּנֶיךָ הָאֵר בְּעַבְדֶּךָ, וְלַמְּדֵנִי אֶת־חֻקֶּיךָ: פַּלְגֵי־מַיִם יָרְדוּ עֵינָי, עַל לֹא־שָׁמְרוּ תוֹרָתֶךָ:

צַדִּיק אַתָּה יְהוָה, וְיָשָׁר מִשְׁפָּטֶיךָ: צִוִּיתָ צֶדֶק עֵדֹתֶיךָ, וֶאֱמוּנָה מְאֹד: צִמְּתַתְנִי קִנְאָתִי, כִּי־שָׁכְחוּ דְבָרֶיךָ צָרָי: צְרוּפָה אִמְרָתְךָ מְאֹד, וְעַבְדְּךָ אֲהֵבָהּ: צָעִיר אָנֹכִי וְנִבְזֶה, פִּקֻּדֶיךָ לֹא שָׁכָחְתִּי: צִדְקָתְךָ צֶדֶק לְעוֹלָם, וְתוֹרָתְךָ אֱמֶת: צַר־וּמָצוֹק מְצָאוּנִי, מִצְוֹתֶיךָ שַׁעֲשֻׁעָי: צֶדֶק עֵדְוֹתֶיךָ לְעוֹלָם, הֲבִינֵנִי וְאֶחְיֶה:

קָרָאתִי בְכָל־לֵב, עֲנֵנִי יְהוָה חֻקֶּיךָ אֶצֹּרָה: קְרָאתִיךָ הוֹשִׁיעֵנִי, וְאֶשְׁמְרָה עֵדֹתֶיךָ: קִדַּמְתִּי בַנֶּשֶׁף וָאֲשַׁוֵּעָה, לִדְבָרְךָ יִחָלְתִּי: קִדְּמוּ עֵינַי אַשְׁמֻרוֹת, לָשִׂיחַ בְּאִמְרָתֶךָ: קוֹלִי שִׁמְעָה כְחַסְדֶּךָ, יְהוָה כְּמִשְׁפָּטֶךָ חַיֵּנִי: קָרְבוּ רֹדְפֵי זִמָּה, מִתּוֹרָתְךָ רָחָקוּ: קָרוֹב אַתָּה יְהוָה, וְכָל־מִצְוֹתֶיךָ אֱמֶת: קֶדֶם יָדַעְתִּי מֵעֵדֹתֶיךָ, כִּי לְעוֹלָם יְסַדְתָּם:

רְאֵה־עָנְיִי וְחַלְּצֵנִי, כִּי־תוֹרָתְךָ לֹא שָׁכָחְתִּי: רִיבָה רִיבִי וּגְאָלֵנִי, לְאִמְרָתְךָ חַיֵּנִי: רָחוֹק מֵרְשָׁעִים יְשׁוּעָה, כִּי־חֻקֶּיךָ לֹא דָרָשׁוּ: רַחֲמֶיךָ רַבִּים | יְהוָה, כְּמִשְׁפָּטֶיךָ חַיֵּנִי: רַבִּים רֹדְפַי וְצָרָי, מֵעֵדְוֹתֶיךָ לֹא נָטִיתִי: רָאִיתִי בֹגְדִים וָאֶתְקוֹטָטָה, אֲשֶׁר אִמְרָתְךָ לֹא שָׁמָרוּ: רְאֵה כִּי־פִקּוּדֶיךָ אָהָבְתִּי, יְהוָה כְּחַסְדְּךָ חַיֵּנִי: רֹאשׁ־דְּבָרְךָ אֱמֶת, וּלְעוֹלָם כָּל־מִשְׁפַּט צִדְקֶךָ:

The Order of Mourning

שָׂרִים Princes have pursued me without cause, but my heart stands in awe of Your word. I rejoice at Your word, as one who finds great spoil. I hate and abhor falsehood, but I love Your Torah. Seven times a day I praise You, because of Your righteous judgments. Great is the peace of those who love Your Torah—they will suffer no misfortune. Adonai, I hope for Your salvation, and have performed Your commandments. My soul has kept Your testimonies, and I love them exceedingly. I have kept Your precepts and Your testimonies, for all my ways are before You.

תִּקְרַב Let my hymn come near Your presence, Adonai; give me understanding according to Your word. Let my supplication come before You; save me according to Your word. My lips shall continually utter Your praise, when You have taught me Your statutes. My tongue shall speak of Your word; all Your commandments are righteousness. Let Your hand help me, for I have chosen Your precepts. I have longed for Your salvation, Adonai, and Your Torah is my delight. Let my soul live and it shall praise You, and let Your judgments help me. I have strayed like a lost sheep, seek Your servant, for I have not forgotten Your commandments.

אלפא ביתא

שָׂרִים רְדָפוּנִי חִנָּם, וּמִדְּבָרְךָ פָּחַד לִבִּי: שָׂשׂ אָנֹכִי עַל־אִמְרָתֶךָ, כְּמוֹצֵא שָׁלָל רָב: שֶׁקֶר שָׂנֵאתִי וַאֲתַעֵבָה, תּוֹרָתְךָ אָהָבְתִּי: שֶׁבַע בַּיּוֹם הִלַּלְתִּיךָ, עַל מִשְׁפְּטֵי צִדְקֶךָ: שָׁלוֹם רָב לְאֹהֲבֵי תוֹרָתֶךָ, וְאֵין־לָמוֹ מִכְשׁוֹל: שִׂבַּרְתִּי לִישׁוּעָתְךָ יְהוָה, וּמִצְוֹתֶיךָ עָשִׂיתִי: שָׁמְרָה נַפְשִׁי עֵדֹתֶיךָ, וָאֹהֲבֵם מְאֹד: שָׁמַרְתִּי פִקּוּדֶיךָ וְעֵדֹתֶיךָ, כִּי כָל־דְּרָכַי נֶגְדֶּךָ:

תִּקְרַב רִנָּתִי לְפָנֶיךָ, יְהוָה כִּדְבָרְךָ הֲבִינֵנִי: תָּבוֹא תְחִנָּתִי לְפָנֶיךָ, כְּאִמְרָתְךָ הַצִּילֵנִי: תַּבַּעְנָה שְׂפָתַי תְּהִלָּה, כִּי תְלַמְּדֵנִי חֻקֶּיךָ: תַּעַן לְשׁוֹנִי אִמְרָתֶךָ, כִּי כָל־מִצְוֹתֶיךָ צֶּדֶק: תְּהִי־יָדְךָ לְעָזְרֵנִי, כִּי פִקּוּדֶיךָ בָחָרְתִּי: תָּאַבְתִּי לִישׁוּעָתְךָ יְהוָה, וְתוֹרָתְךָ שַׁעֲשֻׁעָי: תְּחִי־נַפְשִׁי וּתְהַלְלֶךָּ, וּמִשְׁפָּטֶךָ יַעְזְרֻנִי: תָּעִיתִי כְּשֶׂה אֹבֵד בַּקֵּשׁ עַבְדֶּךָ, כִּי מִצְוֹתֶיךָ לֹא שָׁכָחְתִּי:

Transliteration of the *Kaddish*

Yitgadal VeYitkadash Shemeh Rabba.

BeAlma di-bera chiruteh, ve-yamlich mal-chutey, ve-yatzmach pur-kaneh vi-Karev me-shicheh.

Be-chayechon uv-yomechon, uv-chayeh de-chol bet Yisrael ba'agalah u-bizman kariv ve-yimru (AMEN).

YeHe shemeh rabbah me-varach le-alam ul-almey almaya,

Yit-barach, ve-yishtabach, ve-yitpa'ar, ve-yitromam, ve-yitnaseh, ve-yithadar, ve-yitaleh, ve-yithalal, Shemeh DeKudsha Berich Hu. (AMEN).

Le'elah min kol bir-chatah shir-atah, tush-bechata, ve-nechamata, da-amiran be-alma ve-imru (AMEN).

Al Yisrael ve-al rabanna, ve-al talmidehon ve-al kol Talmideh talmi-dehon, de-askeen be-Oraytah Kadishta, di be'atra haden vedi bechol atar ve-atar, yehe la'na ulhon u'lchon china ve-chisda ve-rachameh min kodam mareh shemaya ve'ara ve-imru. (AMEN).

Yeheh shelama rabbah min shemaya, hayyim vesavah vishu'ah ve-nechama veshezavah urfu'ah ug'ulah uslicha ve-chapara verevach vehatsalah lanu ul-chol amo Yisrael, ve-imru (AMEN).

Oseh shalom bi-mromav, hu ya'aseh shalom alenu ve'al kol amo Yisrael ve'imru (AMEN).

Glossary

Adar – Sixth month of the Hebrew calendar
Adar Sheni – Seventh month of the Hebrew calendar in a leap year
Aliyah – Being called up to the Torah
Amidah – The silent prayer at the center of the Jewish prayer service
Ani Ma'amin – I Believe – a statement of faith
Aninut – Between death and interment
Arvit – Evening prayer service
Avel – Mourner
Avelut – Mourning
Bar Mitzvah – Celebration when a boy reaches the age of thirteen
Bat Mitzvah – Celebration when a girl reaches the age of twelve
Berakhah – Blessing
Bet Kevarot – Cemetery
Birkat HaMazon – Grace after the meal
Bitachon – Trust in God
Chesed – Kindness
Chevra Kadisha – Burial Society
Chodesh – Month
Chol HaMoed – Intermediary days of Sukkot and Passover
Chuppah – Wedding Canopy
Dayan Ha'Emet – True Judge
Emouna –Faith
Gan Eden – Garden of Eden
Gemilut Chesed – Acts of kindness

Haftarah – Prophetic portion read on Shabbat
Halakhah – Jewish law
Hallel – Songs of praise recited on holy days and Rosh Chodesh
Hanukkah – The eight-day holy day that celebrates the Maccabee victory
Hashkavah – Memorial prayer
Havdalah – Prayer recited at the close of Shabbat
Hazkarah – Memorial
Hesped – Eulogy
Kaddish – Prayer recited by mourners
Kavod HaMet – Honor of the deceased
Keriah – tearing one's garment as an act of grief
Kippah – Head covering
Lag La'Omer – 33rd day of the Omer
Levayah – Funeral Service
Matzevah – Head stone
Met Mitzvah – A dead body with no one to bury it
Mincha – Afternoon prayer service
Minhag – Custom
Mishloach Manot – Sending food gifts on Purim
Moed – Holy day
Moed Katan – Name of the Talmudic Tractate which deals with death and dying
Olam Haba – World-to-come
Pidyon HaBen – Redemption of the firstborn son
Rosh Chodesh – New Month / New Moon
Sandak – The man who holds the infant during circumcision
Seudah – Meal
Seudat Havra'ah – Meal of consolation
Shacharit – Morning prayer service
Shalom – Hello and goodbye
Sheloshim – Thirty-day observance
Shema Israel – Prayer recited twice daily
Sheva Berakhot – Seven blessings recited for a bride and groom

under the chuppah, also refers to the seven days of celebration following a wedding
Shivah – Seven days of mourning
Shofar – Ram's horn blown on Rosh Hashanah
Siyyum – Celebration of the completion of a tractate of Talmud
Ta'anit – Fast day
Tachanun/im – Penitential prayers recited twice daily
Tziduk Hadin – Prayer recited for the mourners
Tzitzit – Fringes worn on one's garment
Viduy – Confession
Yizkor – Remembrance
Yom Tov – Holy Day
Zachor – Remember

Bibliography

Primary Works

Tanakh
Mishnah
Babylonian Talmud
Jerusalem Talmud
Rabbi Moshe ben Maimon, Maimonides, *Mishneh Torah*
Rabbi Bahya ibn Pakuda, *Chovot HaLevavot*, "Duties of the Heart"
Rabbi Moshe ben Nachman, Nachmanides, *Torat Ha'adam* Rabbi Yaakov Ben Harosh, *Tur Shulchan Arukh*
Rabbi Yosef Karo, *Shulchan Arukh* and *Bet Yosef*

Contemporary Works

Angel, Rabbi Marc. *The Rhythms of Jewish Living: A Sephardic Exploration of Judaism's Basic Ideas*. Jason Aronson Publishers, 1997.
Ashkenazi, Rabbi Yehuda Shemuel. *Siddur Bet Oved*. Livorno.
Besdin, Rabbi Abraham. *Reflections of the Rav: Lessons in Jewish Thought*. Ktav Publishers, 1993.
De Sola Pool, David. *The Old Jewish Aramaic Prayer, the Kaddish*. Leipzig, 1909.
Faur, Jose, *Hilkhot Avel*. Unpublished Hebrew monograph.
Feinstein, Rabbi Moshe. *Iggerot Moshe*.
Feldman, Rabbi Emmanuel. "Death as Estrangement: The Halakha

of Mourning." In *Jewish Reflections on Death*, ed. Jack Riemer. Schocken Books, 1999.

Frankl, Viktor. *Man's Search for Meaning*. McGraw Hill Publishers, 1979.

Lamm, Rabbi Maurice. *The Jewish Way in Death and Mourning*. New York: Jonathan David Publishers, 1994

Levy, Yamin and Amichai Levy. "Solemn Space: Praying at Cemeteries and the Prohibition of *Loeg Larash*." In *Rav Shalom Banayikh: Essays Presented to Rabbi Shalom Carmy in Celebration of Forty Years Teaching*, eds. Hayyim Angel and Yitzchak Blau. Ktav Publishers, 2012.

Liebman, Joshua. *Peace of Mind: Insights in Human Nature That Can Change Your Life*. Citadel Publishers, 1994.

Solomon, Victor. *Psychodynamics of Grief Management in Jewish Law and Tradition*. Ph.D. New York University, University Microfilms 1981.

Soloveitchik, Rabbi Joseph B. "The Halakha of the First Day." In *Jewish Reflections on Death*, ed. Jack Riemer. New York: Schocken Books, 1974.

———. "Catharsis." *Tradition Magazine*, Spring 1978.

Sutton, Abraham. *Me'ir Or: Hilchot Abelut*. New York, 1999.

Telsner, David. *The Kaddish: Its History and Significance*. Jerusalem, Tal Orot Institute, 1995.

Tochinsky, Rabbi Yechiel Michel. *Gesher Hachaim*. Jerusalem.

Wolowelsky, Joel B. "A Midrash on Jewish Mourning." *Judaism* 23, No. 2 Spring 1974.

Wurzberger, Rabbi Dr. Walter. "Covenantal Imperatives." In *Samuel Mirsky Memorial Volume*, ed. Gersion Appel. New York: Yeshiva University, 1970.

Yosef, Rabbi Ovadia. *Responsa Yabia Omer*.

———. *Responsa Yechaveh Da'at*.

———. *Yalkut Yosef*.

———. *Hazon Ovadia*.

Index

A
Adar, 134, 153
Afterlife, 41, 43
  belief in, 41
Alfa Beta, Psalm 119, 131, appendix II
Amen, 119
  response to Kaddish, 120
Amputated Limbs, 55
  burial of, 55
Amram ben Sheshna Gaon, 121
Aninut, 47–51, 58
  Preparations 49
  When death occurs, 50
  Shabbath and Holy Days, 51, 57
  Summary of laws, 56
Arayat, 126
Arvith service in house of mourning, 119
  motzaei shabbath, 129
Autopsies 52–54
Av, month of 135–136

B
Baby, death of, 153–156
Beliefs, Jewish 35–47
  afterlife, 41–43
  death, attitude towards, 43
  material possessions, 35–40
  moral spiritual purpose in life, 46
  personal growth, 20, 44
  world-to-come, 37, 42
Bibliography, 217

Birkat Hamazon in the house of mourning, 106
  onen, 58
  Seudat Havra'ah, 102
  On Shabbath, 103
  full Hebrew text appendix ii pages 9–12
Body, accompanying requirement, 83
  viewing, 68
Body and soul, 36–37
Brain death, 56
Brit Milah and mourning, 112
Burial Service, 83–86
  absent mourners, 97
  behavior proper, 85
  blessing for, 85
  cemetery, blessing upon entering, 85, 147
  cemetery, departing, 89, 149
  delayed, 93,
  earth shoveling, 84
  filling the grave, 84
  hakafot, circling the casket, 86
  Israel, 93
  kaddish *lechadeta*, 116
  leaving, 86–87, 147
  memorial prayer, 85–86
  no corpse, 94
  pallbearers, 82
  reinternment, 87–88
Burial Society, 58
Business and mourning, 114

C

Calendar cycle and mourning
  practices, 135–142
Candle lighting, 98
Casket, choice, 66–68
Cemetery visiting, 88
Cemetery service, appendix ii, pages
  3–4
  Prayer entering, appendix ii 5
Children attending shiva house,
  114–115
  Keriah, 97–98
  Mourning 93–109
Clothing, rending, 99–103
Comforting mourners, 32–33
Community, support, 25–33, 58
Condolence visit, 28–29
  traditional response, 31
  Timing, 30
  When leaving, 31
Consolation, meal of, 99–101
Converts and shiva, 127
Corpse, honoring of, 49–59
  amputated limbs, 54
  autopsies, 52–54
  behavior, 52–54
  cremation, 69
  eating next to, 52–54
  embalming, 63
  hevra kaddisha, 58, 60–62
  holy days or *hol hamoed*, 135–142

  kohen, 72–73
  organ donation, 54
  shrouds, 64
  transporting, 63
Cremation, 71

D

Dayan Ha'emet, 52
  text appendix ii
Death
  attitude towards, 1–5, 43–45

  baby, 159–162
  brain death, 56
  hearing about, delayed, 98–99
  informing others about, 133
  multiple family deaths, 99
  parent's loss twelve-month restric-
    tions, 145–147
  Rabbi Hanina ben Teradion,
    168–169
  Rabbi Judah's Maid, 165
  Rabbi Meir's sons, 167
  Rabbi Yochanan ben Zakkai's son,
    166
Death and fear of death, 1–5
Disinterment and reinternment,
  87–88

E

Eating,
  house of mourning in 106
Embalming and transport, 65
Empathetic mourning, 95–96
Escorting the deceased, 81–83
  Standing while moving, 82
Ethical will, 23–24
Eulogy 77–79
  holy days, 78–79, 132
  importance of, 77–80

F

Family
  Making peace with
Fasting on day of *Hazkara*
Feldman, Rabbi Emmanuel
Flowers, 67–68
Food, meal of consolation, 101–102
  meat onen, 58
Funeral and funeral service, 75–89
  behavior, proper, 88
  burial, 85–87
  body, viewing, 68
  casket, 66–68
  cremation, 69

distant relatives
eulogy, 77
flowers, 67–68
Israel, in, 93
kohanim, 79–71
Levayath Hamet, 83–84, 89
mausoleum, 69
Recitation of Psalms, 76–77
scheduling, 65
shoveling, 86–87
service, 75
suicide, 71–74
tziduk hadin, 79–80
tzedakah, 70–71

G

Gemiluth Hasadim, xi-xii, 26–28
Ger, Convert, 127
   sitting shiva, 127
   parents of, 127
Glossary, 213–215
God, making peace with, 137
Goodbye, saying 22–23
Grace after meal, 106
   text, appendix
Grave visitation, 132, 150, 154
   psalms read at, 150
Grief, xi-xv, 1–5
   Double, 94–95
   Shiva, 105–112
   sheloshim, 32, 81, 99, 132, 137
   remembering, 141
   confusion, 49, 111
   excessive grief, 150
   multiple family deaths
   recovery and resolution, 2–3, 15

H

Haircutting during shiva, 106–107
   Sheloshim, 142
Hakafot, 86
Halakha, 5–9
   Sephardic 7–9

Halbasha
Hallel in house of Shiva, 139
   In synagogue, 139
Hanukah, 133
Happiness, 1
Hard-boiled eggs, 105
Hashkava, 85–86, appendix ii page
   5–8, 12–13
   Mother's name reference, 85–86
   Father's name reference, 85–86
Havdalah, 130
Hayyim David Halevi, 8, 122
Hazkarah observances, 153
Healing, 19–20
Health and recovery prayer, 161–162
Hevra Kadisha, 53, 60
Holy Days and Hol HaMoed, 129–1136
   Death on, 53, 131–133
   Eulogy prohibition, 132
   Hallel, 139
   Keriah, 95 – 98
   Sheloshim, 32, 132
   Shiva, 132–133
Holiness code, Kohanim, 69–71
   House of mourning, 106–108
   Food in, 106
   Leaving during shiva, 31
   Services, 117–120

I

Intense mourning, 3, 31
Interpersonal relationships, 21–23
Introspection, 20

J

Jacob's deathbed, 24

K

Kaddish, 116–122
   Amen response to, 119
   At the graveside, 121
   Convert and kaddish, 122
   Hatzi-kaddish, 116

History of kaddish, 116–123
How long, 123
Kaddish de-Rabanan, 116
Kaddish le-Chadeta,116
Kaddish Yatom, 116
Kaddish al-Yisrael, 116, text appendix ii page 8–9
Kaddish shalem,116
Laws of kaddish, 121
Reason, 120
Suicide and kaddish, 71–74
Transliteration 211
Kaplan, Rabbi Aryeh, 41
Karo, Rabbi Yoseph, 8, 16
Keriah, 95–98
   Blessing of, 96
   Chol Hamoed, 98
   Garment, 97
   Laws, 96
   Not on time, 97–98
   Parent, for, 97
   Prayer, 9
   Two death, 98
Kislev, 133

L
Ladino Sepharadim, 126
Laundry during shiva, 112
Law, Halakha meaning of, 5–9
   Mourning, xiii
Leap year and *Hazakara*, 147
Leather shoes and shiva, 112
Levayat HaMet, 882–83
Life and afterlife, beliefs, 41, 43
Life introspection, 9, 22
Life telling story, 20–23
Limbs, amputated, 53
Loss, 2
Loving Kindness, xi-xii, 26–28

M
Maimonides (Rambam), xi, 6, 7, 8, 28, 39, 40–44

Amen, 123–124
Body and spirit, 28, 39, 40–44
Nefesh and *Neshama*, 39–44
Marital relations during shiva, 91, 114
Marriage and mourning, 137–139
Material possessions, 1–4, 99
Mausoleum, prohibition, 69
Meal of consolation, 104–105
Mechila, asking for forgiveness, 17, 23, 46
Meditation and reflection texts, appendix 1
Memorial candle, 98, 147
Memorial service, 75, 146–147
   Leap year, 147
   Different time zones, 147
Memories, importance of sharing, 32
Messiah and resurrection, 37–39
Minhag, 6–9
Mi Sheberach Prayer, 14–15
   English, 15
Mishna study in house of mourning, 38, 131
Miscarriage, 154
Mishloach Mantot on Purim, 134–135
   During shiva, 134–135
   During sheloshim, 134–135
   Twelve months, 134–35
Mishmara, 126
Mitzvoth, performing during shiva, 2, 4, 7, 28, 50–51
   Preparation of the deceased, 60–63, 73
   Exemptions for mourners, 50
   Exemptions for pallbearers, 82
   Nihum avilim, 60, 94, 99
   Onen, 58
Monument, erecting, 150–151
Moral purpose, 10, 19, 23
Moroccan Sepharadim, 126
Mourners, 93–95
   Honoring and support, 58, 89–103
   Children, 95–96

Condolence visits xiii, 30–32
Empathic mourner, 91
Holy days and *hol hamoed*, 135–142
Intense mourning, 3, 31
Leaving the house, 31
Meal, serving the mourner, 104
Points to remember, 32
Voluntary mourning, 91
Who is a mourner, 91

N
Necromancy, prohibition, 37
Nefesh Neshama, 39–44
Nihum Aveilim, Mitzvah, 60, 94, 99
Nisan, 135

O
Olam Haba, 41, 43
Onen status, 49–51, 53
    Requirements, 49
    Exemptions, 50
    Kaddish, 50–51
Organ Donations, 54–55

P
Pallbearers, 82–83
Parents, loss of, 88, 101–102, 117, 126
    Converts, mourning for parents, 127
    Stepson kaddish, 126
    Twelve-month observance, 145
Patach Eliyahu, 126
Persian Sepharadim, 126–127
Pesach, 135
    Sitting shiva, 135
    Sheloshim, 135
Pidyon Haben and shiva, 112, 152
Priestly blessing in house of mourning, 72–73
Psalms, recitation of, 78
    1, appendix ii
    15, Appendix ii
    16, Appendix ii
    23, Appendix ii
    49, Appendix ii
    90, Appendix ii
    91, Appendix ii
    119, Appendix ii
Purim, 134–135
    Eulogy, 81, 134
    Megilath Esther, hearing, 134
    Mishloach manot, 134
    Seudat Purim, 134

R
Rabbi Gamliel, 64, 111
Rabbi Eliezer's son's death, 158
Rabbi Judah's, son, 159
Rabbi Joshua's maid, 157
Rabbi Meir's sons' death, 160
Raisin and wine, 105
Rambam see Maimonides
Rechitzah, 60
Recovery, prayer, 14–15
Repent, 16
Rosh Chodesh, 133
Rosh Hashanah, 133

S
Saadia ben Yoseph Gaon, Rabbi, 122
Sephardic Halakha, 7–9
Sefirat Ha'omer, 60
Seudat Havra'ah, 99–103
    Birkat hamazon, 102–103
Seven-day memorial candle, 98
Shabbath, 128–130
    Aliyah to the Torah, 129
    Aninut, 51
    Death occurs on, 49–52
    Funeral arrangements on, 52–53
    Keriah, 53
    Observances on, 52–53
    Private mourning practices, 53
    Public mourning practices, 53
    Sitting low stool on, 52–53
    Zimun, 108

Siddur Rav Amran Gaon, 121
Shacharit services, 118
   Birkat Kohanim, 118
   House of mourning, 118
   Tachanunim, 118
   Uva Lezion, 118
Shaving during shiva, 148
   Sheloshim, 99
Shavuoth, 135
   Tikun Leil Shavuoth, 142
Sheloshim, 142
   Begins when, 143
   Concludes, 144
   Counting, 143
   Excessive mourning, 3, 31, 144
   Restrictions, 143
   Weddings, 143, 145
   Holy days, 32, 132
   Hol hamo'ed, 132
   Social gatherings, 147–150
Shema Israel, 51
   Pallbearers' exemption, 85
Shemini Atzeret, 150
   Shiva and Sheloshim, 132–135
Shemirah and *rechitza*, 62–64
Shivah sitting, 105
   Birkat Hamazon, 106
   Berit Milah, 112
   Business, doing, 109
   Candle lighting, 98
   Chairs, low, 106
   Clothes, 99–103
      Keriah, 97–98
   Concluding shiva, 125–127
   Converts, 127
   Counting, 92–94
   Final day service 14–16
   Greetings, 108
   Grooming, 106–107
   Ground sitting, 110
   Hard-boiled eggs, 101–102
   Havdalah, 130
   House of mourning services, 109

Informing another, 127
Joy, expression of, 110–111
Kaddish, 116–119,
Keriah, 97–98
Laundry, 109
Marital relations, 109
Meal of consolation, 99–101
Mirrors, 113
Pidyon haben, 112
Prayers, 113–116
Shabbath, 123–125
Synagogue, 115, 123–125
Torah study, 111
Visiting the grave after, 127
Weddings, 112
Wine, 101–102
Work, 109–110
Shoes, leather during shiva, 108, 130, 141
   Shabbath, 130
Shrouds, *Tachrichim*, 61
Sivan, 135
Siyyum celebration during shiva, 142
   Erev Pesach, 142
   First born, 142
Soloveitchik, Rabbi Joseph B., 45–46, 51, 79, 123, 136
Soul, immortality, 39–44
Spiritual purpose in life, 22
Suicide. 71–74
   Halakhic Suicide, 72–74
Sukkoth, 139
   Hol Hamo'ed, 139–140
   Mitzvoth of holy day, 139–140
   Onen, 58
   Sheloshim, 149–150
   Sukkah eating in, 139–140
Synagogue services, 118–120
   Sitting in, 120
   Tachanunim, 118
Syrian Sepharadim, 126

T

Takhrikhim, 61
Taharah, 60
Talleth, burial, 62
Tefillin, 50, 88
Temania Apei BeAleph Psalm 119, page 17–21
Terminal Illness response to, 13, 17–24
  See also Viduy
  Ethical will, writing, 23–24
  Facilitating actions, suggested, 17–24
  Life storytelling, 21
  Prayer, praying, 22
  Unfinished business, 20–24
Teshuva, 45–47
  God Making peace, 45
  Introspection, 13–24
  Viduy, 13–24
Thirty days
  See sheloshim, 147–149
  Counting
Tikun Leil Shavuoth, 135–142
Time zones Hazkara, 154
Tisha B'Av and Shiva, 135–136
Tishrei, 133
Torah,
  Halakha, 5–9
  Minhag, 6–9
  Study Torah, 115
Tzidduk HaDin Prayer, 79–80
  Text and translation, appendix ii 12

U

Unfinished business, 16, 21
Unveiling service, 151

V

Viduy, confession, 13–24
  Completion, 19–20
  English text, 17–18
  Purpose, 14–15
  Recitation, 19–20
  Teshuva 20–22
  Text, Hebrew appendix ii page 1–2
Voluntary mourning, 96

W

Wedding and mourning, 112, 137–139
  Death occurs immediately after, 137
  Second marriage, 138
Wine, 101
  Shabbath, 59, 106
Working during shiva, 114
World-to-come, 37–43, 158

Y

Yehuda Ashkenazi, Rabbi, 125
Yom Kippur and Shiva, 133
Yosef, Rabbi Ovadia, 8

Z

Zachor, remember, 141, 147–149
  Excessive grief, 150
  Fasting on day of memorial, 139
  Hazakara observances, 147–148
  Leap years, 147
  Monument, 156
  Unveiling, 157
  Visiting the grave, 155–156
Zimun, 106–107
  Shabbath, 108

Made in United States
North Haven, CT
05 August 2022